ADOPTION OF BASIC FACTORS FOR RURAL-URBAN DEVELOPMENT

Adoption of Basic Factors for Rural-Urban Development

E.D. Setty

P. Krishna Moorthy

AKANSHA PUBLISHING HOUSE

NEW DELHI • GUWAHATI • VISAKHAPATNAM

AKANSHA PUBLISHING HOUSE
4649-B/21, Ansari Road
Daryaganj, New Delhi-110002
Phones: 23268193, 09435116718
Email: ektabooks@yahoo.com
visit us: www.akanshapublishinghouse.com

Adoption of Basic Factors for Rural-Urban Development

First Published 2011

ISBN 978-81-8370-264-5

PRINTED IN INDIA

Published by Akansha Publishing House, New Delhi-110002 and printed at Harmain Offset Press, Delhi.

CONTENTS

Acknowledgements *vii*

Preface *ix*

1. Indispensability of Water for Life 1
2. The Philosophy behind the Neeru-Meeru Programme 10
3. Conservation of Water: Efforts by the State Government 14
4. Operational Means and Methods in Harvesting and Conserving Rainwater 23
5. Integrated Approach to Water Supply and Sanitation Management 37
6. People's Image of Rural Development: Development Implications 60
7. Community Organization and Programme Planning 87
8. People's Participation in Upland Conservation 107
9. Participatory Technology Development and Sustainable Agriculture: A Case from Philippines 125
10. Training as a Principal Factor of HRD Initiative 151
11. Strategies for Developing Entrepreneurship among People 172
12. Extension Education iPn Aid of Agricultural Marketing 210
13. Each Village as a Unit of Rural Development 233

14. Guidelines for Sectoral Development 241

15. Application of Technologies Appropriate to Rural Areas 285

16. The Part Played by NGOs in Rural Development 292

17. Janmabhoomi in Andhra Pradesh: A Clinical Approach to Multi-Sectoral and Segmental Development 306

18. Caste Dynamics in Rural Development 335

19. Rural Sanitation: Need for a Perspective Plan 342

20. Prospects and Problems in Rural Communities Lead to Urbanization in India 350

Index 359

ACKNOWLEDGEMENTS

The authors would like to express deep appreciation and thanks to Sri K. Murali Krishna, who has prepared the material for publication. The first author would like to express his sincere thanks to his wife Vishalakshi, who has been the spirit behind his attempts in writing all these years. He is thankful to Prof. P. Krishnamoorthy (co-author) for his support and encouragement in writing this book.

We gratefully acknowledge the authors and sources from which we have borrowed some material.

We would like to express our profound thanks to Sri M.P. Misra for bringing out this volume.

—*Authors*

PREFACE

If one goes around the villages in India he could witness the stages and the conditions in which several segments of the population live today. Owing to historical reasons more especially of the foreign colonial administration and diverse princely states ruling for some centuries, to a greater extent the villages have been neglected entities in terms of minimal humane standards of living. The problems are multifarious and the needs are enormous. With all commitment, sincerity and attention, the state has been attempting to improve the conditions of living in rural communities for the past fifty years in terms of planned and organized development. Since the problem is so vast and the machinery of development is not properly tuned across the entire chain and in spite of good intensions, owing to laxity in terms of realistic assessment of the problems, needs and resources, we have not been able to achieve development as we visualized. One may point out several lapses. In a way, the development efforts have been something like broadcasting of seed without paying detailed attention to certain segments of population and sectors of development. Though there have been ethnic-wise, class-wise programmes, either owing to lack of resources on the part of the government and initiative and response from the people, we are still moving rather slowly with halting paces in the march towards development. Examining the way in which we have been working all these years, one realizes what is needed today is what we may call a clinical approach to rural-urban development. The present volume based on the extensive field experience of the author discusses the principal factors contributing to rural-urban development. It may be mentioned that some of the aspects discussed in this volume are not new but unfortunately, attention has not been paid to some of the strategies and methods of development. These are some of the missing links in what has gone on so far. As a kind of a remedial measure, the chapters that are contained in this volume focus on and highlight the importance of these missing links and the way to go about making rural urban development a successful endeavour with tangible results.

The introductory part focuses on indispensability of conservation of water, followed by the philosophy behind the Neeru-Meeru programme in chapter – 2. The Chapter – 3 details the efforts made by the State Government in conservation of water. As a follow-up to conservation of water, chapter – 4 looks into operational means and methods in harvesting and conserving rainwater. The chapter – 5 highlights the way to go about in managing rural water supply and sanitation.

Chapter – 6 focuses on people's image of development and development implications. Chapter – 7 details the ways to organize a community for programme planning and implementation. Chapter – 8 looks him to upland conversation detailing the complex relation between forest eco system and human social system. Chapter – 9 brings out participatory technology development between the people and development agencies.

Chapter – 10 highlights, the growing importance attached to the development of the employees in the interest of the organization development. Further, this chapter lays emphasis on human resource as principal factor for any success in organizations. It also briefly describes the fundamental changes in attitudes, approaches, outlook, philosophy, perspective and practices emerging in the personnel area in the form of human resources management. It spells out the important components in HRD and HRM. It stresses on HRD as a continuous process which tries to match organizational needs that of human resources development. Further, this chapter emphasizes the kind of congenial relationships that should prevail between the employees and the management.

Chapter – 11 may be considered as a key chapter which details the approaches to development of entrepreneurship highlighting the sociological aspects, physical conditions, cultural patterns and human resources in promoting entrepreneurship in a given community. It speaks of the kind of barriers and stimulants in promoting entrepreneurship. It spells out four principal factors that matter in EDP namely, organization, infrastructure, resources and entrepreneur himself. It draws the attention of EDP promoters to the need for a successful utilization and blending of these factors which promote entrepreneurship. The different phases that one has go through in promoting entrepreneurship are detailed in this chapter.

Chapter – 12 though the title speaks of extension in aid of agricultural marketing, it could be taken as the marketing strategies for the products of small-scale enterprises. It illustrates the extension methods that are to be employed in generating awareness and securing the means to venture into entrepreneurial activities. Entrepreneurship development in a larger sense is an educational process. Of several problems which may be called factors in the entire field of entrepreneurship development, marketing of products in a competitive world appears to be really a challenging one.

Chapter – 13 on programme planning as a basic and systematic process in formulating plans in meeting people's needs. It could definitely serve as a guide giving directions to the planners the way they have to go about in formulating plans to meet people's needs. Chapter – 14 speaks of the need to take each village as a unit of rural development. This operationally links to what is emphasized in this volume: a clinical approach.

Chapter – 15 covers all the salient areas of development that matter in rural communities. It covers twelve sectors and the problems and needs in each sectors and the way to solve these problems and meet the needs and improve the conditions in each sector so that the combined effect of remedies and improvement synchronize in the wholesome overall development of each rural community. Development envisages introduction of changes, technological or social. There are always problems in making the essential and useful changes accepted by the people. Chapter – 16 provides a successful strategy in introducing changes in rural communities. Local institutions at the field level politico, administrative and development in nature have a greater role to play in initiating, managing and accomplishing changes and they may be rightly called as agents of social change at the community level.

Chapter – 17 highlights the part played by NGOs in rural urban development, we have a very innovative development programme in the name of Janmabhoomi initiated in Andhra Pradesh in 1977. The Government of Andhra Pradesh having analyzed the earlier experiments in rural urban development arrived at a conclusion that there cannot be a global approach to development but it is to be periodic, sectoral development focusing on one or two sectors in a particular period. With this philosophy, the Government of Andhra Pradesh has initiated which is called Janmabhoomi as a clinical approach to multi-sectoral and segmental development.

Chapter – 18 focuses on this approach. Development cannot be mechanical. Social forces influence and operate on any development activity. Caste which is unique in the Indian context for several centuries, though, it is to the decline still plays a significant role both positive and negative in the field of rural development. The life of the Scheduled Castes who are now called Dalits has been a sad story for centuries. They constitute fifteen per cent of the population in India. Though there are several provisions in helping and improving the life of the Dalits, there is a need for special attention to be paid to them. Chapter – 19 recommends a need for perspective plan on rural urban sanitation. Related to rural urban sanitation, conservation and judicious use of water for all needs is a crucial issue.

Urbanization is a growing phenomenon in every country and when it comes to India, it is the pull and push factor that has led to gradual process of urbanization. Chapter – 20 looks into his process of urbanization in India.

—Authors

1

INDISPENSABILITY OF WATER FOR LIFE

Water is one of the most important resources, which is vital for life and for all economic activity. Its indiscriminate use has resulted in a grave situation that threatens to assume gargantuan proportions very soon. The dwindling of forests has led to a decrease in rainfall and made large tracts of land barren and uncultivable. Lack of water has become a major constraint to development. Several investigations have shown that only 9% of rainwater is actually retained as groundwater. It is needless to emphasize the primacy of water for origin and sustenance of life. We move into action when we face problems and scarcity of resources. So long resources are abundant and appear infinite we do not bother about them. Water was once an abundant resource and today especially by action of mankind it has become a scarce commodity. We could see, as a result of man's ignorance and avarice what has happened over the globe in respect to water. Some parts of the planet are endowed with enormous water resources. Some are in a poor state. The planet has gone through lot of transformations. Some areas have become deserts. Within the country the conditions in respect to availability of water or lack of it vary.

Indispensability of Conservation of Water

It is interesting to note that times were when there was no scarcity of land, water and other basic resources for the survival of mankind. Over centuries, with gradual increase in population, land also has become a comparatively scarce commodity. Nobody would have imagined that water would become a scarce and a precious commodity. We have reached a state wherein water has become the principal source and need for agriculture, industry and for human survival. This awakening of inadequacy of water has been rather gradual and we have not suddenly discovered this inadequacy. As everybody knows minus water in a particular area, there is no question of any settlement or survival of people and other species. We may look at the basic details of land and rainfall in India in general and Andhra Pradesh in particular. This will give us an idea as to where we stand vis-à-vis availability of water and the use of water for survival purposes. There has not been any common, general, concerted effort to think, plan and come out with certain basic regulatory and promotional measures in respect to harvesting and conservation of rainfall and also through different means to contribute to the rise in the groundwater level. The state of Andhra Pradesh has taken positive steps in conserving water by several means and measures. However, there have been measures taken by the farmers and the administration of Maharashtra and Madhya Pradesh in conserving rainwater, thus contributing to irrigation and rise the groundwater level. We may say that these efforts have been sporadic. At the national level the Government of India has focused its attention on conservation of water but the efforts and the programmes have not been widespread and intensive.

In India the total land area is 3,290 lakh hectares, of this extent of land 1,170 lakh of hectares receive 100 mm rainfall during the year. Of the total land area, nearly 2/3rds is subject to very low rainfall. On the other hand 1/9th of the land area is subject to floods. One has to understand the organic or functional relationship between the forest area and consequent quantum of rainfall and the way in which the rainwater is conserved and utilized for agricultural and other purposes. Of the total rainwater 41% ends in the evaporation and another 40% of rainwater runs through canals and rivulets. Of the total rainfall, only 10% is used for agricultural purposes and 9% penetrates into earth and it contributes to the water table. In terms of the future requirement for the population of 150 crore in the year 2050, water requirement for the entire country is 1,20,100000 lakh cubic meters. This is the estimate for the year 2050. There has been negligence and out of ignorance and indifference on the part of the people over decades in conserving rainwater and also in maintaining the water bodies, like irrigation tanks and ponds, there is now scarcity of water for irrigation and for domestic purposes. Another major contribution to this scarcity is the phenomenal increase in population. If conditions continue like this we may reach a situation wherein there will be scarcity of water even for drinking. We have reached a point of time wherein we have to take stock of the situation, mobilize resources, move with concerted action in conserving rainwater and using water judiciously in order to maintain the groundwater water table.

While the entire focus is on water and everybody is close to water, it may not be out of place here to briefly speak of water as a resource on the planet.

I. **Ground Water:** is contained in the voids within rocks, i.e., in pores, cracks and other cavities and spaces. It often excludes vadose water which occurs between the water table and the surface. The groundwater that originates from the surface, percolating through the soil (meteoric water) and other sources are juvenile water, generated accruing and coming from deep magmatic processes and connate water which water is trapped in a sedimentary rock since its formation.

   Groundwater is necessary component of most weathering processes and of course its relationship to the geology, water table and surface may lead to the occurrence of aquifers and artesian wells.

II. **Hydrology:** the study of water and its cycle which covers bodies of water and how they change. All physical forms of water – rain, snow, and surface water are to be studied in all their aspects and their use as the way in which water circulates between bodies of water such as seas, the atmosphere and the earth forms the hydrological cycle.

The cycle consists of various stages: water falls as rain or snow of which some runs off into streams and then into lakes or rivers while some percolates into the ground. Plants and trees take up water and lose it by transpiration to the atmosphere while evaporation occurs from bodies of water. The water vapour in the air then condenses to cloud which eventually repeats the cycle.

III. **The Vegetation:** is controlled by the rainfall and varies from sparse, drought resistant shrubs and cactic to sudden blooms of annual plants in response to a short period of torrential rain. If the groundwater conditions permit or the geology is such that an artesian well (Aquifer) is created there an oasis may develop within a hot desert providing an island of green.

IV. **Drainage:** is the movement of water derived from rain, snowfall and melting of ice and snow, over the land and through it in subterranean waterways, which results eventually in its discharge into the sea. The flow of streams and rivers is influenced by the underlying rocks, how they are arranged and whether there are any structural features that the water may follow. Further, factors affecting drainage include soil type, climate and the influence of man.

V. **Humidity:** the amount of moisture in the earth's atmosphere. Absolute humidity is the actual mass of water vapour in each cubic metre of air.

VI. Of the 1.5 billion cubic kilometres of water on earth,

- The oceans hold 93.9 %
- Groundwater 4.4 %
- Polar ice 1.0 %
- With rivers, lakes, the atmosphere and soil holding the reminder.

VII. Water is finite

- Of the world's major rivers only the Amazon (South America) and the Congo (Africa) are judged as healthy.
- Just 2.5 % of the world's water is fresh and the rest is salty.

VIII. Fresh Water

- **Total Global (Water)**
- 97.7 % Salt water
- 2.5 % Fresh water

i) 68.9 % Glaciers & Permanent Snow cover

ii) 0.3 % Freshwater Lakes and River storage. Only this portion is renewable

iii) 0.9 % Other including soil moisture, swamp water and permafrost.

The Waterless Millions

It is alarming to note that Eritrea, Chad, Ethiopia and Madagascar are countries where more than three-fourths of the people have no access to safe water. UNDP statistics say that whereas 28% of the population are without safe water in developing countries, the figure is 41% in least developed countries and 50% in Sub-Saharan Africa. Among Asian countries, the situation is grave in Cambodia (70%) and Mongolia (60%). In India, 19% of the population are without access to safe water.

IX. The following are the kinds of demand for water:

- Drinking water
- Irrigation sector
- Hydropower
- Navigation
- Industries
- Pisciculture
- Recreation

LAND AND WATER SITUATION IN ANDHRA PRADESH

AP AT A GLANCE – GENERAL

- Area 2.75 lakh sqkm
- Population (1999) 75.7 millions
- Density of population 275 / sqkm
- Rural Population 72.92 % (Agr. Based)
- Urban Population 27.08 %
- Population expected 90 million
- By 2020

AP AT A GLANCE – SOCIAL

- Literacy 44.09 %
- Females for 1000 Males 978
- Scheduled Castes 15.93 %
- Scheduled Tribes 6.31 %

AP AT A GLANCE – LAND USE

	(Million ha)	*Per cent*
• Geographical Area	27.50	100
• Forest area	6.25	23
• Barren & Uncultivable land	2.03	8
• Land put to non-agricultural use	2.47	9
• Cultivable waste	0.79	3
• Permanent pastures & grazing	0.78	3
• Land under trees	0.25	1
• Fallow land	4.44	15
• Net area sown	10.48	38

RIVER BASINS

Available TMCPer cent of total utilizable water

Major Rivers		
• Krishna river	811	30%
• Godavari river	1,480	54%
• Pennar river	98	03%
• Other rivers (37 nos.)	357	13%
Total 2,746 (77,794 m.cum)		

IRRIGATION SCENARIO IN ANDHRA PRADESH

Scheme	*Nos.*	*Potential (lakh ha)*	
		Contemplated	*Created*
a) Major	18	15.63	15.60
b) Medium	104	2.70	2.64
c) Minor	12,351	17.92	17.92
Total	12,473	36.25	36.16

d) Well Irrigation

No. of wells	22.5 lakh nos
Ayacut	26.4 lakh ha

GROUND WATER RESOURCES

	TMC	*(m. cum)*
Present utilization	450	12,749
Balance	371	10,500
In command areas		
In non-command areas	247	7,000

IRRIGATION POTENTIAL

Total Potential area available	87.82 lakh ha
Potential created	60.05 lakh ha
Potential utilized	57.45 lakh ha

Reasons for Shortfall

- High conveyance losses
- Lack of adequate and reliable water supply
- Unscientific methods of usage of water
- Bad health of irrigation systems
- Lack of sufficient funds
- Traditional cropping pattern
- Lack of conjunctive use of water.

There is an extent of 275 lakh hectares in Andhra Pradesh. Of this area 150 lakh hectares happen to be barren lacking sufficient irrigation facilities. This constitutes 42% of the total geographic area in Andhra Pradesh. On an average per annum the rainfall is around 8631 tmc.

Besides the traditional sources of irrigation like irrigation tanks, supply canals, there have been other measures also in irrigating fields. As a result of increase in the area under cultivation and increasing population and unscientific ways of using water and as a result of man caused reasons we have reached a stage where water has become a precious commodity not only for domestic, agricultural and industrial purposes but also for drinking. It has become a problem and time has come wherein we have to plan in such a way that we should educate the people, create awareness in them, involve them in conservation of rainwater and save rainwater by other means in order to conserve it in reservoirs, lakes and ponds and also to enrich moisture and increase the groundwater table. The effort is not only for today and it is a long one and an on-going one and by now we have gone through two "NEERU-MEERU" programmes and the 3rd one is in progress and it will continue up to August, 2001. There has been unprecedented mobilization and concerted efforts both by the Government and by the people's associations in desilting irrigation tanks and removing all unwanted plant growth in the supply and irrigation canals. The objective is to increase the land under cultivation, to ensure adequate supply of water for irrigation and for industrial purposes both in rural and urban areas. It is being carried-on on war footing and the water has become a national priority. The government has constituted a water conservation mission.

Indiscriminate use of water both in agriculture (cultivated area) and command areas and as a result of floods causing stagnation of water in pools, the soil is turning salty loosing fertility for cultivation. The total quantum of water that can be expected from rains and groundwater is 118.71 crore cubic metres. Of this water 88% (177 lakh hectares) of cultivable land could be brought under cultivation. However, at present only 55 lakh hectares of land is under cultivation. It constitutes 33% of cultivable land. There is an imperative need to harvest and conserve rainwater and also to improve the groundwater level. At present 9% of rainwater only contributes to the groundwater. The rest of the rainwater is washed away without seeping into the ground for want of barriers to arrest the running rainwater. The principal and immediate objective of Neeru–Meeru programme is to raise the percentage of rainwater that will be absorbed by the ground to 13.5% from 9 per cent.

2

THE PHILOSOPHY BEHIND THE NEERU-MEERU PROGRAMME

For the birth and existence of all kinds of life on the planet the basic requirement is "water" apart from other survival requirements. In the absence of water there is no question of agriculture or any kind of industry or the very existence of life of all species (not to speak of human species). In the earlier centuries in view of limited population and considerable extent of surface on the planet covered by forests, there was sufficient rain, and the scarcity of water either for drinking, domestic, agricultural and industrial purposes was not felt. But, during the days of the past there has been increase in population and decrease in the forest area, which resulted in reduced rainfall and nearly 50% of the land has become degraded and not fit for cultivation as it is now but with irrigation facilities and with augmenting nutrition of the soil with organic and inorganic material such land could be under cultivation for rising crops. Such measures are also being taken not only in Andhra Pradesh but also in other states.

The objective in *Neeru-Meeru* is to pay attention to water which is the primary basis for life. It is not a question of a day or two. The need is perennial and never ending, it is up to the present generation to ensure that they have the imagination and commitment to ensure that they conserve rainwater and contribute by several measures to the rise in the groundwater level. Water is the factor which has no alternative.

It is a commodity which cannot be in large quantities imported except for drinking purposes.

People over centuries by virtue of their traditional mode of irrigation and vast area covered by forest with seasonal abundant rains, the question of scarcity of water did not arise. But today with increase in population, with extended land brought under cultivation and mechanical means used for drawing groundwater, we have reached a threatening state in respect to inadequacy of water for farming and for industrial purposes. And so, gradually the Government and people have to bestow attention on the measures and the means to conserve water, and using of this water judiciously as a precious material.

There is an organic relation between alleviation of poverty and water. It may be mentioned here in general, most of the poorer farmers largely own dry lands and their farming depends on rainwater and also conservation of water in little ponds or irrigation tanks. Scarcity of water for irrigation, mostly affects the poor farmers who own limited land and who cannot afford to go in for electric pumpsets to irrigate their limited land.

It is law of nature that there is a relation between trees and extent of forests and quantum of rainfall. Rains depend on trees, trees depend on rains. If one dwindles, the other dwindles. We could see the cause effect relationship. Man should have prudence to understand this law of nature and he should increase planting of trees, increasing area under forest, protect the forests and trees like something sacred as the means of survival to man and the entire creation. When you speak of trees, we have to see how the people during the Vedic period and even today the forest dwellers consider trees as something sacred. In *Rigveda*, it is mentioned referring to Vanaprastha of the four Ashramas the code of life in respect to Vanaprasthashrama, that the individual dwelling in the forest, is only to eat fallen leaves, fruits, seeds and not to touch the green leaves. One can imagine the stricture imposed on people in their Vanaprasthashrama stage, not to pluck green leaves and not to speak of felling or destroying trees. One can imagine extensive coverage of land with trees during the Rig

Vedic period (2000-1500 BC). In spite of such extensive area covered under the forests, people living in the forest, revered the trees-forests. The importance given to the trees can be imagined during the Rid Vedic period. Trees are our ancestors and cousins. Life depends on them. But today the situation is different. This kind of stricture on food in respect to the Vanaprasthashrama may also be taken as a dietary regulation which would reduce his desire for food. It is preparing the individual to smoothly move into the state of recluse or Sansyasashrama.

While we speak of conservation of water or securing of water it is interesting to note the efforts made by Bhagiratha, a mythological character in getting water to the earth. Bhagiratha, the son of Raja Dilipa who is said to have spent a thousand severe austerities upon a mountain by which he propitiated Brahma and Siva and brought the Ganges to the earth; and with it watered the ashes of the sixty thousand sons of Sagara, who were at once restored to life, purified by the sacred water; all their sins gone and they ascended to heaven. Sixty thousand sons of Sagara sounds allegorical and we may take sixty thousand sons as sixty thousand hectares of land with crops like wheat, and barley (crops during the *Rigvedic* period) and Bhagiratha through his yogic powers stimulated the clouds to rain. Today we have to plant and provide trees and abundant forests to welcome the Rain God. The yagna today is our massive action to save rainwater and conserve every drop of water that falls on the good earth.

During the Vedic period people worshipped the natural elements like Agni, Vayu, Varuna and Prithvi and offered sacrifices appealing to the deified natural elements for abundant rain, and for protecting their crops and cattle. The only means they had in those ancient times consisted of prayers and sacrifices.

Yagnas mattered a great deal during the Vedic period. But today the *Neeru – Meeru* programme is not prayer or sacrifice but committed massive action on the part of the people desilting of lakes, ponds, supply canals, digging of pits and going in for contour bunds etc., for conserving every drop of water. Today we have the technology and innovative ideas to cope-up with the situation, especially the means to conserve rainwater and judicious use of ground water for agriculture and domestic purposes.

Further, it is quite interesting to note when we speak of planting of trees, and afforestation that the non-Christian tribes in Meghalaya as they did for ages, worship Rivers, Forests and Hills. They are nature worshippers as the early Aryans. A river that is worshipped by them is sacred to them and fishing is forbidden from such a river. They consider forest as sacred and they used to offer cocks and hens as sacrifice to the forest. These natural resources sustain their life and so they have been deified.

For a number of centuries, when agriculture activity was limited, the population was thin and when you had extensive vegetation you had adequate rains and nobody felt the scarcity of water either for drinking, domestic purposes and for irrigation. Today, the situation is different in several parts of the world.

When we think of the means for development and progress and attaining prosperity, one means or commodity is water. We can never imagine any progress or development in the absence of water.

3

CONSERVATION OF WATER: EFFORTS BY THE STATE GOVERNMENT

In the past centuries and decades, the traditional irrigation tanks, ponds, wells and rainwater served the purpose of cultivation of crops. Depending on the location, topography of land, geological features and quantum of rainwater, farmers have devised various means and methods of conserving and use of water for irrigation. Keeping in view the traditional manmade sources of water and modes of irrigation, the government have been making concerted efforts to meet the increasing demand for water for irrigation. The devices suggested have been several. The policy of the government is to prevent drought, famine situation and to meet the increasing needs of water in drought prone areas, the Government has introduced what is called 'Watershed Programme'. It was introduced in 1975 by Government of India and recommended to the farmers. Since it was top-down approach it has not evoked anticipated people's participation and further the coordination among the departments concerned was weak and wanting. Some of the watershed projects did not last long.

In the *Neeru-Meeru programme,* we may think of two principal objectives. One is to conserve rainwater by multiple ways for use and also to augment the rise of ground water table. The second one may be called a preventive action preventing deforestation which causes decrease in rainfall.

This preventive action warrants continuous planting of trees and increasing the area covered under forest wherever it is feasible. The gradual increase of afforestation over a period of time, of course within the geographic area available would ensure sufficient rainfall. Activities in respect to fulfilling these two objectives are to be continuous. On one hand, we may have to go in for what is called harvesting or conserving rainwater and at the same time increase area under greenery which would ensure gradual increase of rain. The increase of greenery cannot only be a local but it is to be a widespread activity i.e., an activity which is to be carried on infinitely. Here the responsibility lies with individuals, families and communities of rural and urban settlements. We may have to understand the nature's principle: when the forest areas dwindle the rainfall too will dwindle and this is the beauty and the principle in nature one contributing to the other. Increase of forest area will increase the quantum of rainfall. The increase of rainfall contributing to more of naturally grown trees provided, man does not destroy them. This is law of nature. We do not have an alternative except respecting law of nature and coordinating with the principles of nature. Rainwater is to be harvested and conserved and deforestation is to be prevented.

Though there are several measures in alleviating poverty, assuring water for irrigation purposes to the limited land owning-poorer segments of the farm community is one of the basic measures. Assuring water for irrigation can be taken as one means in alleviating rural poverty.

As we have mentioned earlier, because of man's ignorance and avarice, and lack of knowledge and technology, man has reached a state where the ground water is depleted and the rainwater has not been adequately conserved and this is to be reversed to bring back the ecological balance.

The entire attempt in *Neeru-Meeru programme* is to bring back the balance between nature and water. Man has caused the imbalance between nature and water and that is to be rectified now. This rectification and the remedial measures involve unending periodic activity, year after year, season after season.

The State government has introduced in 1997, the Watersheds with the modified principles of Dr. Hanumantha Rao Committee. This has brought about considerable results in respect to crops cultivated in waste and fallow lands and lands with less fertility. This appreciable result could be achieved motivating, working with and involving the beneficiary farmer groups in the new watershed programmes. It was realized that people's participation is a primary ingredient in the success of the watershed programme. Keeping in view, the importance and contributing factor of watershed mechanism, a ten-year watershed programme was launched all over the State in 1977 in order to bring under cultivation a target area of 100 lakh fallow and degraded land. As a result of this programme by December, 2000, an extent of 27 lakh hectares of wasteland was in the process of being provided with irrigation. Each watershed project is managed by a committee of the local farmers. By this time, there were 5472 watershed committees who were active in realizing the objective of watershed programme. In a similar way, the Joint Forest Management bodies have taken up 16.85 lakh hectares of forest wasteland for development. In this effort – 6705 Forest Protection Samithis have taken part.

Water a National Priority – Need for a Water Conservation Mission

It is quite obvious that water is a perennial need and it naturally deserves first national priority. It is not enough that we declare this in words but the whole idea is to be translated into action. The State government has made a policy decision to remedy the man-made paucity of water owing to his ignorance, avarice and lack of financial resources. The present water situation is a long accumulated abuse, misuse and negligence on the part of man. Based on the lessons learnt from the past and the suggestions and guidelines provided by several experts, the State government has decided to take up harvesting, conserving and use of water as a priority development and welfare activity involving the beneficiary groups at every phase of action.

The approach of the government in the reformative and constructive work has been bringing together various functionally related departments at State, District and Mandal level to work on water resources in the large and small river valleys and formulate an integrated plan of action for harvesting, conserving and judicious use of water for diverse survival and progressive purposes. This *Neeru-Meeru Programme* has facilitated integrating of several activities and creation of work and job opportunities at the District Level. In order to have the benefit of expertise in this sensitive and project of primacy, the State government has established a State level Water Conservation Mission, comprising eminent people.

THE LIST OF MEMBERS OF THE WATER CONSERVATION MISSION OF ANDHRA PRADESH

Sl.No.	*Position*	*Name and Details*
1.	Chairman	Sri N. Chandrababu Naidu, Chief Minister, Andhra Pradesh
2.	Vice-Chairman	Sri S. Ray, IAS, Principal Secretary to Govt. of AP (RD & RE)
3.	Chief Executive Officer	Sri Anil C. Punetha, IAS, Commissioner, Rural Development Department
4.	Member	Sri Anna Saheb Hazare, Ralegao Siddhi, Maharashtra
5.	-do-	Sri B.N. Yugandhar, IAS (Rtd.) Vassan, Hyderabad
6.	-do-	Sri Anil Shah, Development Promotion Centre, Ahmedabad, Gujarat
7.	-do-	Sri Vilasrao Salunke, Paani Panchayati, Pune, Maharashtra

8. -do-	Sri Vasimalai, Dhan Foundation, Tamil Nadu
9. -do-	Sri Rajendra Singh, Tarun Bharat Sangh, Alwar, Rajasthan
10. -do-	Sri B.G. Dhokarikar, Pune, Maharashtra
11. -do-	Sri C.H. Hanmantha Rao, Planning Commission Ex-Member, Hyderabad
12. -do-	Sri T. Hanmantha Rao, Chief Engineer (Rtd.), Irrigation Department, Hyderabad
13. -do-	Sri Y.V. Malla Reddy, Rural Development Trust (NGO), Anantapur
14. -do-	Sri Crispino Lobo, WOTR, Ahmednagar, Maharashtra
15. -do-	Dr. D.P. Rao, Director, NRSI, Hyderabad
16. -do-	Dr. Nagender Swamy, Villagers In Partnership, Mahaboob Nagar

DISTRICT LEVEL WATER CONSERVATION AND USERS COMMITTEES

Sl.No.	*Designation*	*Position*
1.	Minister	Chairman
2.	District Collector	Executive Officer
3.	Members of Parliament	Ex-Officio Members
4.	Chairman of Zilla Parishad and District Central Municipality	Members
5.	Mayor of Municipal Corporation	Member

6.	A Prominent Industrialist, nominated by the District Collector	Member
7.	Two Water Conservation Technologists, nominated by the District Collector	Members
8.	Chairmen of Best Watershed Committees, Vana Samrakshana Committees, Water Committees	Members
9.	D.P.A.P. Project Director (or) D.R.D.A. Project Director (If there is no DPAP)	Convener

MANDAL LEVEL WATER CONSERVATION AND USERS COMMITTEES

Sl.No.	*Designation*	*Position*
1.	President or Special Officer of Mandal Parishad	Chairman
2.	MLA belonging to the Mandal	Ex-Officio Members
3.	Nodal Officer	Member
4.	Two Local NGOs or Social Workers, nominated by the District Collector	Members
5.	Three Best Presidents of Self-Help Groups, nominated by the District Collector	Members
6.	A Prominent Industrialist, nominated by the District Collector	Member
7.	Mandal Parishad Development Officer	Convener

MUNICIPAL LEVEL WATER CONSERVATION AND USERS COMMITTEES

Sl.No.	*Designation*	*Position*
1.	Chairman or Mayor of Municipal Corporation, Municipality, Town Panchayat	Chairman
2.	Nodal Officer	Member
3.	MLA (s) , belonging to the Municipal area	Ex-Officio Members
4.	Three Local NGOs or Social Workers, nominated by the District Collector	Members
5.	Three Best Heads of Self-Help Groups of D.W.C.U.A., Presidents of Neighbourhood Committees, nominated by the District Collector	Members
6.	A Prominent Industrialist, nominated by the District Collector	Member
7.	Municipal Commissioner	Convener

VILLAGE PANCHAYATI LEVEL WATER CONSERVATION AND USERS COMMITTEES

Sl.No.	*Designation*	*Position*
1.	Sarpanch of the Grama Panchayat	Chairman
2.	The Best Head of Self-Help Group of Watershed Committee, DWCRA, W.U.A.S., Vana Samrakshana,	Chairman
3.	Leaders of All Self-Help Groups and Officers at Village Level	Members
4.	Village Development Officer/ Village Administrative Officer/ Village Executive Officer	Convener

Objectives of Water Conservation Mission

a) To develop a draft vision for conserving and judicious use of water in the State.

b) To formulate effective plans and methods for conserving water.

c) To formulate a time-bound action plan for conservation of water.

d) To implement the conservation and use of water with the coordination of all functionally related departments.

e) To carryout water conservation programmes economically.

f) To encourage local people's part in water conservation.

g) To monitor and assess continuously the water-conservation programmes

h) To obtain people's views and suggestions on the ways, means and methods in respect to water conservation.

The Neeru-Meeru Programme is one of a significant State sponsored popular actions in conserving and using of water. It is an important activity for the present and for infinite period of time and this programme may be reckoned as a very substantial and significant component and contribution towards VISION-2020. Achievement in many of the sectors of development depends upon water as a basic resource. With inadequacy of water for domestic and agricultural and industrial purposes, it would be almost impossible and an Herculean task in realizing VISION-2020.

Conservation of rainwater by several means and measures has been there in other states in India at the local community level and regional level. Andhra Pradesh is the only State in India may be a pioneer state especially in taking up on massive scale this programme. On one hand it is education to the farmers, warning them and creating in them seriousness in conserving water, and judicious application of water for irrigation and other purposes, taking to new kind of technology in conserving and using water and at the same time, encouraging the use of indigenous or the native practices of water conservation on the part of the farmers.

It is really imaginative and extremely commendable the present and futuristic package of programmes of development such as, Vision-2020, Janmabhoomi, Neeru-Meeru, conceived, diligently, earnestly pursued, guided and administered by the Hon'ble Chief Minister of Andhra Pradesh Nara Chandrababu Naidu. We may say, Janmabhoomi and Neeru-Meeru may be considered as contributory factors to some extent in realizing Vision-2020. Here, in Neeru-Meeru, we have conception, planning and action.

Though the communities for centuries have been managing the local water system, the present movement augments, standardizes and regulates the system of water resource management. As water is very basic commodity for existence, people have taken this programme very seriously.

We have reached such a desperate point where you cannot delay and postpone. The situation will become more deplorable. It needs immediate attention. The attention in action and mode of the action that is being taken-up now is in the right and desirable direction. Action programme right from the State level down to the village level is very clearly delineated. The action flows from apex level to the ground level and also moves from ground level to the apex level in a systematic way. Two-way communication.

Neeru-Meeru programme is a concerted, coordinated community action with stimulus, material and financial assistance provided by the Government with the spontaneous involvement of people's representatives and official machinery in the massive desilting of lakes and ponds in the 3rd Round of Neeru-Meeru. Perhaps this is the first time in the history of the State even in India and of the world wherein simultaneous action on the part of the thousands of communities all over the state is carried on in order to conserve rainwater.

4

OPERATIONAL MEANS AND METHODS IN HARVESTING AND CONSERVING RAINWATER

The Groundwater Department of Andhra Pradesh has provided the following guidelines to harvest and conserve the rainwater.

I. Introduction

Groundwater is an important source of water supply throughout the year. Its use in irrigation, industries, drinking both in Municipalities and rural areas continues to increase. The dependence on groundwater is increasing rapidly over the past two decades, especially, due to urbanization and industrialization and extensive use in irrigation/agriculture. Added to the uses above, the scanty and erratic rainfall is resulting in reduction in storage in surface reservoirs. The demand is so high that the ground water levels are getting depleted resulting in drying up of dug wells and bore wells in several places. Apart from this, sealing of permeable soil zone is gradually increasing due to construction activities thereby resulting in reduction of area for percolation of rainwater into the sub-surface and increase in surface runoff. Therefore, there is an urgent need to take up rainwater conservation/ harvesting methods to the extent possible on a large scale which would subsequently help to recharge and maintain groundwater balance.

Artificial recharge is the process of augmenting the natural infiltration of rainwater into the underground geological formation by some artificial methods. As the main source of groundwater recharge is rainfall, methods are suggested to collect and store run off water from roof tops of the buildings, road surfaces, municipal parks, school play grounds, open lands and run off water flowing in the natural streams etc., for artificial recharge. The choice of any particular method is governed by local geological, topographical, geomorphological, structural, hydro-geological conditions and ultimate water use. The State Groundwater Department suggested simple, low cost rainwater harvesting methods. The department has rendered the technical guidance necessary for location of rainwater harvesting structures. In addition, the details of the structures to be implemented by various organizations, the design and performance, guidelines for selection of structure, precautions to be followed during construction are to be adhered strictly.

II. Guidelines for Selection of Recharge Structures:

- Recharge structures should be designed and constructed in favourable geological conditions i.e., permeable soils followed by morrum etc. The structures should not be taken up in impervious clayey soils, rock and steep sloppy areas.
- Recharge structures should be preferred for recharging to depleted aquifers with deep water table. They should not be taken up in the shallow water table areas. The depth to water level should not be less than 5 to 6 m. in post monsoon period.
- Recharge structures should be taken up with unpolluted surface water only. Adequate precautions should be taken to prevent entry of polluted urban surface runoff water, sewerage water into recharge structures.
- Recharge structures should be planned and taken up in areas experiencing intensive ground water development for various uses and they need not be taken up in areas where groundwater development is negligible.

- All existing kuntas and tanks in and around the urban agglomeration areas are to be protected against encroachments and should be converted as percolation ponds and tanks. The polluted drainage and other industrial pollutants should not be allowed to let into these tanks.
- Groundwater recharge through shafts is preferable in steep slope areas.

III. Methods of Artificial Recharge:

The Groundwater Department has rendered the technical guidance for location of Rainwater Harvesting Structures for collection of roof top water and road top water through recharge pits/ trenches, abandoned wells/bore-wells for recharging groundwater. All these measures are to be taken up in residential zones with restricted open areas. There still lies scope for harvesting of surface runoff water flowing in the natural stream before entering the municipal zone. Structures like gully plugs, rock fill dams, check dams garbion structures, contour trenches and contour bunding etc., are the possible measures for impounding rainfall runoff water and recharge to groundwater table.

Category	*Broad classification and areas*	*Feasible Rainwater Harvesting Structures*
I.	Residential zones with restricted open areas (Independent houses, apartments, institutions, etc.,)	Pits, Trenches, Shafts, dried up dug wells, bore wells, storage sumps, recharge pit, etc.,
II.	Large Open areas, Industries, Cantonment Areas	Gully Plugs, rock fill dams, check dams, continuous contour trenches, staggered contour trenches & recharge pits for rainwater harvesting from roof tops etc.

IV. Design Aspects of Recharge Structures

The number, type and dimensions of recharge structures are to be designed as per site-specific requirements and available water source. The natural recharge through soil due to rainfall takes place first by absorption of the water up to its capacity and vertical drainage from the moist soil. The infiltration capacity of the highly permeable soils would be around 2 cm/hr. But beneath the soil occurs disintegrated rocks generally called as morrum. The intake capacity of water in morrum is found to be very high around 20 cm/hr (as per test results). This principle is the basis of the design of recharge pits. Roof water is diverted into the recharge pits for subsequent percolation towards groundwater table. The volume of the voids in the filter media is taken as one third of the volume of pit and this is designed to match with collection of rainwater for 20 mm rainfall event. The high rate of percolation through morrum layers makes it possible to take up recharge pits in a small area to compensate for loss of natural recharge to the soil covered by built up areas.

Category-I

Commonly runoff water from rooftops is let off into the drain canals. Instead of this, the outlets can be connected through a pipe to a storage tank and let into trenches/pits filled with filter media or existing open wells/bore wells etc., to serve as recharge points.

a) Recharge through Pits

A minimum of 6 Cum. Volume of recharge pit/trench is recommended for a catchment area of 100 Sq.M. and multiples thereof for large areas. Pits are dug deeper and away from the building foundations where the soil is more compressible. Commonly pits with 1.0 m dia and 2 to 3 metres depth are recommended.

Actually, the rainwater harvesting process consists of three stages (i) collection of rainwater, (ii) filtering of rainwater through a filter media and (iii) percolation of rainwater into the ground.

b) Recharge by Water Spreading and Pit Method.

This method is applicable to the houses having larger plain areas with high permeable soils. The run off water from the rooftop can be diverted into the bare soil or garden in the premises of households. Apart from this a longitudinal trench of 1.00 to 1.5 m depth with a width of 0.50 to 1.0 m may be dug and filled with well-rounded pebbles, gravel and sand in order to store excess run off water during rainy days that eventually percolate. The topsoil may be loosened before monsoon for better recharge.

c) Recharge through Shafts

Groundwater recharge through shafts is preferable in the steep, slope areas because water spreading and pits might create springs or water oozing in the neighbouring houses located on the down slope. The shafts are deep pits with a width of 1 m. length of 2 m. and depth of 10 to 15 m. preferably terminating above the aquifer level. The shafts may be cased or uncased near the top layers but are rock filled with permeable soil, which facilitates more effective and faster percolation and mitigation of biological and chemical pollutions. Shaft construction is rather expensive.

d) Recharge through Wells:

Recharge through wells involves direct introduction of rainwater through a settling sump to the underground formation. These wells are commonly used both as production as well as recharge wells. The rainwater from the rooftops can be used directly for washing and other usages. Industries, multistoried residential buildings and government organizations can implement this method as they depend mostly upon groundwater sources. The bore wells used for groundwater drawal can also be used for recharge with a valve control between the storage tank/setting pits and bore well.

e) Recharge through Bore wells

Because of severe depletion of groundwater levels many of

the open and shallow bore wells have dried up. Therefore, the people are discarding these wells and preferring deeper bore wells adjacent to these dried up wells. These dried up wells can be utilized as recharge wells by connecting them to the water outlet pipes from the rooftops. A pit can be constructed around the bore or adjacent to the bore and roof water can be diverted into the pit. Slotted pipe with coir pack has to be used so that the sand and silt will not enter the slots.

f) Storage Sump and Recharge Pit

In independent houses and apartments where there is sufficient open place, we can have recharge pit/trench with storage sump for rainwater harvesting and storage. Excess rainwater after filling the sump shall be conveyed to the recharge pit for groundwater recharge, like this, the rainwater collections may continue for direct use for a period of 4 to 5 days. In 100 Sq.M rooftop area, apart from 2 Cum. Sump, a pit/trench of 6 Cum. is to be constructed. Recharge of rainwater of 55,000 lts. Per year could take place which is sufficient for 5 members for a period of 100 days. Water stored in the sump could serve day-to-day requirements.

In places where there is hard rock or clayey soil within 2 m. depth from ground level, these pits are not useful because of their non-permeable nature. In such places, only storage sump of 4 Cum. Capacity is used.

g) Recharge in the Apartment Areas

The roof of apartments are drained by several pipes. The water drained by some pipes can be used for growing garden crops. The remaining pipes can be connected to recharge pits or trenches located in the premises. The existing bore well can also be recharged.

h) Recharge of Waste Water near the Hand Pumps Through Pit

The water which goes waste near the drinking water hand pumps can be diverted into recharge pits. But washing of clothes and cleaning of utensils is to be restricted at the platform round the hand pumps. The advantages of diverting the wastewater near the hand pumps are (i) Recharge, (ii) Surroundings will be kept clean and (iii) Avoidance of mosquito problem.

i) Street Recharge Pits and Trenches

The storm run off generated within an area can be utilized for recharging by diverting it into suitably designed structures near pavements, parking plots, municipal parks, play ground, stadiums, air ports etc., and earmarking some open places exclusively for the purpose. Collection of storm run off into local depressions, unused tanks can serve temporary storage of water and subsequent infiltration and recharge.

The design of recharge structures has to be accomplished with sufficient number of recharge pits and trenches filled with gravel. The location of these recharge structures should be close to the place where storm run off water is collected posing problem for traffic and disposal. Pavements can be utilized for collecting road run off and for recharging groundwater. An infiltration trench of 0.5 m. wide and depth of 1 to 1.5 m. back filled with porous material and large perforated pipe to distribute storm run off rapidly and to hold more water serves as a best recharge facility. Infiltration pits of 1 m. dia and 2 to 3 m. depth can also be taken up along the street corners and connected to trench. These structures are to be taken up in clean environments only.

Category-II

Large areas owned by Educational Institutes, organizations are endowed with clear-cut drainage courses and vacant land. Rain water harvesting in vacant land can be achieved by urban forestry, forestry with broad furrow method, continuous contour trenches, staggered trenches, whereas the runoff flowing in the stream courses can be detained at several locations by constructing bunds of small depths to detain water flow and spread over large stream channel section area to facilitate groundwater recharge. These structures, apart from being low cost variety, are very effective in the sense that runoff water generated on many of the rainy days can be detained and allowed to percolate. These structures are classified as gully plugs, rock fill dams, check dams depending on the size of the structure and its location in the catchment.

a) Gully plugs are to be constructed across the first order streams with less than one metre width and half metre height. Stone pebbles and earth are used in the construction. If these materials are not available, plastic bags filled with sand can be heaped to form gully plug. Several gully plugs can be constructed along the stream at such interval that the streambed drops by 05 m. to 1.0 m. in between.

b) Rock fill dams are to be constructed across the 2nd order streams with width around 2 m. and depth of 0.5 m. locally available large boulders are to be used to withstand speed of the flowing water. To fill up the gap between the boulders smaller size stones as well as earth material can be used to prevent leakage of water.

c) Check dams are to be constructed across the streams having width exceeding 3.0 m. and depth of one metre and more. The catchment area of such streams could be 0.25 sq. km. To 2.00 sq. km. All the rainfall incident in the catchment of the streams should not be impounded like irrigation tanks so that the riparian rights are not infringed and also that submergence problems are minimized. Therefore, check dams are to be constructed across the streambed up to a height of 1.0m. All the excess stream flow would be passing over the top of the check dam. The construction material comprises of C.R. masonry of first sort, laid over plain cement concrete foundation. On either side of the check dam abutting the streamsides, there shall be wing walls with C.R. masonry laid on P.C.C. rough stone paving is essential on either side of the stream to maintain its section intact. Earthen bund leads with rough stone pitching may be provided on either side, if the site condition requires. The check dams are to be preferably located upstream of bore wells/ open wells supplying water to the municipalities.

d) Sunken ponds are suitable to impound surface runoff over flat and gently slopping terrains. Sunken ponds are formed by excavating and removal of soil cover and part of morrum to create thereby a storage space and the recharge to groundwater made possible thorough weathered rock at a faster pace of dissipation. Depending on the site situation about 5 x 5 m. size or 3 x 8 m. size pond with 3 to 5 m. depth may be made. The edges of the pond may be prevented from collapsing by stone pitching. Selection of suitable site is an important phase in the planning and construction of a pond.

   The site selected should ensure that the catchment is neither too small nor too big. Too small catchment may not contribute sufficient water to the pond while too big a catchment may result in rapid siltation of the pond. Catchments with well-protected conservation measures will contribute less silt to the ponds. Other aspects like area with minimum undulations and free from soil problems like salinity / alkalinity and stoniness are to be considered in selection of pond site. For the drainage of excess water from the pond, emergency spill ways/ outlets are to be provided. The ponds may be provided with controlled inlets of the chute spillway type so that gullying does not occur at the inlet portion. The capacity of the inlet should be sufficient and suitable.

e) **Continuous Controur Trenches and Staggered Trenches**

If the large areas endowed with existence of hillocks the runoff from such hillocks and hill slopes rainwater harvesting can be done by constructing CCTs or STs. Forest plantations can be clubbed with the programme of CCTs.

f) Percolation Tanks

The Irrigation Department have already issued a manual of construction of percolation tanks.

V. Computation of Additional Recharge to Groundwater

Roof top collection and diversion to recharge pit factors considered for 100 sq.m individual house and 500 sq.m. apartments.

- Roof top area.
- Rainfall 20 mm in single event.
- Total annual rainfall 778 mm.
- Percent rainfall considered for harvesting is 70% of annual rainfall i.e., 555 mm.

Sl.No.	*Description*	*Individual Houses*	*Apartments*
1.	Roof Top area	100 Sq. M.	500 Sq. M.
2.	Available rooftop water for 20 mm. Rainfall.	2.0 Cum.	10.0 Cum.
3.	Available rooftop water for additional recharge per annum @ 70% of total annual rainfall.	55 Cum.	275 Cum.
4.	Available rooftop water for additional recharge from 2000 houses of 10 Sq. M. each	1,10,000 Cum.	

If two thousand such units are constructed, the additional recharge to groundwater can meet the requirements of 2,000 families for 100 days.

VI. Cost of the Recharge Pits/Trenches

The volume and estimated cost of recharge pit / trench for different rooftop/catchment areas are furnished hereunder.

Sl.No.	*Rooftop/catchment area in Sq.M.*	*Volume of recharge Cum.*	*Estimated Cost Rs.*
1.	40	2.5	2,000
2.	100	6.0	4,500 (Rs. 750/- per Cum)
3.	500	30.0	25,000/-

VII. Advantages of Rainwater Harvesting

- Build up in groundwater levels.
- Rejuvenation of dried up wells.
- Improvement to the yields of wells.
- Improvement in the quality of groundwater through dilution.
- Helps in reducing incidation of roads and flood hazard.
- Saves future generations from water scarcity problem.
- Collection of rooftop water into a sump and recharge pit facilitates direct use of rainwater apart from recharge to groundwater. This helps in reducing the water bill and huge investments or purchase of water through tankers in scarcity areas.
- The structures recommended for rainwater harvesting are simple, economical and eco-friendly.

VIII. Precautions to be Followed while selecting & Constructing the Recharge Structure

A). In case of collection of rooftop & road top water.

i) To clear off doubt whether the rocky layer beneath the soil is permeable or not, it is advisable to dig a pit

1x1x1.5 m. deep and fill up with water. If the water seeps over a day or two, it is feasible to go for recharge structures.

ii) Recharge structures are not required in shallow water table zones, i.e., the water level less than 5 m. in November.

iii) Commonly runoff water from rooftops are let off into the drains. Instead of this the outlets can be connected through a pipe to a storage tank and let into gravel filled trenches/pits, existing open wells/bore wells etc., to serve as recharge points.

iv) Recharge water should be clean and free from contamination. Urban surface run off water flowing on roads with lot of sediment load and pollutants should not be allowed for direct recharge.

v) While recharging through open shafts/wells the source water is to be sent through a silt filtering pit/silt-settling chamber.

vi) While harvesting road top water, a filter pack comprising of layered filter media with a grating may be introduced in the vent from catch pit to recharge pit.

vii) The recharge pit/trench is to be provided with brick lining of 45 cm. Height at the top 30 cm. Below ground level and 15 cm. Above gravel level to debar entry of waste material into the structure. The height of wall can be more if loose soils are so deep.

viii) The lined portion of the pit can be left empty to accommodate more water. If needed, an additional precaution with protective porous concrete covers or wire mesh may be provided as per site requirements.

ix) Avoid constructing the recharge structures near dustbins, toilets, solid waste dumps.

x) Road top rainwater recharge structures are to be planned and taken up cautiously in unpolluted and hygienic catchment areas only.

xi) In order to arrest impact of flow on filter media a splash pad is to be placed on top of the filter media.

xii) The earth material excavated for making a pit/trench should not be allowed to be left near the structure. The excavated material should be carried away and dumped somewhere else.

xiii) Roof to be kept clean by end of May.

xiv) The first rainwater not to be diverted to pit.

xv) Brick pieces are not to be used as layer in the pit.

xvi) Domestic sewerage waters are not to be utilized unless treated depending upon local conditions.

B). In case of storm runoff and stream courses

- Many existing stream courses are either cut off or diverted by rapid construction activity in and around the city. The storm runoff may be diverted into the nearest tanks or depressions which will create recharge. The collection of storm run off in unused tanks can serve for temporary storage.
- Desilting of the streams approaching the reservoirs & tanks to facilitate accumulation of run off water.
- Domestic sewerage waters can be reclaimed after soil aquifer treatment depending upon local conditions, quality of water and also feasibility.
- Adequate precautions for not letting sewage and effluents into the stream courses are to be taken.
- Roof top collection with filter media need not be resorted in large areas since it is the costliest than rainwater harvesting structures on watershed approach such as rock fill dams, check dams, etc.

Conclusion

Groundwater exploitation is inevitable in urban areas. But the groundwater potential is getting reduced due to urbanization resulting in over-exploitation. Hence, a strategy to implement the ground water recharge, in a major way, need to be launched with concerted efforts by various Government and Non-Government agencies and public at large to buildup the water table and make the groundwater resource a reliable and sustainable source.

The successful implementation requires people's participation and acceptance. Support and participation for which canvassing through pamphlets in English, Telugu and Urdu languages, organizing of similar workshops at district and mandal levels and through audio-visual publicity are being carried on. Accordingly, technical guidance was given by conducting gramsabhas and workshops during Janmabhoomi. Resident welfare associations, builders associations and contractors were also trained. At district level, Deputy Director, Groundwater Department will provide technical guidance.

In each Municipality concerned Municipal Engineer/town planning officer etc., will coordinate and guide the rainwater harvesting activity and also technical assistance. The site selection by either Engineer/Geologist/Volunteer self help group persons will be in a report form with diagrams. This will give rational approach to arrive at the sizes of the structures recommended.

5

INTEGRATED APPROACH TO WATER SUPPLY AND SANITATION MANAGEMENT

While focusing attention on harvesting and conserving rainwater and going in for various devices for percolation of rainwater in order to have rise of groundwater table, we may have to pay attention to the day-to-day use of water. Further, environmental sanitation is closely associated with the availability and use of water. Conserving water is one thing, utilizing and managing the use is another. The following pages outline an integrated approach to water supply and sanitation management.

I. Water supply and sanitation and their management are an integral part of a rural community and they cannot be isolated from the culture or way of life of a people. An integrated approach to WSS management raises a series of questions before one can think of what the approach should be. Some of the questions are:

i) What are the conditions and problems prevalent in a rural community with respect to WSS?

- the physical nature of the problems, cluster, linear, dispersed type of dwellings
- nature of the soil
- sources, adequacy, distance, and means of supply, storage and use of water

- size of population, its ethnic and class structure and social stratification
- sanitary conditions.

ii) What is the present nature and level of WSS in the community?

iii) What is the community's perception of sanitation?

iv) What do they consider as insanitary?

v) The causes they attribute to insanitation?

vi) What is their level of awareness of insanitation?

vii) What have they done to improve sanitary condition?

viii) Assuming that the people are aware of sanitary problems, what are the reasons for their not alleviating the situation?

ix) How does the community organize and manage WSS?

x) What are the physical, economic, social, technological, organizational and managerial requirements to ensure a better/ satisfactory level of WSS?

xi) What are the kinds of resources available within the community?

xii) What are the kinds of resources that need come from outside?

xiii) What are the external agencies that are to provide/ facilitate with the requisite resources?

xiv) In what manner have the WSS activities been carried out by the development agencies thus far?

xv) What is the experience and attitude of the residents of the community vis-à-vis the WSS activities of the development agencies?

xvi) What is the level and nature of integration of WSS activities that obtains now?

xvii) What are the missing links? Where does the lacuna lie?

II. Keeping in view the ensuring of general health and welfare of the community through WSS, what kind of an integrated approach is necessary?

III. The elements in the integrated approach:

i) Physical: housing, use of the precincts of the house, cattle shed, kitchen, backyard, disposal of waste, the environs, the source, supply, protection, adequacy and use of water, and its disposal.

ii) Technological: improvements/innovations and their maintenance in respect to WSS.

iii) Economic: the cost of improvement, maintenance, the local resources, the anticipated external support, the individual/ community affordability

iv) Cultural: values attached to WSS, habits of people in the use of water, defecation and waste disposal, attitude towards environmental sanitation and level of tolerance to insanitary conditions.

v) Organizational: who will organize and manage the WSS activities at the community level? Who from external agencies?

IV. What should be integrated at the community level?

- needs
- interest
- initiative
- activities
- groups
- resources
- leadership

V. What is to be integrated at the external agencies level? How to integrate and the problems of coordination?

- programme planning
- programme implementation
- programme evaluation

VI. The suggested approach is a holistic, integral, composite one linking physical, technological and institutional components: housing – environs – water – sanitation – toilets – waste disposal – the user.

VII. The organization and management of WSS at the community level is dependent upon and influenced by the following aspects of the community:

i) Awareness

ii) Pressure of the need

iii) Resources – material, human

iv) Composition of the group

v) Size of the group

vi) Social structure

vii) Structure of power and authority

viii) Kind and strength of existing organizations / institutions in the community

ix) The kind and strength of local – institutional leadership

x) The degree of influence from outside the community

xi) Channels and pattern of inward and outward communication

xii) Cultural orientations, values, attitudes of people towards sanitation, use of water and maintenance

xiii) Economic level and affordability

xiv) Occupations and professions of the groups.

In this context it may be relevant to briefly look into community organization the concept, objectives, benefits and some of the organizations at the rural community level. We may remember that an existing organization may be utilized for a specific new activity. An organized community, in terms of groups, institutions, functions and responsibility is a machinery that may be used for diverse purposes. It does not deny the need for a specific organization or special organizing for a specific activity. The thrust of the question is on organizing the community and revitalizing the existing institutional infrastructure at the rural community level.

(i) *Community Organization*[1]

It is important for a worker to have a complete understanding about the community with which he works. By making a sociogram of the community, he can work out the pattern of communication and then understand who influences whom and to what extent. The question is often raised as to how best agency workers can assist the people in dealing with recalcitrant individuals and groups whose sole purpose is to block progress. This needs a careful examination and it brings us to the question of skills involved in working with groups and communities. The worker has to understand what exactly is the cause and the real cause may be different from what appears on the surface. The worker may have preconceived notions. He can look for the answer by studying the power structure within the community and the vested interests it upholds. It has also its processes such as decision-making, communication, social and cultural linkage and boundary maintenance. A social compass would provide valuable guidance to the extension worker and if he understands the elements and processes operating in it, he will very easily map out the interrelations of various factors. The components of the social compass comprising of such things as community, governmental structures, education, religion, family, social class, health, communication, etc., can be analyzed in terms of its elements and processes.

Community organization is a method by which an individual is influenced through the group in which he works. This group provides him the "fields" and it is by understanding the "field forces" that affiliations and alignments of individual members are identified and interpreted.

(ii) *Community Concepts*

The word community signifies different things to different

people according to their interpretation. In some places ethnicity and religion may come to the mind whereas in other countries various social communities are mentioned. Community refers to a group of people inhabiting a given geographical area and having some kind of common activities or some degree of common life, irrespective of their social, religious or social differences. It is not confined to any of the various restricted fields of community life on the basis of religion, caste, race, language or profession but one that envelops the whole life of the whole community.

(iii) *Definition*

Community organization has been defined as a process initiated to bring about and maintain an adjustment between social welfare needs and social welfare resources in a given geographical area. As a disciplined method "community organization seeks to bring about a social climate in which it is easier to resolve group conflicts and initiate cooperative activity for the common good of the community".

Community organization work concentrates its efforts in narrowing down the areas of conflict and enlarging the areas of cooperation. In short, the negative and destructive aspects of competition is sought to be replaced by the positive and constructive aspects of cooperation.

(iv) *Central Objective*

The objective of "community organization" as a method of social work activity is, one of helping the communities to recognize and realize their needs and aspirations. First, there has to be an awareness about their problems and secondly there must be willingness to work together towards these common objectives.

In any area, there will be problems of some sort and resources both in men and materials and "community organization" seeks to rouse the latter for the solution of the former. There is invariably a gap between what facilities a community has and what it would like to have, in other words, between achievements and aspiration. It is the task of "community organization" to narrow down and bridge this gap between social welfare needs and social welfare resources of a community.

(v) *Specific Objectives*

(a) *To obtain consciousness of community:* For harmony and progress of the community, a sense of "we" feeling, a sense of belongingness is to be fostered among the members of a given community. Such a sense of "we" feeling and interrelatedness make the members feel that they constitute a unit by themselves, a social entity as distinct from other communities. Just as self-consciousness is essential for the individual so its importance to the community. The process of integration rests primarily upon definite self-consciousness of the community.

(b) *To Satisfy unmet needs:* Common needs which individuals and groups are unable to satisfy for themselves could be met by the collective action of the community. It may be in any sphere, political, economic, social or cultural. Collective action is the basis for community integration and community mobilization. Determination of the needs of the community is therefore one of the first steps.

(c) *To obtain social participation as a means to socialization:* The ultimate goal of all human association is the development of better personalities by the individuals concerned. A community is composed of various groups in which its people associate. One of the chief handicaps to community action is the number of families and individuals who do not belong to any formal organization, who live a relatively isolated social life associating with their own families and neighbours. The best index of the socialization of the members of a community is the degree of their participation in its organizations.

(d) *To obtain social control:* Community organization is to obtain social control through community spirit and loyalty. Social control becomes possible by the development of community spirit, by loyalty to the community and by symbols which express the common objective of community activity. Sociologists have called these three factors – morale, collective representations and *esprit de corps* (common spirit pervading the group).

(e) *To Coordinate groups and activities:* In a given community there may be several interest groups and their interests and activities may come in conflict. Community organization is necessary in order to prevent conflict and promote efficiency, cooperation and coordination. This is important in a small community. Proper adjustments are necessary. Efficiency may be promoted and ends attained if coordination can be carried out to the point of active cooperation.

(f) *To prevent the community from the introduction of undesirable influences and conditions:* It is not enough to promote community betterment from within, for the community must be able to defend itself from the aggression of undesirable influences. Many a community has found that it can work together for the elimination of a drinking place or any other nuisance to the physical and social health of the community.

(g) *To cooperate with other communities and agencies to obtain common needs:* Frequently, the community is too small a unit to achieve certain desired ends on its own. To obtain them, it is necessary to cooperate with neighbouring communities to obtain a bus line, water facilities, schools, colleges, etc.

(h) *To establish a means of obtaining consensus:* As for having their needs accomplished, it is easily done by coming to a common understanding. In a small rural community, it is obtained by gradual crystallization of public opinion through casual conversation at any shop or public place where people gather usually. Sometimes hearsay, gossiping distort the facts and promote disagreement rather than consensus.

(i) *To develop leadership:* Leadership for any group or collective activity is a must. Potential leaders in the community are to be identified, their talent recognized and developed. Local initiative and local leadership are essential for building up a self-reliant and self-confident community. It is not a question of spoon-feeding, the external agency alone functioning, but creating opportunities so that the local leadership is fully developed and employed for the growth of the community.

Benefits of Community Organization

(a) Group thinking and common good,

(b) Division of labour and responsibility,

(c) Recognition of individual merit,

(d) Community work, and

(e) Group efforts are more effective than individual efforts.

A Measure of Community Organization

Community organization should not be conceived as a relationship which can be set up and which can be abolished. It is rather a process of establishing relationships which will always be in a state of becoming analogous to the growth of personality or character in the individual. One measure of community organization is the degree to which organizations and interests are willing to cooperate in activities or objectives for the betterment of the common welfare, for which they are not primarily responsible and in which others will take the lead.

Another measure is the ability to have competition in politics or business without conflict and the ability to discuss matters with a division of opinion but with tolerance and with united support for the objectives sought.

The degree of socialization of the community is the best measure of its organization. The better a community is organized the more it serves the needs not only of its adult individuals but also of its potential members.

It has been very well summarized that the goal of community organization is enlisting everyone in the community activities so that each individual shall register effectively, that is, shall achieve self-expression and status in community service.

From a behaviouristic standpoint the measure of community organization is the degree to which the members, individuals or groups of the community act collectively for common welfare.

Statutory and non-statutory organizations like Village Panchayats, cooperative societies, special interest groups like DWACRA, Self Help Groups, Vana Samrakshana Samithis, Vidya Committees, Water Users Associations, Water Shed Development Committees etc., constitute some organizations at the rural community level.

Facilitating Community Organisation[2]

A generic description of the process of facilitating community organization in a population group is depicted in Fig.1. Each step in the critical pathway is needed for achieving stated objectives.

- *Meeting population leaders*: The critical entry point for the worker at which the process of confidence building begins.
- *Gathering information (community diagnosis)*: Demographic, socio-cultural, topographic, and health data may all form a part of the information gathered. Information also serves to broaden dialogue and include women.
- *Identifying existing structures*: organizations capable of serving as vehicles of community development are

identified and the worker seeks to strengthen, mobilize and coordinate them for the subsequent steps. Most communities present several candidate organizations, such as councils of elders, development committees, or saving and loan associations.

- *Selecting priority problems*: The worker assists the new organized group to agree on a set of problems of greatest importance to the population. Community diagnosis also helps to define these problems.
- *Choosing one problem to work on*: From the problem set the group selects the one to attach first of all. Usually the problem chosen will be the most pressing to the dominant faction or the most amenable to local solution.
- *Informing the people about the problem*: By means of explanation, demonstration, and auxiliary materials the workers and others seek to raise the level of knowledge of, and sensitivity to, the problem and its ramifications.
- *Assessing local resources*: Money, labour, materials, and technical expertise may all be needed to adequately address the problem selected. The extent to which they can be obtained locally is ascertained.
- *Setting staged objectives*: The solution to the problem, whatever it may be, can usually be divided into several stages and to each attached a concrete objective, a time for achieving it, and a sense of what it takes in labour, materials, and expertise to reach it.
- *Setting responsibilities and time schedules*: The staged objectives, attached time frames, and resources requirements, are identified with individuals and groups within the population, to whom are given the responsibilities for execution.
- *Implementation*

- *Evaluation*: Achievements are matched against objectives. Problems are identified as well as success and used as platforms for launching a new critical pathway.

It may be noted that "with each successful organized community effort the cooperative and collaborative attitudes and practices of the community are broadened and deepened. Likewise, unsuccessful efforts have profound demoralizing effects".

FIGURE 1: THE GENERIC PROCESS OF FACILITATING COMMUNITY ORGANIZATON: A CRITICAL PATHWAY

Each step is necessary to achieve objectives

Meeting Population Leaders

Gathering Information ↓

Identifying Existing Structures ↓

Selecting Priority Problems ↓

Choosing One Problem To Work On ↓

Informing The People About The Problem ↓

Assessing Local Resources ↓

Setting Staged Objectives ↓

Setting Responsibilities And Time Schedules ↓

Implementation ↓

Evaluation Of Results ↓

Rationale

The appropriateness of the community organization process to water and sanitation programmes resides in two conditions for the success of these programmes:

- If water supply and sanitation facilitates are to function properly they must be maintained and repaired in a timely and correct manner. Maintenance and repair can be assured in most rural communities of developing countries only by an organized and trained constituency.
- If the health and social benefits of improved water supply and sanitation facilities are to be obtained, then the population must participate in an organized way to properly use and protect water, and to incorporate essential personal and domestic hygiene associated with excreta disposal, food handling, and infant and child care.

Maintenance and Repair of Facilities

The appalling rate of breakdown of water supply and sanitation facilities in rural areas of the developing world is well known. Few developing countries are able to provide sufficient numbers of maintenance personnel or the institutional and material support needed to maintain a widespread network of water supply and sanitary installations. Most water supply ministries are seriously hampered by shortages of trained personnel, lack of transport facilities, deficient material supplies and overly centralized organizations. Ministries of Health, the usual repositories of responsibility for sanitation, suffer even more in the usual case from these organizational maladies.

Responsibility must therefore, devolve upon communities themselves at least for the long-term maintenance and repair of facilities. Women must necessarily play important roles in this regard. The success of community maintenance programmes is dependent on how well communities are organized. Community organization is in turn conditioned by a number of other factors.

Achievement of Health and Social Benefits

Even if the water supply is safe and in working order, and the excreta disposal facility properly installed, a host of behavioural factors may intervene to mitigate potential health and social benefits.

In the case of water supply, factors associated with water drawing, transport, and storage may bring about contamination of the source or the household supply. Even more importantly, use of excreta disposal facilities needs to be reinforced by personal hygiene: hand-washing, bathing, and washing and protecting food after preparation. A sustained approach to these matters depends on organization of supportive community structures, and networks of peer support for behavioural change.

Conditions for Successful Facilitation of Community Organization

Ideally, community organization goes on without the influence of the worker or any other external assistance. In fact, population groups may quite properly be said to have their own intrinsic organization, i.e., the innate ability to deal with defined problems. Yet in practice normal social structures of many communities may have deteriorated and function very poorly at best when challenged with such matters as technological change. Colonial policy, leadership factors, urbanization, disease patterns, and traditional systems of assigning status have been cited among those correlated with variations in adaptive community behaviour.

For water and sanitation the conditions for successful facilitation of community organization need to be made more explicit. Four conditions appear relevant:

(a) Trained personnel

(b) Information about the community (community diagnosis)

(c) Integrated approaches among sectors

(d) Available technology and information

Trained Personnel

Personnel need to be armed with skills of three types: diagnostic, supportive, and evaluative. Diagnostic skills relate to the ability to delineate the communities within populations that represent the main social units. Leadership, decision-making and communication patterns, as well as the physical, demographic, economic and health characteristics of the population should be assessed. The worker should be enabled to gather data that will be immediately useful in guiding his/her action without spending undue time or effort in doing so. In essence what a worker needs to know is how he/she can operate within the resources and constraints of a given community to generate optimum participation in the planning, installation, maintenance, and repair of water supply and sanitation facilities. The categories of what information is needed are explained below.

Supportive skills extend from establishing trust to guiding and facilitating group discussion, and providing continuous support and empathy to individuals and social structures until they become independently viable. We may think of a list a number of subsidiary supportive functions:

- Creation of favourable group settings for community leadership to emerge and develop.
- Reconciliation and mediation of conflict or potential conflict, where there is a threat to continuity to community organization.
- Maintaining contact between community structures and their progress on the one hand and external government or agency action on the other.
- Acting as a resource link for village and external resources.
- Knowledge and appropriate use of technical back-up resources.
- Assurance of a continuity of surveillance and monitoring of water and sanitation facilities.

Evaluation skills pertains particularly to understanding the relevance of programme evaluation to continuous programme improvement and effectiveness, and to stimulating the participation of the people of the community in the design and application of evaluative procedures as a means of developing greater commitment on their part to the programme. Community workers should also be able to do simple process evaluation of events, activities, and the characteristics of local participation as well as simple outcome evaluation of change in knowledge and behaviour.

Information about the Community

By means of simple observations and selected interviews the community worker should be able to gather a modicum of data sufficient to make the diagnosis of community capacity to participate mentioned earlier. Data items selected from the following categories should be incorporated into a simple instrument feasible for use by community workers.

i). *Physical features of the community*

a. Topography

b. Types of soil

c. Water table

d. Types and location of water sources

e. Meteorological and climatic features

f. Availability of natural resources

ii). *Biologic features*

a. Water quality

b. Common disease vectors

c. Prevalent water and excreta-related diseases

iii). *Economic features*

a. Assets

b. Access to resources

c. Liabilities

d. Economic infrastructure

iv). *Demographic features*

a. Distributions

b. Ethnic composition

v). *Socio-cultural features*

a. Beliefs about water and excreta

b. Water use

c. Excretion patterns

d. Local skills

e. Existing local organizations

f. Relationships to outside organization

g. Leadership patterns

h. Communication patterns

i. Decision-making patterns

j. Previous self-help experience

Integration of Approach among Sectors

Specific reference to health workers has been deliberately avoided in the discussion above in order to emphasize the intersectoral nature of both water and sanitation programmes and the concern with facilitating community organization. Several sectors depend upon the success of community organization for the achievement of their objectives at the periphery of the population. Among them are agriculture, education, public works, and health. In a sense, facilitating community organization is the primary objective for each, more important in the long run than achieving any specific technical objective. If pumps are installed but break down, whom do they benefit? If latrines are constructed but are not maintained, who will use them? If a primary school is built but teachers refuse to live in the village, how will the children be taught?

A feeder road constructed but not maintained may not result in increased access to markets. If one worker undermines or fails to contribute to the success of the community organization others may not be able to achieve their objectives. Workers need to be able to refer "felt-needs" from one organization to another to another and to feel a sense of accomplishment in success achieved outside their particular sector. Figure 2 illustrates these relationships. As depicted, the community organization process is at the centre. Each community level worker contributes to the process while making specific technical inputs.

These inputs need to be made at appropriate points in the process. The figure indicates that the community organization is a dynamic cyclical process. Each successfully completed project in fact enhances the ability of individuals and social structures to work together and strengthens local ability to analyze and solve problems. With each turn of the cycle, as it were, the capacity of the community to absorb new technical inputs and face new adaptive challenges increases.

Thus a community at one point may be able to successfully complete and maintain an open well with a bucket and pulley and though what was learned in both a technical and organizational sense, be able to move on later to the installation and maintenance of a handpump, or even later to the maintenance of a feeder road.

These interrelationships need to be operationalised in joint intersectoral policy-making, joint middle level management, and joint training programmes.

Available Technology and Information

If community organization is to issue in successfully installed and maintained water supply and sanitation facilities, then community members must have access to adequate and appropriate technology, and information on how to use it. Personnel in public education, public works, health, agricultural, and other services may be the purveyors of both technology

Fig. 2. THE COMMUNITY ORGANIZATION PROCESS:
Community Organization: Planning -Evaluation

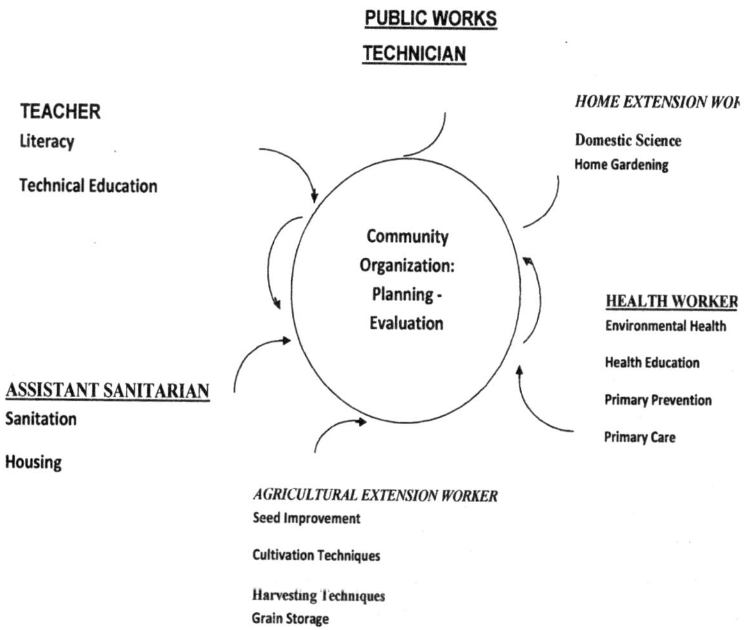

and information. The results of community diagnosis should indicate which of available technologies are economically affordable, socially acceptable and technically maintainable for both water supply and sanitation. Careful analysis of previous local experiences of organized problem solving, particularly the most recent experiences will help to determine whether the information and technology introduced at a particular point in the community organization cycle can be absorbed and adapted by the local organization.

A good case in point is that of villages in the South Cameroon, which at the onset of efforts to stimulate community organization installed temporary protection of springs using strictly local materials, but later were able to commit funds and labour to a more permanent protection. The introduction of more sophisticated technology close on the heels of the initial success was a key strategy. An important element in this transfer of technology was the introduction of a technique of splitting rock. The project chauffeur, who had learned the technique on trips to another region of the country, taught the villagers how to pour cold water over a heated rock. This technique facilitated spring box construction.

Information on the use of the many varieties of water supply and sanitation technology is unfortunately in short supply. Most available manuals are written in English and use language and images too technical for practical use by community members. Needed are manuals generously illustrated with non-technical drawings and a minimum of written explanation.

Greater emphasis needs to be placed on the development of demonstration models.

Outcomes of Successful Facilitation of Community Organization

Case histories drawn from Africa illustrate three major benefits of effectively stimulating or facilitating the local community organization process:

1. Reinforcement of local management capacities
2. Enhancement of participation
3. Increased probability of programme success

The first, taken from a village in the South Central Cameroon, illustrates the catalyzing effect or efforts to facilitate community organization on local ability to manage water and sanitation facilities. This village with about 1500 inhabitants in five hamlets, was one of four selected as pilot villages in the AID/OCEAC Public Health Training Project (1972-76). Four years prior to the onset of the project, this village had experienced a remarkable reversal of what had been a deteriorating relationship between the older and younger generations. Through the establishment of dialogue between the generations on a number of important issues, a reconciliation took place which the Project inherited.

A village health committee took shape readily in the central hamlet. Despite having no technical experiences with the protection of springs or the construction of latrines, the committee was able to organize the temporary protection of one spring and the construction of over 40 properly covered pit latrines. Later the spring was protected in a permanent manner, and plans were laid for pumping water from the spring to an elevated reservoir and thence by gravity to a community standpipe. In all, 43 pit latrines were constructed (out of 50 households) and in use. At a later date, the committee had calculated the costs of putting in similar systems in the other hamlets. The health committee had become a community water and sanitation planning board.

A second South Cameroon village presented in 1972 a distressing picture of a predominantly/dependent population (elderly or very young), widespread endemic disease, and virtual absence of water source protection or excreta disposal installations. Leadership was confined to the hands of a few clan leaders surrounding a rather weak elderly traditional chief.

Community leaders agreed to form a health committee, but spring protection and latrine construction progressed little beyond the talking stage, except for a single pit latrine at a clan leader's.

The committee, however, provided a forum in which many others besides village elders participated. Discussions of issues surrounding environmental protection, direct health education presentations, and the baseline medico-social survey, exposed many, including women and youth to new technology and new information. In the second year of the project, with continued efforts to strengthen the committee, other latrines began to appear and protection of four springs moved ahead apace. Facilitation of community organization had a salutary effect on both the characteristics and the extent of participation.

We may think of a framework for analyzing participation as an impact of the community organization process described above. In simplest terms, this framework cossets of two parts: (1) the *dimensions* of participation in terms of what it consists of, who participates and the characteristics (the how) of participation; and (2) the *context* of participation, comprising characteristics of both the *project* and the environment in which the project is implemented.

One could be sure of a steady reduction in the prevalence of intestinal parasites as community leaders took hold of the long-term management of latrine construction and use, albeit and the incentive of periodic vermifuges played an important role. In the same Cameroonian village reported earlier community leaders on the basis of their success with the management of the water supply, took advantage of a change in Cameroonian land tenure laws that allows for optional individual or communal ownership of land, to develop a community-wide landholding. The Malawi enhancement of organization at the community level was prelude to a successful long-term maintenance programme.

Thus whether one is speaking of health or social benefits or simply the proper functioning and use of water and sanitation facilities, improved organization at the community level appears to be an essential ingredient in the mix.

Conclusion

Experience to date points, therefore, to community organization and to whatever can be done to stimulate and enhance this process intrinsic to local population groups, as an imperative to the success of water supply and sanitation programmes among most rural populations of developing countries. Organized individuals and social structures appear to be essential for both the proper function of facilities and the achievement of health and social benefits. Certain conditions, however, are needed for facilitation of the process: *personnel* trained in community diagnostic supportive, and evaluative skills, *information* about the community to guide facilitation, integration of approach among services standing to benefit from successful community organization, and *technology and information* the continuous cycle of local development. Finally, successful facilitation of community organization produces in practice certain benefits: improved local management of water and sanitation facilities, enhanced participation by community members, and increased probability of project success in both an operational and an outcome sense.

REFERENCES

1. Setty, E.D. 1970, *Community Development and Extension in India"*, Gandhigram Rural Institute, Gandhigram, South India.
2. WASH Technical Report No. 7, June 1981, WASH Coordination and Information Centre, 1611, N. Kent Street, Room 1002, Arlington, VA 2209, USA.

6

PEOPLE'S IMAGE OF RURAL DEVELOPMENT: DEVELOPMENT IMPLICATIONS

Many things can be said about various approaches to rural development in developing countries. It is interesting to note that any approach to rural development in developing countries can be described as a process of change from the traditional ways of living of rural communities to progressive ways of living; as a method by which people can be assisted to develop themselves on their own capacity and resources; as a programme for accomplishing certain activities in fields concerning the welfare of the rural people.

All the efforts, under the nomenclature "rural development" can be categorized as a method, as a programme, as a movement and as a process. When viewed as a process, the objective of such efforts becomes the change that takes place in the people socially and psychologically. As such, the fact as to what people think about development, that is, their vision, imagination and their perception of the development activity becomes quite important.

As it is well known the whole attempt in rural development is to introduce something new in the life of the people or bring about some modification in the way of life of people. It amounts to a basic process of change, introducing change and people accepting the change and the change that is introduced is expected to be sustained and internalized by the individual and the group (Setty, 1988a). In view of such a change to be accepted and internalized by the community, the image of development based on the perception of the people as regards the change to be introduced assumes importance. In our discussion of the proposed change and the people accepting the change, two terms need to be understood clearly. These are, "perception" and "image".

Perception and Image

Perception is the phase of operations that takes place after receiving information but one that is well-nigh distinguishable from it. It refers basically to the manner in which a person experiences the world. Information receiving is only the beginning of the functioning of the part of the sub-system we refer to as the organism. Something must happen to the inputs as they are received, altered, and then sent along to other central information processing phases. The organization of inputs into an arrangement that has meaning for the person is the experience called perception.

What we perceive depends a great deal on not what is out there but what we ourselves bring to the situation–our own needs, drives, or predispositions. The process of selection is present, but this is very much a changing one; it is very creative and dynamic.

Our perception proceeds along established lines, along a rut that has been pretty well fixed in our past. In this sense, a biased perception of people and events has been called a stereo-type. Stereotypes is a term first used by Walter Lippmann, who wrote about them as being "pictures in people's heads". These pictures determine the perception of others in ways that may vary widely. The prejudgment of others based on their membership in certain groups is a common example, for instance, "Japanese are industrious and Americans are free-lancers".

Stereotypes are nothing but generalized impressions of others that become rigid and laden with negative values. They cause difficulties and misunderstanding when they lead us to ignore behaviour of others that is inconsistent with our expectations for them. They may be corrected by exposing them to reality, but finding that reality is often a problem. Learning what members of the target group think about themselves is one way of correcting our stereotypes about them, although we should recognize that self-percepts (auto-stereotypes) also have their biases.

As it is well known, the human organism is able to interpret and react to patterns of stimuli; it is able to extract information from the changing array of stimulation provided by the environment. As such, what becomes important for a planner or an agency engaged in developing a rural community is to consider, respect, value and learn from what people think about development. Kenneth Boulding defined this process as Image — "the sum of what we think we know and what makes us behave the way we do". Miller, Galanter and Pribram (1971) structured the concept of "image" for their major contribution on 'Plans and the Structure of Behaviour' (1960), with a recognition as to the fact that "the image (is a man's) knowledge of the world. His behaviour depends upon the image. Meaningful messages change the image".

Chadwick (1978) provides us with an explanation of planning behaviour in the most general sense. This is also the most basic explanation of planning in relation to the nature of a human-being and environment.

He starts his argument by pointing out how important communication between man and his fellow citizens and, between man and his environment is for daily survival. Information communicated to fellow men and the environment provides the basis to react against unfavourable conditions threatening man's existence. This knowledge of the world results in an image of it and ultimately in a plan to act upon expected threats. Since such plan depends on an image of the world, i.e., an accumulation of knowledge that the organism has learned about itself and its world including values as well as factual materials organized by concepts and relationships, it changes also the content of the image through action upon specific elements of this image. There is an interdependence of plan and image. Plans must be included in the image before we can decide which plans can be implemented. Changes in the image we hold of the world, result from plan implementation. Images of the world are, of course, part of our plans because they provide the basis to plan. According to Chadwick planning is a process, a process of human thought and action based upon that thought. This is a very general human activity.

Chadwick made a pertinent statement that planning is done by human-beings for human-beings. To understand this we must first refer to the limitations of the human mind insofar the storage of learned experiences, i.e., assimilated information, is concerned. Information that is screened by the human mind is evaluated against a set of parameters to sieve relevant from irrelevant or non-sense information. This process is, of course, again determined by previous experience that may be acquired or culturally inherited (i.e., through the school system presented as relevant to the society of this particular individual). Secondly, information may only be acceptable against a rather short term planning horizon: in other words daily needs may prevail over long term considerations in accepting information and thus building the image.

The human mind basically works through a process of abstraction, analogy and comparison. Abstracting from details and case-specific characteristics, an analogy between phenomena is accepted through comparison, and actions are based on plans that have yielded favourable results in the past when applied to these comparable problems, to tackle new problems.

But as it should commonly be known, human beings are not always and not in all situations acting in the described rational manner. Chadwick rightly pinpoints how "the discursive mind that is orderly, intellective, calculating, is the same mind that is intuitive, disorderly, non-intellective, incalculable". Thus, the human mind is capable of creating images that are not found in his environment.

Therefore, it is not necessary to go always by what people think since, their image of development may be at times, unrealistic, too narrow or too ambitious. However, when one looks at different components which together form people's image of development, one can visualize the fruits that the "image" may bear. The possible contents of people's image of development may be economic, social and political elements. The sources of image maturing and development may be (i). Information, (ii) Observation, (iii) Intuition, (iv) What people were told or promised to expect, (v) What people perceive as desirable in their life, occupation or profession, or a matter of social or political right, (vi) People's own defining of a decent, meaningful life, (vii) The successful/rewarding or unsuccessful/ unrewarding experiences of the immediate neighbourhood. Such images are then dependent on age, sex, knowledge levels, the kind of job people are engaged in as well as, social interaction.

We plan to meet common felt-needs. However, in reality, hardly any attention is paid to what is the image of development on the part of the people. Thus, there is always a gap between what people got and the shape in which they got. The usual tendency of the people is to simply accept whatever comes forth from the development agency or the change agent. They may accept such things with reluctance, but they may not be happy about them. Seldom do they express their dissent. Seldom does the agency attempt to go indepth to find as to what people really want, what is their image of growth and development. The vast majority of rural people still constitute to some extent, Freire's (1972) "culture of silence", with no voice, no access and no involvement.

Why Image is so Sacrosanct

The people in any rural community are the basic or primary resource in rural development. Every thing centres around the people in any effort to develop the community. The people in general comprise the target population, the clientele, the beneficiaries, the men and women, the old and the young, the formal and informal leaders in the community, people of different segments and strata of the community, depending upon the specific development programmes and activities (Setty, 1988b).

Assessment of people's needs, identification of the problems and the study of the physical and natural resources and the extent to which the available resources have been exhausted–all form the initial steps to be taken while preparing a programme for developing such a community. The change agent must determine to what extent people on their own can meet their basic needs.

It follows that an assessment of the natural resources that the community is endowed with and a study of human resources, existing skills and the potential to be developed, has to go along with the assessment of people's needs.

Planning for rural development in developing countries in the true sense consists of two interdependent phases. One is the setting of overall rural targets for the production of different commodities according to the primary consumption needs of the rural people, of agriculture, or industries, or building up of stocks of exports, etc., and the national capacity for outlay needed for achieving these targets. The second phase emphasizes the careful laying down of the tasks to be carried out by the production units according to their own requirements, potentialities, and the specific environmental and economic situation in which they are located, in order to ensure that the plan resources will be utilized with maximum efficiency towards the achievement of the targets (Bhattacharya, 1983).

In order to understand how all this is operationalised, a country illustration is immediately called for. India serves as an appropriate illustration.

After Independence in 1947, India adopted a Federal Constitution. There are at present 25 States and 7 Union Territories. The system of national planning for economic and social development was adopted in the early 1950s. The Planning Commission prepares blueprints of plans and programmes in consultation with the State Governments and the Central Ministries. A time-frame of five years has been adopted for concrete plans for the long term projections. The Five-Year Plans are broken up into annual action programmes for implementation. In so far as the programmes of rural development are concerned, the primary responsibility for implementation is with the State Governments. The Central Government provides coordination, technical guidance, training and research inputs, in addition to monitoring the progress of implementation and evaluating the impact of major programmes. The Central Government also extends financial support to all-important programmes. In recent years, the Government of India has geared its efforts towards maximizing people's participation in the development process.

People's participation, in a broader sense is viewed as people's total involvement with development agencies in deciding the programmes and activities, fixing up of priorities, taking initiative and carrying out the projects as partners with the contribution of their ideas, interest, material, money, labour and time. In this context, people's image of development becomes quite important. In order to secure maximum participation of the people in carrying out a programme or a particular activity, it becomes quite imperative for any development agency to seek answers to the following questions, namely:

(1) What do the people think about development?

(2) What kind of development they want or anticipate?

(3) What do they know about the resources, they are endowed with?

(4) In what way do the people intend to make use of such resources?

(5) What do the people think that their community can do?

(6) What do the people expect from the development agency?

The answers to these and similar other questions will bring out objective facts that are important and must be treated so;

though they are not the whole story. "Attitudes and opinions are facts too, and so are the emotions and values of people" – observes Raper (1953) in case of rural Taiwan. It is in the realm of these more subjective phases of life that the greatest opportunities lie for the furtherance of development activities. For, it is within these aspects of life that may be found the best understanding of what the people really want, and the best guidance for developing programmes that will secure their fullest cooperation.

Following four illustrations would substantiate our argument for people's image vis-à-vis rural development. Considering agricultural development as a key to rural community development in India, many innovations regarding improved seeds, chemical fertilizers and advanced farm implements were introduced during past few decades, through a number of development programmes aimed particularly at the village people. However, since most of such programmes failed to meet what people precisely wanted, the innovations proposed to them were not accepted by the village people. The gap between what people wanted and what they got was so wide that it reduced the efforts of the development agencies to merely futile attempts. The illustrations that follow reflect upon the incongruence over the "want: get" ratio in the development process.

Illustration One

The village people may acquire additional bits of information through communication, however, they may not be able to relate them to any of their felt-needs. Water-sealed latrines, smokeless ovens, and sanitary wells with attached bathing enclosures have been demonstrated to the village people often enough, but a serious and sustained effort has not yet been made to convince them that these should be adopted in the villages. Similarly, in the case of agricultural development, awareness of the farmers in respect of several improved implements and practices has been considerably increased, but their adoption has been marginal, for the village agriculturist has not yet identified them with his requirements.

Illustration Two

The concept and mode of communication under certain development programmes may be such that it would fail to convince the village people of the advantages of an innovation (perceived in terms of economy, efficiency, and ease of mastery), of its feasibility (viewed with reference to their resources and needs), and of its cultural compatibility. For example, agriculturists are conscious of the desirability of using only good and healthy seed. With a view to facilitating multiplication of good seed, a simple implement – the dibbler – was introduced by the agricultural extension agents in India (IADS, 1981). Although, its efficiency was demonstrated adequately, the dibbler did not gain wide acceptance as envisaged. One need not have to make much of an investment in acquiring this implement, for it could be made locally and was relatively inexpensive. However, it required heavy investment in labour and time; the method of its use being slow and labour-consuming, it was given up as uneconomical.

Illustration Three

Frequently we come across an unhappy history of similar developmental activity. This naturally makes the people cautious-if not suspicious – in trying the innovation proposed under a programme again. In some part of India there is a prejudice against chemical fertilizers, because, in the first instance, either the wrong fertilizer was recommended (without any consideration of soil or crop) be its correct dose and proper application were not clearly explained or demonstrated to the village people. Extension workers returned to the village with more fertilizer and better information regarding its proper application only to find that in view of the earlier failures the village people were extremely reluctant to try it again. This story was repeated in some parts of the country when the extension agents recommended an improved seed that was not suitable for the soil or climate of a particular area.

Illustration Four

The timing of carrying out certain activities under particular programmes is important. In one development block of the State of Bihar, India, as a part of the malaria eradication programme, all the houses were sprayed with DDT. This was a well-intentioned step, but its timing was unfortunate. Spraying was done early in October, and soon after, according to local custom, the houses were whitewashed for the Deepavali festival (Hindu festival of lights). In the process, the efficacy of DDT was substantially lost. Naturally, the experiment did not succeed in eradicating mosquitoes from the houses (Lerner, 1972).

In all the four cases cited above, the picture would certainly have been different and better had the development agencies listened to the people, shared their views, before launching respective activities.

Image-led Participation

The standard approaches to rural organizations and development have left increasing number of people outside or clinging desperately to the margins of segments of local and national economies. Human welfare has too often been considered as either an autocratic side-effect or as charity, competing with development investments for productive resources. Thus, development analysts and planners have been reluctant to provide for more than a minimum of rural people's participation, and governments and inter-governmental organizations have been loathe to consider structural and process changes required in existing socio-economic systems for effective participation to be possible.

Thus, in many countries, increasing number of rural people are found to be without any secure means of livelihood. Yet many national cases and innumerable micro-development projects for agricultural and rural development, bear witness to the important role of people's organizations to successfully mobilize continuous, intelligent and productive efforts of rural people. They also reveal that growing mass poverty is simply the result of lack of access to opportunities to participate in development.

The 16-country study attempted by FAO and Rural Organizations Action Programme (ROAP) for the involvement of the poor in development (1979) bears a testimony to the fact that development-oriented systems have too frequently concentrated exclusively on economic growth and the skills and knowledge required by managers of that growth. Many essential human dimensions of development have been neglected i.e., those of people's organizations and "human capital" development in the form of people's knowledge and skills required for masses of people to participate.

Drawing from development as essentially a humanizing process, participatory development must be consciously based on people, their needs, their analysis of issues and their decisions. In other words, participatory development must rely on people's own image of development. It also implies an implicit faith that people, whatever the condition of their poverty and oppression, can progressively transform their environment with the help of, but not dominated by, external agents. In essence, participatory development demands that rural people move from being objects to becoming subjects of development projects (Oakley, 1991).

The underlying assumption is that rural people are able to initiate development but that the very nature of development interventions to date has denied a practical opportunity for them to do so. While few would disagree with these sentiments, the implications for project practice are profound. Chambers'(1983) suggestion of "putting the last first" aptly sums up what is required and he rightly points to the major transformation that would be required on the part of "development professionals" to pursue a participatory approach. Tilakaratna (1987), in his impressive work on the role of the development worker in participatory rural development, argues that these workers can become the major stumbling-blocks to authentic people-led development because of their tendency to impose their "own biases, values, visions and attitudes on the poor". This important principle of people-led development calls the attention of the rural development professionals to rural people's own ideas about development, their values, attitudes, their own vision of the world.

Rural people are not normally constrained from participating in development simply through apathy or inertia; hence the importance of studying the forces which prevent their participation. In this respect, Cernea's (1985) study of the sociological dimension of development projects illustrates clearly how a lack of understanding of these dimensions frustrated projects' efforts to involve rural people. Of particular importance is the need to understand possible reactions on the part of the elite groups which may wish to see project participation on a broader basis (Paul, 1987).

Development projects normally proceed through a pre-established sequence of stages around which different objectives and inputs are correspondingly organized (Oakley, 1991). The experience of participatory projects suggests that this sequence needs to be re-examined. Projects with economic or other material objectives invariably place these objectives in the forefront and trust that people's participation will ensue; other projects, however, see participation as an objective in itself and, in the sequence of project activities, give initial and equal emphasis to the activities designed to strengthen the basis of this participation. In a review of rural public works projects in Nepal, Pradhan (1979) recognized the importance of this sequence of activities and showed how a lack of attention to developing the basis for people's participation caused these projects to fail to involve the local people. Rahman's (1989) review of a number of participatory projects in Africa similarly confirmed the importance of starting a project by building up people's confidence and abilities as the basis for their participation.

As Tilakaratna (1987) observes, an outsider who comes with ready-made solutions is worse than useless. He must first understand from the community people what their questions are and help them articulate the questions better, and then help them find solutions. Outsiders also have to change. He alone is a friend who helps them think about their problems on their own. Tilakaratna's observation can be best construed with an explanation to people's image of development.

The critique of Sen and Das (1987) on social forestry in India is a pointer to our present argument on people's image of development. The present practice of planning and management of community forestry in the States of India hardly fulfills the conditions of participatory programmes. Villagers are rarely consulted at the preplanning stage, and the preparation of a feasibility report, and selection of site and species is generally done by the local forest officials. The village Panchayat or similar agencies offer the land (often with no or half information to their members) for plantation activities by the forest department. During the initial years till its handover to the Panchayat, the villagers do not have any responsibility but to remain as passive spectators.

To continue with the forestry illustration, Romm's (1986) hypothetical illustration of community forestry project emphasizes our line of argument that the people themselves are the key factors in a village system and their aspirations, beliefs, knowledge of resources, their expectations– all need to be valued for the success of any development effort.

Talagune's description of the "type" of dialogue between the change agent and the community people supports the claim to reverse the traditional style of project implementation. In the traditional approach to development it is well known that the administrators of development projects and the beneficiaries do not sit on the same side of the table. In fact, they sit at different levels, the former being always at a higher level. What follows, therefore, is quite inevitable. Each looks at each other with suspicion. To the official, the villager is lazy, ignorant, un-resourceful and irresponsible. To the villager, the official is conceited, unsympathetic, unconcerned and corrupt. Each does not take the other into his confidence. Instead of getting together they continue to stay apart (Talagune, 1985).

Nyerere's vision of the development of rural people also

emphasizes the need to value people's own image of development. As Nyerere views, rural development is the participation of people in a mutual learning experience involving themselves, their local resources, external change agents and outside resources. People cannot be developed, they can only develop themselves by participation in indecision and cooperative activities which affect their well-being. People are not being developed when they are herded like animals into new ventures (Nyerere, 1968).

Very close to "people's image of development" is the newly emerging concept of Farmer Participatory Research (FPR). Farrington and Martin's (1987) review of this concept and its practice sees FPR as helping both to build farmers' knowledge into research activities and to ensure that new farming technologies are relevant to farmers' needs and their own ideas.

When we look at Bruneau's definition of a community, the need to understand people's image of development becomes further clear. Bruneau (1986) views community as primary groups associated because of class or territorial proximity. In these groups the people meet, exchange ideas and support one another. The groups offer their members the possibility to interact, discuss and in fact become communities. The members speak in their own words, using their own terms to express their own ideas and interests. By so doing they eliminate the need for spokesmen with different class and educational backgrounds who have traditionally represented the people. Following from this and because of the focus by the members on their own interests expressed in their own words, the possibility for critical reflection on their environment is encouraged, which in turn may lead to an understanding of the deeper causes of poverty and inequality. The change agent then, can certainly rely on and draw from this strength of the community.

Following case study on Malaysia's Price Subsidy Scheme for Padi (Abbas, 1984) using coupons supports our arguments for people's image of development.

Padi is the Malay word for unhusked rice. The Price Subsidy Scheme for *Padi* (PSSP) was a part of a broader national agricultural development programme of Malaysia. The major policy adopted by the government was (a) *Padi* prices be increased without increasing the price of rice; and (b) *padi* price increases be given in the form of subsidies for production inputs, and on actual increase in the prices of *padi*. The overall objective of the PSSP was to increase the income of the *padi* farmers so that it was at lest on par with the National Poverty Line of $ 270 per month. The scheme was officially launched by the government on January 10, 1980.

On January 23, 1980, just two weeks after the launching of the PSSP, a large crowd of *padi* farmers and their supporters gathered in front of the State Secretariat Building of Kedah to express their dissatisfaction with the PSSP, *Padi* prices and other related things.

A look at the *padi* planters' views provides the explanation as to what went wrong. While the government correctly identified the urgent need to increase *padi* prices, it did not ascertain the level of prices that the farmers felt desirable. As it was, the government decided on a top price of $ 30 per *pikul* (1 *pikul* = 605 kilograms) for long grain *padi* plus $ 2.00 subsidy whereas what the farmers wanted was a top price of between $ 36 and $ 40 for long grain *padi*.

The farmers felt that these prices were justified. They said that what they were asking for was not much. In their experience, the question was, one "*kati*" (one hundredth of a *pikul*) of "*taugeh*" (bean sprouts) which takes about four days to produce costs about 40 cents a "*kati*" (or $ 40 a pikul). So why cannot *padi* which takes about six months of continuous labour and care to produce be priced at 40 cents a "*kati*" also?

The farmers also could not comprehend the reasons for introducing the coupons. They were told that it was to teach them the value of thrift, i.e., to save some of their income. But they said that they needed all the money they could get from their labour to pay for their daily needs. With the income that they were getting, they could not afford to save. The majority of them preferred cash. The farmers also preferred to here news about PSSP or for that matter, news about any government project affecting their lives, directly from government officers or Members of Parliament and State Assembly men, or, if possible, Ministers, rather than from their village heads and other local leaders. To them the government officers and elected representatives had more credibility. Also they could get immediate clarification about anything that they found vague or confusing from the decision makers. The implementation of the PSSP did not take cognizance of this preference. The Malay case thus proves that farmers' choice, preferences and expectations demand attention of the policy makers, planners and administrators.

In changing rural socio-economic environment new technologies may play a vital role through developing new ideas and attitudes. However, anything new, being new alone, may not be appropriate to the local circumstances. The introduction of new technologies generates new types of expectations and attitudes among the community people. If these technological innovations introduced are not in line with the community's needs, expectations and at the same time not related to the local situation then they are not well received and the objectives behind their promotion stand defeated. Amatya (1987) demonstrates the importance of understanding the implications of such new technological adoptions to local communities. His illustration of mechanization of farming operations such as use of tractor in land preparation by large number of farmers in rural Nepal, is a pointer to the planning based on local needs.

Mayfield (1986) documents Dr. Y.C. James Yen's work with the illiterate poor of China to illustrate "rural people development". In this regard, Dr. Yen's words, "Go to the people, live among the people, learn from the people, and plan with the people", are taken seriously. The people's school approach proposed by Mayfield makes the point that government must come to accept the fundamental importance of true local political expression as essential to the development process. He concludes that "rural development is people development". Its sources are found within the cultural sinews, the religious traditions, and the sacred values of people. Such values are often articulated by men and women who have looked beyond the flickering shadows of Plato's cave and are unique in their ability to convey to their fellows new meaning and purpose.

Weitz's study (1971) challenges many of the plans and priorities that have characterized development efforts over past few decades. In doing so, it prescribes a new and revolutionary approach with a concern for the attitudes, customs and values of people in the developing world.

Fugui (1981) goes a step further and singles out people as the masters of development. Natural resources are only useful because people are there to use them. People have the ultimate power to choose the kind of development they want. People can reason out what is good in their environment and what is bad. As discussed earlier, it is not necessary to go always by what people think, since their image may be at times, unrealistic, too narrow or too ambitious. Laksono (1988) illustrates this arguments well with the help of an anthropological study of the hamlet of Gimbal on southwestern slope of Mount Merapi volcano in Central Java. He compares and assesses responses to the volcanic threat to Gimbal by two different parties, the national government and the villagers themselves. The government's response has consisted primarily of attempts to resettle the villagers on one of Indonesia's outer islands. The villagers' response has consisted of trying to remain on the volcano and adapt to its hazards, using local systems of knowledge to both monitor (empirically) and explain (ontologically) the volcanic activity. These differences in the perception of the same problem as illustrated by Laksona show that each view has its own validity. Under such circumstances a compromise is to be reached. This certainly is not an easy task for the planners.

When people are forgotten, things go wrong. When people's needs and demands are neglected or forgotten, the resources, promotional organizations, physical and economic infrastructure– all are reduced to ineffective energies. Thus, apparently there may be development – tangible substantive achievement as a result of the amount of money spent, but it may be miles away from what the people really want. The villagers of Vemandampalayam, a South Indian village, present the best case of the people forgotten (*The Hindu*: 18 November, 1989, news item with heading "21-year wait for a pucca road", as reported from Erode, dated 7 November, 1989).

The villagers of Vemandampalayam Panchayat under the Nambiyur Panchayat Union in Gobi Taluk of Erode District in Tamil Nadu, presented a petition in 1968 to the Collector of the undivided Coimbatore District, for laying of a road between two villages covering a distance of two kilometers. This was requested because the existing road was very narrow and not even fit for pedestrians use. Thus, the villagers were required to walk a distance of five kilometers to reach another village via Vemandampalayam. The request for laying of the said road was honoured only after 21 years, a number of reasons might have caused this delay, but no doubt, neglect is the major one.

It is worthy to note how development agencies, by listening to people, by watching and observing them can learn lessons that rural people have learned for themselves, often as the result of painful experience, as to how best to organize themselves to manage their resources. It helps the agency recognize the range of local conditions to which it must be able to adjust its intervention.

The potential for increased crop production from the use of irrigation water has motivated groups of farmers in different societies to cooperatively find the means to bring water from streams to their fields. Utilizing their intimate knowledge of the local terrain, they locate the most appropriate site for diverting water from a steam and the routes for delivering the water to their fields. Because construction of the irrigation infrastructure often relies fully on manual labour, this usually extends to over a few years.

In the Philippines, communal systems exemplify the indigenously developed irrigation systems. These farmer-owned and managed systems individually serve less than 1,000 hectares, but as a group they irrigate about half of the total irrigated lands in the country, or about the same area of land covered by systems owned and operated by the government. The prevalence of communal systems throughout the country indicates that farmers in widely dispersed communities have worked out similar solutions for managing a critical resource.

The management of irrigation confronts farmers with a variety of questions regarding water distribution, system maintenance, paying for operating costs, and conflict management. In many communal systems the farmers have evolved answers to these questions over several decades. In the process they have developed many management methods well suited to the constraints of their particular system and its environment. It is documented how public irrigation programmes in the Philippines benefited from studying how self-formed irrigator groups organize themselves for system operation and maintenance.

How Rewarding is the Image

In the past decade or so, there has been a growing interest and concern, especially in the developing countries about the need for popular participation in planning and development. It has been realized and widely accepted that a better dialogue needs to be created between the planner and the planned and this is possible only if the planners go to the people, creep into their proclivities and find out about their wants and needs.

Knowing people's ideas, opinions, attitudes, solutions is providing them an opportunity to secure their involvement. It may not always be possible to act according to the people's image of development, but to know it is necessary.

The knowledge as to the ways in which people want to develop their community will reveal the possibilities as to whether the proposed change shall be sustained and internalized by the community or not. Their expectations in seeking help or assistance from the external agencies and their faith as to what they think they can accomplish shall expose the strengths and limitations of the community. Appel (1988) illustrates how planners may utilize the strengths of the local community including its knowledge of the local ecosystem and its potential for adaptation for the management of social change.

As Dube (1958) points out, it is necessary to consider the village people's view of change. Do they consider it necessary and desirable? Then it is useful to find out their attitudes toward the promoters of change. Do the people trust them? Or do they have misgivings about their motivations?

As the present day technology becomes increasingly complex, it depends more and more upon accurate perceptual discriminations by human beings. Here is the need for applied research.

The radar operator must be able to distinguish the brief visual blips on the radar screen that indicate the approach of aircraft. The sonar operator must discriminate between the echoes returning from a school of fish and those from a submarine. The pilot monitors an elaborate panel of instruments and makes appropriate adjustments. The astronaut must make countless acceleration that alter his normal functioning. Similarly, a rural development planner must know what people think of development, what way they want things to be done and what the development agencies think what people need, should have and should do. Rural development professional expertise calls for an understanding of the clientele system, involving and working with them for their sustained development.

Accepting local residents as collaborators in order to be able to make use of the reservoir of knowledge and skills which have evolved to ensure survivability in the local environment with all its cycles, fluctuations and recurring catastrophes, is an important and rarely taken step. Contact with locals cannot be confined to elite. This is because elite are themselves buffered from the consequences of environmental fluctuations which impact their poorer neighbours so severely, and may not have the detailed knowledge those poorer sectors of the population if the full range of survival skills is to be tapped (Boulding, 1989). This is quite a job for the change agent.

The human resources of a particular rural community are the energies, skills, talent and knowledge of people which potentially can or should be applied to production of goods and rendering of service. Thoughts, motives, beliefs, feelings, aspirations and culture of people can be taken as the components of such human resources. In this context, the analysis of people's likely attitudes to development would help in solving the human resource problems for rural communities. For an understanding of the people within their culture, within their context of opportunities and for knowing the flexibility of their thinking and their capacity to exercise initiative, their image of development is expected to serve as a guide for the planners. However, in reality this "people's image" of development has always been neglected so far.

In this context, it is interesting to note what Schumacher (1973) observes on development:

"Development does not start with goods, it starts with people, and their education, organization and discipline... An entirely new system of thought is needed, a system based on attention to people, and not primarily on attention to goods", for goods will look after themselves. Schumacher's observation can only be construed at best with an explanation of people's image of development.

Implementation of any development programme is like organizing a symphony. Many instruments play a part. Failure of any one instrument creates a discordant note. Similarly, when things go wrong with people or when planning goes astray from the client group's perception, the costs are higher and the objectives defeated.

Image and the Logistics of Indigenous Knowledge

There is no denying of the fact that the success of a development project often depends on local participation. Familiarity with indigenous knowledge can help change agents understand and communicate with local people. The indigenous knowledge system has an important bearing on the images that people carry in their heads. What is this indigenous knowledge?

Indigenous knowledge is local knowledge. It is the knowledge that is unique to a given culture or society. This knowledge is the information base for a society (Warren, 1989). It is dynamic, changing through indigenous creativity and innovativeness as well as through contact with other knowledge systems. Such knowledge is passed down from generation to generation, usually by word of mouth. Such a knowledge system represents successful ways in which people have dealt with their environment. Indigenous knowledge thus serves as a guiding force for the local community's behaviour and helps in shaping the mental maps in the heads of the members of the group.

Anthropological studies not only help identify community patterns of dealing with conservation and change, they also identify the kinds of mental maps with which individuals in households in particular communities work. The Para-scientific knowledge about local soil variation and local ecosystems already inside the heads of traditional farmers, the knowledge of how certain types of inter-planting can serve the functions both of protection from parasites and of soil building, of how multi-year crop cycles can rebuild exhausted soil, is very important for technologists to learn about and take account of in considering the introduction of productivity-enhancing technologies. The same applies to the general understanding of the problem of resource degradation on the part of agricultural societies in general. The health-maintaining knowledge of local healing herbs carried in the heads of rural women is important for health specialists to know, as are the mutual aid networks known primarily to women which enable household crises to be managed.

In relation to population policy, the complex household calculations about trade-offs between "quantity" and "quality" of children, about extended-family investment in migrant labour to ensure diversification of economic resources, and about extended family resource allocation in terms of land and other forms of capital, that go on inside the heads of the uneducated poor, rural or urban, need to be understood before effective assistance with population control can be designed. It is for example clear that historically societies have managed to control population size when there was a clear perception of the need to do so, long before modern fertility control technology was introduced.

There have been several non-documented instances wherein the shepherds or the herdsmen who trod miles and miles in search of pastures in particular regions have proven more knowledgeable than the overseers, surveyors and engineers in understanding the slope, variations in soil types, growth of vegetation, availability of ground-water and so on in a given region.

The anthropological development literature is full of case histories of how community structures have operated to initiate innovations in the context of community perception of advantageous opportunities, and also full of case histories of how community structures have operated to oppose innovation proposed by outsiders when community perception has been that the innovation would be disadvantageous.

Since most of the new technologies which come from the laboratories of the scientist and the technologist must by definition, be introduced by outsiders to the community in question or the client community so to say, understanding the criteria that communities bring to the evaluation of innovations, and the processes by which those criteria are utilized by the community in making action decisions, can be very important and rewarding.

The shared mental maps of men, women, children and the elderly in each household need to be included as variables along with individual mental maps, since many significant behaviours and action choices take place at the level of the household.

A major corollary to the people-led nature of participatory development is the principle that people's knowledge is as appropriate a basis for development actions as that knowledge brought in by professionals (Oakley, 1991). This assertion has given rise to reorientation of some development practice and the incorporation of local knowledge into development projects. For too long, it is argued, external forces have not only controlled the means of material production, but also the means of knowledge production and, in particular, the power to determine what is valid or useful knowledge. While in certain fields such as health care, artisan production and irrigation control, local knowledge has to a limited extent been recognized, until recently development projects have rarely sought deliberately to incorporate people's knowledge into project design and planning. Intellectually there are arguments to establish the scientific basis of people's knowledge just as professionals bring scientific knowledge to rural areas; there are even arguments that rural people should be "intellectually self reliant" from outside experts. Certainly, as Oakley remarks, participatory development argues for the recognition of the creative tension between two knowledge streams, namely rural people's essential knowledge and the formal knowledge introduced from outside.

Conclusion

Since its historical evolution dating back to the seventeenth century when voluntary efforts were initiated to serve the mankind, the term rural development has undergone several vicissitudes and continues to be a debatable subject of strategic importance. We have not yet reached a satisfactory stage. Much remains to be done.

The expertise inside the heads of target populations, particularly when they are uneducated and poor, is continually underestimated, resulting in a failure to build up resources already available for innovation, and a futile offering of resources that cannot be utilized under local conditions.

The need is to get down to the people, get into their frame of thinking, understand their priorities, formulate programmes and projects congruent and inconsonance with their image of development, of course with an injection of innovations and technologies that would accelerate people's development in the real sense. Such an approach would give planners a direction for planning. Planning then can be expected to be closer to reality, closer to what people think and want.

REFERENCES

Abbas Fadil Azim, (1984), "Malaysia's Price Subsidy Scheme for Padi Using Coupons" in *Studies in the Management of Rural Development Projects—Cases from Asian Experiences,* Vol.1, Southeast Asia, edited by Gabriel U. Iglesias and Romeo B.Ocampo, Asian and Pacific Development Centre, Kaula Lumpur, pp. 79-108.

Amatya Udaya Bahadur, (1987), *Adoption of New Technology and Its Social Impact on Rural Communities in Asia – A Country Study of Nepal,* Centre for Economic Development and Administration, Tribhuvan University, Nepal.

Appel G.N.(1988), "Costing Social Change" in *The Real and Imagined Role of Culture in Development—Case Studies from Indonesia,* edited by M.R. Dove, University of Hawaii Press, Honolulu.

Bhattacharya, Sib Nath, (1983), *Rural Development in India and other Developing Countries,* Metropolitan Book Co., Ltd., New Delhi.

Boulding Elise, (1989), Cultural Perspectives on Development: *The Relevance of Sociology and Anthropology, in Alternatives,* Vol.XIV, No.1, January, pp.107-122.

Bruneau, T.C.,(1986), "The Catholic Church and Basic Christian Communities" in *Religion and Political Conflict in Latin America,* ed. By D.M. Levine, University of North Carolina Press, Chapel Hill.

Cernea, M., (1985), *Putting People First: Sociological Variables in Rural Development,* Oxford University Press, Oxford.

Chadwick G.,(1978), *A Systems View of Planning: Towards a Theory of the Urban and Regional Process*, 2nd edition, Pergamon Press, Oxford.

Chambers, R.(1958), *India's Changing Villages; Human Factors in Community Development*, Cornell University Press, Ithaca, New York.

FAO, ROAP, (1979), *Participation of the Poor in Rural Organizations– A consolidated Report on Studies in Selected Countries of Asia and the Near East and Africa*, FAO, Rome.

Farrington, J., Martin,A.,(1987), *Farmer Participation in Agricultural Research: A Review of Concepts and Practices*, ODI,London.

Friere, P., (1972), *Cultural Action for Freedom*, Harmondsworth, Penguin Publishers, Middlesex.

Fugui Leslie, (1981), "People as a Resource for development" in The Roat *Out—Rural Development inSolomon Islands,* Institute of Pacific Studies, Solomon Islands.

IADS, (1981), Assessing Farmers' Needs in Designing Agricultural Technology, in *IADS Occasional Paper,* International Agricultural Development Service, New York.

Laksono, P.M.,(1988), "Perception of Volcanic *Hazards: Villagers Versus* Government Officials in Central Java: in *The Real and Imagined Role of Culture in Development – Case Studies from Indonesia. Op.cit.*

Lerner, Daniel and Schramm Wilbur (ed.), (1972), *Communication and Change in the Developing Countries,* East-West Centre Press, Hawaii.

Mayfiedld James,B., (1986), *Go to the People—Releasing the Rural Poor through the People's School System*, Kumarian Press, Connecticut, USA.

Miller, G.A., Galanter, E. and Pribram, K.H., (1971), Plans and the Structure of Behaviour, Henry Holt and Co., New Year, 1960, as cited by Chadwick George in *A Systems View of Planning,* Pergamon Press, Oxford.

Nyerere, J.,(1968), *Freedom and Socialism,* Oxford University Press, Dar es Salaam.

Oakley Peter, *et.al,* (1991), *Projects with People, Practice of Participation in Rural Development,* International Labour Office, Geneva.

Paul S., (1987), Community Participation in Development Project, Discussion Paper No.6, World Bank, Washington DC.

Pradhan, P.(1979), "Baglung Suspension Bridges: Outcome of People's Participation in Nepal", in *Rural Development Participation Review*, Vol.1, No.1, pp.13-14, Cornell University, Ithaca.

Rahman Md. A., (1989), *Glimpses of the Other Africa,* WEP Working Paper, ILO, Geneva.

Raper, Arthur F., (1953), *Rural Taiwan-Problem and Promise,* Chinese-American Joint Commission on Rural Reconstruction, Taipei.

Romm Jeff (1986), "Framework for Governmental Choice" in *Community Management: Asian Experience and Perspective,* ed. By David C. Korten, Kumarian Press, USA.

Schumacher, E.F.,(1973), *Small is Beautiful: A Study of Economics As If People Mattered*, Blond and Briggs Ltd., London.

Sen, D., Das., P.K.,(1987), The Management of People's Participation on Community Forestry: Some Issues, ODI, London.

Setty, E.D.,(1985), People's Participation in Rural Development: A Critical Analysis, *The Indian Journal of Social Work,* Vol. XLVI, No.1, April, pp.74-75.

Setty, E.D., (1988 a&b), *Field Approach to Integrated Rural Development,* Seminar Paper, Asian Institute of Technology, Bangkok, Thailand.

Talagune, A.B.,(1985), *Operational Aspects of the Change Agents Programme*, Ministry of Rural Development, Colombo.

Tilakaratna S., (1987), *The Animator in Participatory Rural Development: Some Experiences from Sri Lanka*, ILO, Geneva.

Warren, Michael D.,(1989), In-dij' e-nes knowledge: A Definition, Editor's Note, *CIKARD News*, Centre for Indigenous Knowledge for Agriculture and Rural Development, Iowa State University, Ames, Vol.1, No.1, February.

Weitz, Raanan,(1971), *From Peasant to Farmer–A Revolutionary Strategy for Development*, Columbia University Press, New York.

7

COMMUNITY ORGANIZATION AND PROGRAMME PLANNING

In this chapter, we may look into community organization as a process, social structure and functional grouping of people and programme planning which are germane to people's participation in rural development.

Community Organization

Organizing the target Community is a prerequisite and a concomitant activity in securing its involvement in any development or service functions. All rural communities have certain levels and kinds of organization. Community organization is a continuous process with birth, growth, decay and disappearance of social and cultural institutions of diverse nature. It is a dynamic social process with changing patterns and institutions in the life of a community.

The organization and management of any developmental activity at the community level is dependent upon and influenced by the following aspects of the community.

(a) Pressure of the need,

(b) Awareness,

(c) Resources-material, human,

(d) Composition of the group,

(e) Size of the group,

(f) Social structure,

(g) Structure of power and authority,

(h) Kind and strength of existing organizations/institutions in the community,

(i) The kind and strength of local-institutional leadership,

(j) The degree of influence from outside the community,

(k) Channels and pattern of inward and outward communications,

(l) Cultural orientations, values, attitudes of people towards certain development initiatives and aspects,

(m) Occupations and professions of the group, and

(n) Economic level and affordability.

We may briefly look into community organization, the concept, objectives, benefits and some of the organizations at the rural community level. We may remember that an existing organization may be utilized for a specific new activity. An organized community, in terms of groups, institutions, functions and responsibility is a machinery that may be used for diverse purposes.

It does not deny the need for a specific organization or special organizing for a specific activity. The thrust of the question is on organizing the community and revitalizing the existing institutional infrastructure at the rural community level.

What is Community Organization?

It is pertinent to note that a worker must have a complete understanding about the community with which he works. By making a sociogram of the community, he can work out the pattern of communication and then understand who influences whom and to what extent. The question is often raised as to how best agency workers can assist the people in dealing with recalcitrant individuals and groups whose sole purpose is to block progress. This needs a careful examination and it brings us to the question of skills involved in working with groups and communities. The worker has to understand what exactly is the cause and the real cause may be different from what appears on the surface. The worker may have preconceived notions. He can look for the answer by studying the power structure within the community and the vested interests it upholds. It has also its processes such as decision-making, communication, social and cultural linkage and boundary maintenance. A social compass would provide valuable guidance to the extension worker and if he understands the elements and processes operating in it, he will very easily map out the interrelations of various factors.

The components of the social compass comprising of such things as community, governmental structures, education, religion, family, social class, health, communication, etc., can be analyzed in terms of its elements and processes. Community organization is a method by which an individual is influenced through the group in which he works. This group provides him the "fields" and it is by understanding the "field forces" that affiliations and alignments of individual members are identified and interpreted exactly.

What is Community Concepts?

Infact, the word community signifies different things to different people according to their interpretation. In some places ethnicity and religion may come to the mind whereas in other countries various social communities are mentioned. Community refers to a group of people inhabiting a given geographical area and having some kind of common activities or some degree of common life, irrespective of their social, religious or social differences. It is not confined to any of the various restricted fields of community life on the basis of religion, caste, race, language or profession but one that envelops the whole life of the whole community.

Meaning and Definition

Community organization has been defined as a process

initiated to bring about and maintain an adjustment between social welfare needs and social welfare resources in a given geographical area. As a disciplined method "community organization seeks to bring about a social climate in which it is easier to resolve group conflicts and initiate cooperative activity for the common good of the community".

Remarkably community organization work concentrates its efforts in narrowing down the areas of conflict and enlarging the areas of cooperation. In short, the negative and destructive aspects of competition is sought to be replaced by the positive and constructive aspects of cooperation.

Central Objective

Infact, the objective of "community organization" as a method of social work activity is, one of helping the communities to recognize and realize their needs and aspirations. First, there has to be an awareness about their problems and secondly there must be willingness to work together towards these common objectives. In any area, there will be problems of some sort and resources both in men and materials and "community organization" seeks to rouse the latter for the solution of the former. There is invariably a gap between what facilities a community has and what it would like to have, in other words, between achievements and aspiration. It is the task of "community organizations" to narrow down and bridge this gap between social welfare needs and social welfare resources of a community.

Specific Objectives

(a) *To obtain consciousness of community:* For harmony and progress of the community, a sense of "we" feeling, a sense of belongingness is to be fostered among the members of a given community. Such a sense of "we" feeling and interrelatedness make the members feel that they constitute a unit by themselves, a social entity as distinct from other communities. Just as self-consciousness is essential for the individual so its importance to the community. The process of integration rests primarily upon definite self-consciousness of the community.

(b) *To Satisfy unmet needs:* Common needs which individuals and groups are unable to satisfy for themselves could be met by the collective action of the community. It may be in any sphere, political, economic, social or cultural. Collective action is the basis for community integration and community mobilization. Determination of the needs of the community is therefore one of the first steps.

(c) *To obtain social participation as a means to socialization:* The ultimate goal of all human association is the development of better personalities by the individuals concerned. A community is composed of various groups in which its people associate. One of the chief handicaps to community action is the number of families and individuals who do not belong to any formal organization, who live a relatively isolated social life associating with their own families and neighbours. The best index of the socialization of the members of a community is the degree of their participation in its organizations.

(d) *To obtain social control:* Community organization is to obtain social control through community spirit and loyalty. Social control becomes possible by the development of community spirit, by loyalty to the community and by symbols which express the common objective of community activity. Sociologists have called these three factors – morale, collective representations and *esprit de corps* (common spirit pervading the group).

(e) *To Coordinate groups and activities:* In a given community there may be several interest groups and their interests and activities may come in conflict. Community organization is necessary in order to prevent conflict and promote efficiency, cooperation and coordination. This is important in a small community. Proper adjustments are necessary. Efficiency may be promoted and ends attained if coordination can be carried out to the point of active cooperation.

(f) *To prevent the community from the introduction of undesirable influences and conditions:* It is not enough to promote community betterment from within, for the community must be able to defend itself from the aggression of undesirable influences. Many a community has found that it can work together for the elimination of a drinking place or any other nuisance to the physical and social health of the community.

(g) *To cooperate with other communities and agencies to obtain common needs:* Frequently, the community is too small a unit to achieve certain desired ends on its own. To obtain them, it is necessary to cooperate with neighbouring communities to obtain a bus line, water facilities, schools colleges, etc.

(h) *To establish a means of obtaining consensus:* As for having their needs accomplished, it is easily done by coming to a common understanding. In a small rural community, it is obtained by gradual crystallization of public opinion through casual conversation at any shop or public place where people gather usually. Sometimes hearsay, gossiping distort the facts and promote disagreement rather than consensus.

(i) *To develop leadership:* Leadership for any group or collective activity is a must. Potential leaders in the community are to be identified, their talent recognized and developed. Local initiative and local leadership are essential for building up a self-reliant and self-confident community. It is not a question of spoon-feeding, the external agency alone functioning, but creating opportunities so that the local leadership is fully developed and employed for the growth of the community.

How to Measure Community Organization

Community organization should not be conceived as a relationship which can be set up and which can be abolished. It is rather a process of establishing relationships which will always be in a state of becoming analogous to the growth of personality or character in the individual. One measure of community organization is the degree to which organizations and interests are willing to cooperate in activities or objectives for the betterment of the common welfare, for which they are not primarily responsible and in which others will take the lead.

Another measure is the ability to have competition in politics or business without conflict and the ability to discuss matters with a division of opinion but with tolerance and with united support for the objectives sought.

The degree of socialization of the community is the best measure of its organization. The better a community is organized the more it serves the needs not only of its adult individuals but also of its potential members. It has been very well summarized that the goal of community organization is enlisting everyone in the community activities so that each individual shall register effectively, that is, shall achieve self-expression and status in community service.

From a behaviouristic standpoint the measure of community organization is the degree to which the members, individuals or groups of the community act collectively for common welfare.

Statutory organizations like village councils and non-statutory organizations like cooperative societies, special interest organizations like farmers forums, youth clubs, recreation clubs, dramatic associations, women's clubs etc., constitute some of the community organizations.

Statutory Village Council

A village-statutory body may go under different names-village council, village development committee and so on. For instance, in India, the village panchayat functions as a statutory body at the village level. The members of the panchayat are elected by the adults of the panchayat area. It is one of the three basic institutions at the village level (the other two being the village cooperative and the village school). It is the lowerst tier in the three-tier structure of the Panchayati Raj. Being the basic unit of democracy at the village level, the panchayat will mobilize all the available human resources for works of community benefit, mobilize savings for development work, in addition to discharging administrative and judicial duties.

It is through this institution, therefore, that the socio-economic programme of the village is to be achieved, through agricultural production plans and other general plans. The panchayat will thus not only be the self-governing body at the village level but also the principal institution for self-development. It will organize through cooperatives, the development of necessary credit and supplies, arrange for the education and cultural needs of the village through the village school.

The village panchayat will broadly attend to the (a) drawing up of plans in keeping with people's aspirations and wishes; (b) executing approved plans; (c) mobilizing local resources, human and material, to supplement whatever resources may become available from the state and other sources; (d) bringing about a progressive increase in people's participation and (e). arranging constant evaluation of its own work by way of stock-taking.

The Village Cooperative

The cooperative is the basic economic institution at the village level. The principles underlying the cooperative movement are implied in the objectives of the community development programme. In fact, from the very beginning of the community development programme, due emphasis has been placed on the application of cooperation to various aspects of rural life.

A cooperative society, it may be pointed out, is a union of persons, voluntarily united for utilizing reciprocally their own resources for their common benefit. Its basis is an association of persons and not capital. The emphasis of the cooperative movement thus is on the character of man and not on his property. By its very definition, a cooperative organization must be open to everybody desirous of becoming a member and must work on democratic lines at all levels.

Formed on voluntary basis and on the principles of equality, the cooperative movement promotes mostly the economic interests. Its pivotal point is the principle of self-help and thrift, which means making the best use of time, energy and wealth.

There are several types of cooperatives:

(a) Credit cooperatives,

(b) Service Cooperatives,

(c) Joint Farming cooperatives,

(d) Tenant farming cooperatives,

(e) Better farming cooperatives,

(f) Collective farming cooperatives,

(g) Purchase cooperatives,

(h) Production and sale cooperatives,

(I) Insurance cooperatives, and

(j) Marketing cooperatives.

Every form of human economic activity and any collective function where the individual or a few individuals or a few sections of the community alone cannot accomplish the task, a cooperative does the job. It ensures individual's growth and the welfare of the community not the one at the cost of the other.

The Village School

The village school is an important institution, through

which the community could be organized for meeting its educational and intellectual needs. The village school has to play a significant role of providing leadership for the community; for a school becomes a community school in as much as it derives its programmes from the problems of the people whom it serves, and draws upon all the available resources in an attempt to solve them. It is also to be a community center for the village as a whole and render assistance in the establishment of adult courses including adult literacy, provide recreational programmes, help in the improvement of health and sanitary conditions and introduce all other measures which are conducive to inspire the community and thus contribute to a better living.

A school must function as a miniature community- a community within a community reflecting almost all the facets of the community life. The idea is to organize the community's civic life inside the school, trying to correlate the classroom instruction with that of the community activities.

The school, in addition to being linked with the community in general, should also be closely associated with other community associations, organizations and agencies, particularly the panchayat and the cooperative and other associate organizations such as the Youth Clubs, Women's Clubs, etc.

To enable the village school to be a vital link in the life of the community, the leaders of the community have to take active interest and become involved in the programmes of the school. Participation by the community leaders in the programme of village school is very vital.

Youth Clubs

The Youth Club is an associate organization at the village level. The purpose of organizing such Youth Clubs in the villages is to develop young people into better farmers and citizens by equipping them with best skills, attitudes, habits and values of life as to make them intelligent, well-informed and useful citizens at whatever level they function.

In the community development movement, the youth organization can be a living force only if the youth become active agents in carrying out the community development activities in their areas.

Objectives of Youth Clubs

The specific objective of Youth Clubs is to develop the youth in physical, mental, moral, spiritual and social aspects of life and to channel their energies in the right way for the balanced development of the individual and the welfare of the community. The specific objectives can be:

1. Developing the qualities and skills of leadership so that they may be helpful in the development of the community,
2. Providing them with opportunities for building up their character and health,
3. Providing them with technical information about improved practices in agriculture, home economics, so that they may become leaders for others,
4. Teaching them the value of research and developing in them the scientific attitudes towards the problem confronted at the individual and community level, and
5. Inculcating in them the cooperative way of life and social responsibility.

These objectives are to be achieved on the principle of learning by doing and earning while learning. There are individual and group projects the individual and community interests are met.

Farmers Forums, Women's Clubs etc.

As in the case of Youth Clubs, the Farmers Forums and Women's Clubs are associate organizations at the village (they could be at higher levels also) level fulfilling the needs of farmers and the women-folk. Dissemination of scientific farming practices among the farmers is an important function of the Farmers' Forums. The Women's Clubs strive to make the women-folk understand the outside world better and arouse interest and initiative in them to take active part in the affairs of the community and the nation. The activities of the Women's Clubs of literacy, social education, home management, childcare, kitchen gardening, sewing and other economic activities centre around better homes, better farms and better communities.

Local Social Institutions

Sometimes organizations and institutions are used interchangeably. Institutions are a resource and a means to understand, interact and involve people in any development activity. We have to see how best the institutions could be utilized for the development of the client community. It is interesting to think for a moment how a society has emerged over a period of time and how it functions at a given moment of time. Society, in one sense, consists of individuals as aggregate units and, on the other hand, it speaks of the network of enduring relationships that exist among the individuals. A society has devised certain ways and means for meeting the individual and the collective needs and wants of the group. Institutions in the sociological sense are patterns of behaviour often accumulated over generations. These patterned ways of living or institutionalized ways of behaviour meet the physical, biological, social and psychological needs of people. The norms in the group over a period of time get established as enduring patterns of living. These institutions provide the guidelines which facilitate the life of the group. The institutions are the lubricants of the human collectivity.

Member of Several Groups

The individual is developed by the group and it is the individual who forms the group. Every man is bound into a family and will belong to a family throughout his life. An individual is a member of several groups at a given moment of time; member in the family, office, club, friendship circle, and political party. A man becomes a group member without deliberations or he joins a group by choice or he is forced to be a group member in some situation.

An individual influences and he is influenced by several groups. He is held by several institutions and he is obligated to several groups or associations. It is the institutions which guide, promote or protect the interests of the individual and the group. In a given community, we may come across different types of institutions and groups. They are: family, race, sex and age-groups, various nationalities, political, economic, occupational, artistic, ethical, religious, educational, scientific, philosophical, philanthropic, recreational etc. One such resource that could be utilized to involve the community and introduce and sustain any kind of change is the network of local institutions. Earlier, we have looked into some of the political and economic institutions. We may look into some more social institutions. These institutions constitute the fabric of community organization.

Social Institutions

Under social institutions come the family, the kinship circle, the caste, the tribe and various sects among the castes and tribes; under the religious institutions come the church, the temple, the mosque and the other religious organizations which have some enduring influence on the behaviour of people; under educational institutions come the school, college or university. We may likewise think of different associations or organizations which are related to recreational, political and other aspects of life.

The whole attempt in rural development is to introduce something new in the life of the people or bring about some modification in the way of life of people. It amounts to a basic process of change, introducing change and people accepting the change and the change that is introduced and the group. An individual may react to change in two ways: he may accept or reject it. The individual or the given local community has learnt to live certain pattern of life over a period of time and has tried to maintain an equilibrium however inadequate it is. Once it is used to a particular pattern of life it will have the tendency to continue the *status quo*. Anything new that is attempted will be a disturbing factor to the individual or the group.

In view of the ways in which an individual has been socialized in group-living as a part carrier of culture, he is obliged to several individuals in decision-making or in his accepting a new idea. Whether it is a question of change in dress, food, a new practice, a school or career, shifting from one area to another, whatever may be the activity, the individual does not always decide for himself and he depends on several individuals within the family, the kinship circle and the community. He looks for the approval or appreciation of the members of the group in which he lives. Even though he is convinced of the change suggested to him by the change agency, he seeks the approval or the support of the people within his social sphere. Unless we influence his social environment, secure him the support that he is looking for, it would be difficult for him to accept the change. On the other hand, the power to influence people in decision-making or in modifying their behaviour whether this power is power of legitimate authority, power of influence or power through coercion, it is the institutional leaders in a given community who function as gate keepers and regulators of the group ethos. It is imperative on the local institutional leadership behind these institutions. He may have to work through these institutions and institutional leaders in order to introduce a change and make the change adopted and sustained by the group.

Institutions and organizations in the community may or may not have a direct bearing on or a functional relationship to an economic or social activity in question. The tribal council, the caste/ethnic council, the religious institutions, for example, deal mostly with social aspects of the community, but as traditional and deeply rooted institutions, they influence and control the behaviour of people. The change agent may try to make use of these existing institutions and customs to communicate to the people.

A well-organized community promises better and effective participation in development activities and an important prerequisite to increase, secure and sustain people's participation in any realm of development is community organization.

Against this background of community and its organization which provides the arena and milieu for any development planning at the community level we may look briefly into some salient aspects of programme planning in rural development.

Programme Planning

The central objective of rural development is to develop in the people the ability to make a better living and to live a more satisfying life. This implies a series of changes in the ways of the people, their practices and methods. These different changes to be introduced in the clientele communities should be properly planned, executed and evaluated, so that they are in the desired direction and meet the needs of the people. In developing countries the needs of the people and their problems far outweigh their capacities and the resources. Therefore, the best use of men, materials and resources is necessary to achieve quick and lasting results. This requires careful planning.

Planning is the systematic way of assessing the existing situation i.e., identifying the needs and interests of the people, appraising the available manpower and material resources, setting of general and specific objectives, fixing priorities and targets, working out sound procedures and proposing solutions to meet the needs of the people on the basis of the people's experience and results of scientific studies and research.

A plan of work is thus an outline of activity so arranged as to enable efficient execution of the programmes. It tells what, when, where and by whom the programme shall be carried out. The term programme indicates focus, priority, and design.

Any sound programme has as its basis the needs of the people for whom the programme is meant. The needs of the people constitute the core around which successful programmes are built. The needs are those which fill the gap between the existing situation and the desired situation. The existing situation can be determined by the conduct of a study or a survey of the field. The study should reveal facts about the clientele group, their attitudes and outlook, their level of information and progress, to whom the clientele look for leadership and what they think their needs are. The desired situation can be decided on the basis of research finding, functional and official leaders. Determining what ought to be or what the desired situation is, is the process of consciously deciding the objectives or programme targets. This work must be a cooperative venture of all concerned.

We may say that designing programmes for rural development is one of the most difficult tasks confronting RD workers. This is so because planners must avoid programming that has super-imposed characteristics and instead, assure programmes that have roots among the people. Programme planning is basically a process of making decisions that will carry into the future. Decisions have to be made about what the present situation is, how it could and ought to be changed and what means can be used to accomplish the new and more desirable situation. Good planning for social development requires the ability to sound decision-making about the objectives the programmes should seek to attain, and what courses of action are most likely to achieve them. The ability to plan requires:

1. an understanding of the nature and function of planning,
2. skill in formulating planning procedures,
3. skill in identifying problems and needs,
4. ability to decide on significant objectives and goals,
5. skill in formulating means and wise courses of action to attain objectives, and
6. skill in involving key leaders in the planning process.

Some guides to planning:

1. Effective rural development programmes must have clear and significant objectives.
2. To achieve the broad purposes of socio-economic development requires planning at the top level and also at lower levels.
3. A number of crucial questions about programming must be asked and their answers taken into account in the planning process.

These questions are:

(a) To whom and to how many people is the programme important?

(b) In what way is the programme significant to people-economically, socially, morally?

(c) What is the relative importance of programme objectives?

(d) Who thinks the programme is important-the nation, State, catalyst agency, clientele community?

(e) Who arrived at the programme objectives?

(f) On what amounts and kinds of information is the programme based?

(g) Who is acquainted with the programme and its purpose?

4. The most effective social development programme result when there is general agreement among the clientele group, catalyst institution and other liaison agencies on three important items. They are:

(i) a basic philosophy regarding programme development,

(ii) A clear policy that reflects the basic philosophy, and

(iii) a workable procedure that gives general direction but provides ample latitude for adjustments needed to meet local situations.

5. Programmes are most effective when based on adequate and current facts pertaining to local conditions as well as those related to national and regional situations.
6. Selection of a relatively small number of the most significant needs singled out for major attention contributes to the effectiveness of socio-economic development programmes.
7. Skilful involvement of progressive community leaders is fundamental in planning social development programmes.
8. Programmes that are planned for longer periods of time than one or two years tend toward greater effectiveness.
9. Programmes in social welfare programming that assure fairly close integration of problems related to the occupation/profession, the home and the community appear to contribute to their soundness and effectiveness.
10. Programme planning must take into account cultural values and the social system.
11. Programme content must be determined with care and preciseness.
12. The interpretation of the programme to officials and non-officials and to the general public is an essential step in successful programme planning.

Professional Abilities Needed by Planners

Planning effective programmes for community development requires a number of high-level professional skills. Needed abilities include understanding and skill, in at least the following broad areas of competency:

1. Understanding of the nature and role of the national and state level/rural development organizations.
2. Knowledge and understanding of technology related to

subjects with which the programme is to deal.

3. Ability to clarify the objectives of a programme and to take them so that they are useful in guiding its execution.
4. Ability to organize activities.
5. Skill at seeing the relationship between principles and practices.
6. Skill at enquiry.
7. Skill in human relations.

In sum, the measure of success achieved in free-choice societies by public programmes to promote social development is in direct ratio to the extent to which the programme is built around people's needs and consequently, is an effective influence in helping meet their needs.

To accomplish these desirable ends effectively requires a carefully structured programme at all levels that meets the following criteria:

1. It must focus on the felt-needs and interests of the people.
2. It must be developed through joint participation of village leaders, catalyst institutions, taking into account the recommendations of the rural development organizations at the State and National levels.
3. It must focus on problems that are most important since it cannot be all things to all people at the same time.
4. It must be flexible, but with a "backbone" that gives it stability and continuity.
5. It must provide for a system of priorities in line with local needs, interest and resources.
6. It must be balanced that is, it contains items of assistance for all major social, economic, age and sex status groups.

7. It must have objectives that are attainable within the economic, social and mental capacities of the people through education with a minimum government aid.
8. It must be developed, understood, conducted and judged as an educational instrument for helping people learn how to help themselves.
9. It must be highly significant economically, socially and morally to a relatively large number of people in the clientele community.
10. It must provide satisfaction for the people who participate. The central objective of rural development may be stated as one that helps each individual, each family and each local community achieve the highest level of living that it is capable of economically, socially and culturally by means of aided self-help through education.

8

PEOPLE'S PARTICIPATION IN UPLAND CONSERVATION

People's participation as we have discussed earlier is pervasive and a highly desirable political and social component in all spheres of community development. In this chapter, as an illustration, we shall look into people's participation in upland conservation.[1]

Uplands and Uplanders: Prevailing Situation

All lands which have slopes exceeding 3 per cent and which generally occur at elevations of more than 600 metres could be regarded as "up-lands". These so-called upland areas are characterized by a mosaic of diverse micro-environments. Soil types, slope, drainage, and even rainfall vary within each of them. This mosaic of land resources is matched by equally similarly varied cultures of people who occupy such lands.

Upland conservation, thus, deals with two interlocking or complex systems: the forest ecosystem and the human social system. Interactions between these two systems largely determine the success or the failure of upland conservation projects. An understanding of people and how they behave in relation to trees is a requisite to rational utilization of uplands. No sensible forester would initiate a tree planting programme without first assessing such ecological factors as soil, climate, topography before choosing the species to be planted, the spacing etc. Similarly it is necessary to assess the human factors in seeking people's participation in upland conservation as this affects programme implementation.

There are two principal types of upland inhabitants: those who belong to tribal or ethnic communities, and low-landers who have migrated into the mountains. This distinction is important because of essential differences between the two communities, especially in terms of environmental attitudes and behaviour, and values regarding land ownership and use.

An increasing number of lowlanders have turned to upland forests, as a result of population growth in the lowlands, economic dislocation, or because large-scale development projects required their dislocation. They also have relatively greater access to education, health and governmental bodies, and to the marketplace. These make them more visible as well as more open to development programmes compared with indigenous ethnic groups.

When competition over resources is among groups of different ethnic backgrounds—say, lowland migrant groups versus indigenous hill tribes—it is not unusual that staking of claims are done with intimidation and coercion. The history of the upland community is replete with cases where indigenous occupants have been victims of manipulation by powerful outsiders seeking cheap labour, land, minerals and timber resources.

Farming is the primary occupation of uplanders. For almost all upland farmers, however, production of the main food crops typically rice, corn and / or root crops is subsistence-oriented. Periodic surpluses are bartered or sold, especially during lean months when prices rise. Multiple cropping is practiced, with crops grown either in series or in combination, again for subsistence purposes. Depending on climate, ruggedness of terrain, length of farmland use, these secondary crops commonly consist of fruits (bananas, mangoes, citrus, etc.), coffee, tobacco, abaca and coconut.

Nutrition researchers agree the typical upland diet is inadequate. Malnutrition is thus a problem. Protein from animal sources is also deficient, among many tribes, because of the scarcity of forest game; pigs, cows, chicken, and other domestic animals. As a whole, then, upland diets are inadequate in both quality and quantity.

Given the subsistence nature of upland farming and the farmers' need for additional income (particularly cash), it is not surprising that upland farmers engage in a variety of secondary economic activities. Livestock and poultry is common with a few household animals reserved for home consumption during rituals, feasts and other special occasions. The rest are traded or sold. Handicraft products, formerly used exclusively in households, are now also sold to itinerant traders or in lowland markets. These include: blankets, pottery, brooms, beadwork, carvings, baskets, and mats. Forest products such as fuel wood, ferns, orchids, mushrooms, and honey may also be sold to lowlanders.

To sum up, the prevailing situation of uplanders is characterized by several inter-related factors. Among them are:

(a) lack of secure land tenure;

(b) low productivity of land due to soil degradation;

(c) inadequate access to upland technology (lowland technology is often super-imposed on upland settings e.g., tribal people now opt for mono-crop grain production, never a part of their tradition);

(d) inadequate infrastructure;

(e) lack of marketing experience and inadequate distribution systems (most uplanders end up exploited as their produce is often under priced and consumer items overpriced);

(f) lack of credit access to production;

(g) weak community organizations and willingness to take risks;

(h) increased population pressures;

(i) traditional imbalance in resource distribution; and

(j) natural calamities.

Deforestation and Degradation of Uplands and the Consequences

There is now evidence available quantifying the extent of deforestation and its consequences. Studies by FAO pinpoint the current rate of tropical deforestation in the region at around 2 million hectares per annum. If this trend persists, more than 20 million hectares of forest cover could disappear between now and 2000.

Annual rates of deforestation are the highest in Indonesia (over half a million ha); followed by Thailand (400,000 ha); Malaysia (230,000 ha); India (150,000); Laos (125,000 ha); Myanmar (100,000); Nepal (84,000 ha); Vietnam (65,000 ha) etc. Deforestation in these countries has occurred due to a multiplicity of reasons including shifting cultivation. Among the causes are:

(i) *Unorganized and spontaneous encroachments:* These are by low-landers. They manifest the relentless build-up in demand for cultivable land, by increasing numbers of landless and unemployed rural poor. This form of deforestation is most prevalent in Thailand and Philippines. In Nepal, population pressure in the hills is force-feeding migration streams to the "Terai" areas and encroachment into forestlands.

(ii) *Organized forms of settlement:* Generally government sponsored, these are more common in Indonesia, Malaysia, Sri Lanka and, to a lesser extent, in Nepal. Examples: Indonesia's transmigration programmes and conversion of forestland into oil palm and rubber plantations in Malaysia.

(iii) *Loss of forest land for other uses:* Construction of irrigation and hydro-electric projects (observed in almost every country) claim forest land, and often displace upland communities on a significant scale.

"Deforestation" is defined as removal of forest cover followed by changes in land use from "forest" to other uses. "Degradation" is the phenomenon where the "forest use" is maintained but the vegetation is despoiled and the soil badly affected.

Improper methods used in exploitation of forests and excessive removals result in degradation. Forest roads represent forest areas taken out of production either permanently or temporarily. Studies in Sarawak established that temporary open space and bare soil (skid trails, roads, landings etc) could be as high as 40 percent of logged-over area. In varying intensities, this type of degradation appears in some 44 million ha. Of logged-over forests of insular Southeast Asia.

Degradation of tropical forests is accelerated by the demand for fuel wood. Nepal provides a typical example of degradation due to excessive fuel wood and fodder harvesting. This process has lead to severe soil erosion and deterioration of forested areas into wasteland. Destructive landslides and flash floods, exemplified by the Bangladesh deluge of 1988, are the stark result of a problem that cannot be contained within national borders.

In farming system of tropical Asia, particularly of South Asia, animals provide food and draught power. These are essential to the functioning and stability of rural economics. But they also overgraze. The problem is specially acute in India which is estimated to have 15 percent of the World's cattle, 46 percent of its buffaloes, 17 percent of its goats and 4 percent of its sheep. Grazing intensity is high in most of the upland forest areas of India.

Incessant lopping of trees by grazier, with no time allowed for regeneration of lopped trees, has reduced vast forested areas to an unstable low scrub in the Himalayan zone. In Nepal, leaves make up about 40 percent of the annual feed of a buffalo and about 25 per cent for a cow. In addition to depletion of vegetative cover, trampling by cattle hardens the soil. This prevents forest regeneration, and causes soil erosion in several parts of the Indian subcontinent. Fire is another agent of forest degradation in the Asian region. Most forest fires are set off by man; to clear land for shifting cultivation, to facilitate collection of minor forest produce, to smoke out bees and rats, etc.

In South Asia, forest fires are generally started by grazier to burn the tough old grass and induce fresh shoots when the first rains fall. Forest fires degrade existing assets, inhibit regeneration that bring on soil erosion. In the tropical high forest areas repeated forest fires induce far-reaching ecological changes. Hence the dominance of *Imperata cylindrical, Thema triandra, Chrysopogon aciculatus and Capillipedium parviflorum* due to frequent occurrence of fires and overgrazing. This perpetuates a grass-fire-grass cycle. In certain parts of the Philippines, this cycle prevents any plant succession.

As a consequence of deforestation and degradation, the biological system is at the threshold of collapse in some parts of the region. Water and soil conservation problems are growing in severity. Human beings searching for arable land, fodder and fuel wood have stripped much of the protective cover over land in catchment areas of rivers. The result is silt-laden rivers with their capacity for providing irrigation water seriously impaired. The Yellow River of China, for example, sweeps away 1.6 billion tons of soil into the ocean each year. The Ganges disgorges 1.5 billion tons of soil into the Bay of Bengal, and the Brahmaputra carries 726 million tons of soil each year. The Indus river is laden with 435 million tons of soil.

The list is long and the end is not in sight. Rehabilitation of upland areas should, therefore, be at the top of the agenda of most developing countries in the region.

To help rehabilitate degraded upland areas, strategies should be pursued which ensure that poverty alleviation and environmental protection complement each other. To this end, increased investments, incentive mechanisms, environmental awareness programmes and measures to identify target populations and seek their full participation, deserve highest priority.

Current Approaches to Upland Conservation: An Overview

The degree to which individual upland communities depend upon forests varies greatly. In some communities the dependence of people on forests for fodder, energy, shelter, employment and income is almost total. This is the case with traditional tribal communities in parts of India, Indonesia, Laos, Philippines, Papua New Guinea, Sarawak etc. Other communities use trees simply as a source of fuel and fodder and protect the land to maintain environmental stability on which continued food production depends. This is predominantly the case in the mountainous areas of Bhutan, China, Nepal, Pakistan etc.

No matter what the perceived needs are, it is now well recognized that forests play a vital role in determining the total productivity and living standards of upland communities. Consequent upon this recognition was born the need to find new ways to satisfy the urgent requirements of the rural people for the goods and services of forestry sector.

However, any new system must first give due recognition to the prevailing life styles of upland communities. New measures that ignore these life styles invite failure. In fact, many forms of upland conservation introduced in some countries of the region, often lacked this focus.

In China, mass reafforestation in mountain areas was taken up under the "three norths" programme involving food for work. In India, various soil conservation measures, integrated watershed management, establishment of village woodlot, strip plantations, social security forestry, school nurseries, and raising of nurseries by school children were among the programmes carried out. In Indonesia, intensified system of soil conservation and agro-forestry are being practiced. Such income-generating activities as bee-keeping, raising of fodder grasses, and medicinal plants were encouraged. In Laos, through a package of food, tools and technology, shifting cultivators in Laung Probang province are being taught of terrace uplands. In Nepal, the conservation activities were carried out mainly through local bodies (Panchayats). In the Philippines, major projects undertaken in uplands were: forest occupancy management projects; communal tree farm projects; and the family approach to reforestation projects. In the Republic of Korea village forestry associations were constituted to implement forestry programmes.

In Northern Thailand, the Royal Watershed Management Projects initiated by His Majesty the King of Thailand, is an example of an integrated approach to upland conservation. To understand the complexity of this approach, some details of this project are given here.

This Royal Project seeks to promote the economic growth of Isu, Karen and Haw hill tribes by organizing permanent settlements for them. Activities, are carried out by several government agencies in a coordinated manner, among them the Royal Forest Department; Narcotics Suppression Committee; Ministry of Interior; Public Welfare Department; Department of Education; Department of Agriculture; Department of Livestock Development; Border Patrol Police, and the National Economic and Social Development Board. All these agencies have one common objective: to stimulate environmentally sound and proper land use and improve living standards of forest communities practicing shifting cultivation. These activities include: resettlement, agricultural development, and in particular diversification of crops, housing improvements, medical programmes, family planning, rehabilitation of addicts, education for children and adults, vocational training such as cottage industry training, and infrastructure development like road construction and water resources management. Together, these activities allow the hill tribes to diversify the product mix, raise livestock, and engage in side-line occupations. In an attempt to discourage the hill tribes from cultivating opium, the project introduced the growing of commercial crops, such as flowers and vegetables. A well-organized delivery and marketing system was set up.

The project also trains farmers in correct land use practices.

They are taught, for instance, that only lands with gentle slopes should be used for annual crops. Steeply slopping lands are to be used for tree cash crops, such as tea, coffee and for fruit or trees. Areas with over 50 per cent slope should be used for forest plantations or should be kept permanently under forest cover. Farmers learn to take soil conservation measures, set up small irrigation schemes, improve agricultural practices, select crops to be planted and engage in agro-forestry. Forestry field workers developed a number of conservation practices to prevent soil erosion. The most effective but most expensive of this is complete bench terracing. Simpler and less expensive methods have also been introduced such as intermittent or convertible terraces, hill ditches and contour bunding. For tree crops, orchard terracing was introduced.

Role of Government in Enhancing People's Participation

Several measures on a broad front-institutional; technological and economic-need to be initiated and continued with increasing momentum to ensure that people's participation becomes reality.

Institutional Measures

The more important institutional measures required to accelerate the process of people's participation deal with:

(i) training of staff;

(ii) informal and formal education and re-education;

(iii) extension services;

(iv) security of land tenure;

(v) a system of incentives;

(vi) promotion of local organizations;

(vii) decentralized decisions;

(viii) appropriate linking mechanisms; and

(ix) government policies and legal instruments;

Training of Staff

Upland conservation programmes, based on people's participation, are in some ways a fundamental departure from conventional forestry. To execute these programmes successfully the staff involved should be trained to develop, not only expertise in the most appropriate forestry technology, but more important correct attitudes and skills to communicate with the people. Education and training received by the foresters should be specially designed and re-oriented. If a forester is to play a significant role in serving people's participation, he will need:

(i) Knowledge, insight, and understanding of rural structures, culture and needs and aspirations of rural societies;

(ii) Knowledge of the nature and extent of available natural resources, their alternative uses, and availability of indigenous technologies to develop them;

(iii) Knowledge of forestry technologies as applied to upland conservation, and ability to disseminate this knowledge to rural people;

(iv) Knowledge of interactions between social systems and forest ecosystems and consequences of those interactions;

(v) Ability to work as a team member, accept group responsibility and accountability, and capacity to listen and accept ideas of others;

(vi) Ability to lead, motivate, innovate, and to solve problems;

(vii) Ability to cooperate and work with horizontal organizations in a spirit of mutual respect and understanding;

(viii) Ability to monitor and evaluate programmes and to obtain feedback; and

(ix) Ability to collect data and keep records and to use them effectively.

Upland conservation programmes are notoriously difficult to implement. Achieving people's participation is easier said than done. Therefore, in designing a national programme the best choice may be to start small and expand with experience. Initially the focus should be on demonstrating the approach, utilizing services of staff with outstanding personal qualities and technical abilities.

Education

Informal or formal education and re-education are important for creating awareness, positive attitudes, values and motivation; stimulating self-confidence and self-reliance; expanding "aspiration frontiers" of the rural poor; improving participation capabilities of target groups through generating respect for, and faith in, people's power. Re-education is also relevant for government officials, politicians, and social leaders for acquiring new skills and orientations.

Education /re-education processes involve inclusion of forestry in school curricula; leadership training to enable people to take their own initiatives; non-formal education for women; field level workshops and seminars for farmers and community members to encourage articulation of their problems; a system of social communication and campaigns for effective dissemination of information; forestry education and demonstration centers for imparting skills of management to the community.

Extension Services

Governments in the region are now generally aware of and accept the need for promoting upland conservation. But many countries do not have well-organized forestry extension systems. For the success of upland conservation programmes it is crucial to constitute separate functional units for carrying out forestry extension activities. Forestry extension activities should be integrated into the general rural extension services wherever possible.

Extension agents are to help local communities take the greatest possible advantage of opportunities for high productivity so as to augment family income. They pave way to introducing government services in an integrated manner. Adviser, teacher, analyzer and organizer, these are the essential roles of an effective forestry extension agent. He may not perform all of them in all situations, but each role is a legitimate and interlocking part of his task. In the final analysis, the work of the extension agent has a human dimension: it is to enrich the lives of people.

Security of Land Tenure

Security of land tenure and right to the use of trees are important to promote people's participation in upland conservation. Unless the farmer is assured that the trees will remain his property at harvest time, he is unlikely to cooperate. In many situations, therefore, it may be difficult to introduce forestry/agro-forestry on uplands prior to a more far-reaching reform of land tenure or change in land use.

Where landless people have already occupied and are using common lands, governments can encourage more productive use of land by assuring security of tenure. Where people have doubts over the ownership and control of the land they farm, they will withhold the long term commitment necessary to promote upland conservation.

Even if land tenure is secure, forestry legislation in several countries prescribe procedures involving prior permission for transport and marketing of forest products. These often act as a disincentive to growing trees by farmers. Laws, therefore, need to be re-examined and, where necessary, appropriately modified.

A System of Incentives

When available land is needed for producing food and/ or cash crops, many farmers do not see any reason for planting trees, particularly when returns can be expected only some years into the future. Introduction of packages of incentives, allowing farmers to benefit more from trees, would be needed. Some of the incentives that can be considered are:

(i) Supply of seeds and seedlings, including transport cost either free of charge during the initial period or charging a nominal fee;

(ii) Allocation of land and an assured title or guarantee of tenure;

(iii) Provision of tools and equipment and supply of fertilizers;

(iv) Credit on liberal terms;

(v) Guaranteed markets;

(vi) Food aid such as the "food for work" programme under the World Food Programme;

(vii) Provision of infrastructure like village roads, schools and dispensaries, water supply etc;

(viii) Facilities to enable women to participate in the work (i.e., child care centres).

Promotion of Local organizations

Promotion of local organizations, as well as improving the effectiveness of existing self-help organizations, is vital for sustainable participation. These would enable local people to reach out and effectively use services that are delivered. The existence of a delivery system to provide incentives is not adequate by itself. It has been demonstrated, time and again, that because of their influence and access, rich farmers tend to monopolize benefits provided by delivery systems. The weak and the poor are bypassed.

Therefore, there is a need for local level organizations to strengthen the capacity of the poor farmers to take advantage of incentives provided by governments. Strengthening of receiving systems can best be achieved through promoting local level organizations and associations in which, through united action, small farmers and disadvantaged groups can gain access to services provided by government.

Experience in small farmer development work shows that a trigger for development, at village level, is organization into small homogeneous groups of about 10-15 farmers or heads of families. These informal groups with similarity of income, problems and aspiration, organized from below, can better receive government services.

Local institution-building is a lengthy and complex process which must take into full account the real distribution of social, economic, and political power at local levels. A long and careful sequence of steps, designed to build the capabilities of local institutions and confidence of people in them, may be necessary before effective devolution of programmes can take place. Some of the local level organizations involved in forestry in the region are: the Panchayats in India and Nepal; the Village Forestry Associations of the Republic of Korea; the Tree Farmers' Associations of the Philippines; the Tree Cooperatives in parts of Pakistan; the Forest Villages of Thailand etc.

Decentralized Decisions

Decentralization of decisions- especially financial decision- by government agencies will reinforce local level participation. At the same time, unnecessary proliferation of local branches of central bureaucracy are avoided. Responsibility for projects should be delegated to local organizations, wherever feasible.

Appropriate Linking Mechanisms

Appropriate linking mechanisms, such as joint councils of government and community representatives enable governments to share responsibility with people's organizations and NGOs in such activities as monitoring and evaluation of programmes and assessment of the viability of proposed activities. Consultation with people may take more time. In many countries, uplanders lack political support. They are the "voiceless" people. In a variety of ways they are disadvantaged and are left out of the mainstream. Despite all plans to the contrary, it is commonly observed that policies tend to favour the already-advantaged; stress urban over rural areas, flood plains over uplands; concentrate rather than redistribute income and use external resources and benefit external parties.

Very often there is a surface hum of development activity. Superficial sings of growth are in evidence in uplands. Because the investment is from outside, and "developers" also from elsewhere, returns also leave the area. Little benefit accrues locally. Policies that allow local communities to retain a share of forest revenues and vest them with authority to spend such revenues on local development can help build participatory activities rapidly. Legal instruments for resource control and conservation need to be realistic. Procedure related to implementation of policies should be simple, and clearly understandable to the people.

Technological Measures

These measures involve generation of new and improved technology and its use for development. Technology should be appropriate and adequate to attract people's participation including innovations to overcome physical constraints.

Applied research with active involvement of farmers can focus on pressing problems related to species, sites, plant mixtures, planting, tending and tree management. These help integration of forestry with other forms of land use for obtaining best possible results.

Economic Measures

Economic measures are those meant to ensure adequate incentives, credit facilities, delivery of inputs, markets and marketing arrangements. Availability of credit or other financing facilities, such as rural banks with a flexible system of collateral requirement or revolving funds for collateral free loans for groups, is crucial in meaningful participation. A system of price supports for wood, as is done for certain agricultural products will be needed in some cases to encourage tree planting.

There are often no local markets for wood and wood products. While planning tree-planting projects, it is therefore necessary to analyze the market situation and explore new markets so that investment involved is assured of adequate returns. Another possibility, in favourable situations, is to link wood production with processing industries through appropriate integration. It may also be possible to capture far-away markets through organized cooperative marketing.

Role of Non-Governmental Organizations (NGOs)

Experience shows that upland conservation programmes fail due largely to rural people's inherent mistrust of governments. There are very real and deeply-embedded community-government barriers. Thus, rural communities develop defence mechanisms to ward off external intrusions.

In the past, there were virtually no upland-farmer government interactions at the local level. Relations of forestry services with local people were mostly authoritarian in nature. In this context, NGOs can help bridge the government on the one hand and the rural people on the other. Many changes will certainly be brought about by the governments themselves. But NGO action can reinforce official action and hasten changes that governments to see and countries so desperately need.

In Asia, hundreds of NGOs are operating at the local levels dedicated to constructive action. Their operations are generally limited in scope. But they are usually carried out by a core of adherents who live among people. A serious weakness with many NGOs is the *ad-hocism* associated with their work. To some extent, this seems unavoidable, as it stems from an uncertainty in their resource position (funds, men and materials). NGOs also have a tendency to work in isolation from each other. This results not only in wastage and duplication but also in the failure to conceive the effort as a movement. External factors have also limited functioning of these organizations. Resistance from vested groups is a major hurdle. When any voluntary effort meets some success, it also meets with opposition from those who wield some power, as they feel that their own power base is being eroded. Another limitation which organizations face is the apathetic attitude or lack of cooperation from the local government officers concerned with development.

Programmes of NGOs in the Asia-Pacific Region cover a wide spectrum of activities: agriculture, health, construction of wells, developing village and cottage industries, dairy farming, spinning and weaving, adult education etc. Forestry is a late entrant into this list. Nevertheless, in recent years there has been a surge of NGO activities in the fields of environment and forestry.

An internationally known example of an NGO campaign to protect the forests of Himalayas is the *Chipko* (hug the trees) movement. Dasholi Gram Swaraj Mandal (DGSM) is the NGO behind this movement. Over the past 18 years, the Mandal, spread the message of forest conservation through innumerable foot marches, meetings and discussions. They gained widespread public support, specially that of women in the hill districts. The *Chipko* movement has spawned in its wake several NGOs in India who are engaged, not only in environmental awareness campaigns, but also in constructive action to rebuild forest resources with people's participation. Eco-development camps and afforestation camps, conducted by NGOs, are now a common feature in the Himalayan region of India.

Conclusion

To win and retain people's participation, it is essential for upland to be seen as central to human interests and aspirations. As a dynamic concept, it can incorporate different social, institutional and land ownership systems wherein people come forward to cooperate in an organized manner in conserving and sharing the benefits from forests.

Much theoretical knowledge on people's participation in upland conservation exists. However, practical measures needed to promote participation still lack definition and widespread acceptance. There is a greater need to look into the following aspects:

(i) The ways in which consequences of upstream degradation/

conservation can be expressed in terms of productivity of land, rural employment, income generation, energy production, water supply, and social welfare and stability;

(ii) The required capability, content and the techniques of conservation extension needed to mobilize people's participation; and

(iii) The incentives which can trigger people's participation leading to greater local control over natural resource management and conservation, security of tenure and increased productivity.

NOTE

1. The material in this Chapter is adopted from *"People's Participation in Upland Conservation"* by Y.S. Rao, Senior Programme Adviser (Forestry), FAO, Bangkok; undated mimeograph. The author gratefully acknowledges the source. Dr. Rao died in the Bombay bomb blast on March, 12, 1993.

9

PARTICIPATORY TECHNOLOGY DEVELOPMENT AND SUSTAINABLE AGRICULTURE: A CASE FROM PHILIPPINES

Introduction

For the past five decades, rural development remained as the top priority/agenda in most of the programmes and projects implemented in developing nations. Many programmes had been implemented to increase income of the rural people employing several strategies such as farmers organization, women's club and youth mobilization with the hope of attaining sustainable development among them. It was seen that there is a need to increase agricultural productivity because it was foreseen that rural development could not be attained when agricultural production could not be improved above the other factors. Hence, agricultural development was considered as the top priority.

One of the major development initiatives implemented in developing nations to increase income among the rural poor was the "Green Revolution" programme. It was assumed that with this kind of programme meaningful rural development could be attained. This programme was implemented based on the conventional approach to agricultural development called "Transfer of Technology" (TOT).

This approach was based on the top-down and paternalistic idea that scientists are more knowledgeable and aware of the rural situation compared to the rural people. Therefore, "improved" farming techniques were introduced based on the knowledge generated in the research institutions and agricultural universities. Believing their knowledge to be superior to that of the farmers, scientists decided what changes were needed, tried them out under controlled conditions and passed the results on through extension services (Waters-Bayers, 1989).

Some of the innovations resulting from conventional agricultural research have been applied by richer farmers but few have been widely adopted by small farmers. Reasons for these were sought in supposed characteristics of the small farmers, such as ignorance, laziness and conservatism or the support services, such as poor extension services and lack of credit facilities, but seldom in the characteristics of the innovations themselves. In fact, the ones most benefited by these high yielding varieties were the rural elite who were big landowners. This was so, because the new varieties recommended were dependent on high levels of agricultural inputs and on favourable and reliable climatic conditions and, or, irrigation. To support the programme, physical infrastructural facilities were provided such as irrigation and credit facilities. But who benefited with this kind of ambitious rural development effort? Only the few big low-land farmers comprising only about 15-20 per cent of the total local population in the Philippines. Hence, rural development in its real sense failed because agricultural development initiatives were not able to improve the living conditions of the target population with the less fortunate 75 to 80 per cent of small farmers. This is because, vast majority of the farmers in developing nations practise mainly rainfed farming, often on poor soils in areas of high climatic variations, and face high production risks.

Against this experience (that Green Revolution technology was proven unsuitable for farmers in marginal environments), there is a need to reorient our approach to rural development, more so in case of agricultural development programmes. There is a need to reverse the process. It should be "farmer first" not "farmer last". In line with this, Waters-Bayers (1989) recognized the importance of indigenous knowledge and innovation compared to TOT approach because it was found that most agricultural technology used in the developing nations was the outcome of the informal innovations by subsistence farmers. Besides, some scientists began to recognize the rationality behind the small farmers' techniques as the ecological dangers of many large-scale projects (such as irrigation schemes) and modern farming techniques (such as the use of chemicals and monoculture) became more obvious.

Hence, the participatory technology development approach for sustainable agriculture was developed as an offshoot of the failure of the conventional approach of research and development, and extension. This is a new approach which seeks full participation of the clientele in developing technologies adoptable to their actual farming circumstances.

The Process of Participatary Technology Development (PTD)

There are three main phases in PTD viz., planning, implementation and embedding of technology. Planning phase involves analysing the situation, identifying problems, setting priorities, and choosing priority solutions to investigate or test. While implementation deals with designing trials to investigate and to test potential solutions, carrying out trials, and monitoring and assessing the results. Embedding the technology, on the other hand, is the sharing of results with other farmers and scientists, and helping create the necessary social and economic infrastructure to sustain the application and further development of the technology.

A. Planning Phase

Planning phase has two main stages, namely : diagnosis and design.

1. *Diagnosis*

This is the first stage in PTD approach. This stage is carried out by eliciting and gathering information in the community in order to determine the main problems and their causes; and potential solutions, using the Rapid Rural Appraisal (RRA) techniques.

Moreover, as a first step toward participatory situation analysis, the scientists must learn local conditions and practices, so as to gain a basis of communication with the farmers. During this process, it is important that they would be conscious of the conflicts in interests between different local groups (such as farmers and traders), between different levels of administration, and between local, regional and national interests.

In collaborative research, discussions and field observations together with individuals and group of farmers allow the scientists to help the farmers specify their needs and wants, analyse constraints in achieving them, and identify possibilities improving their situation. This often involves an historical approach in which farmers recall past changes in crops, cultivation techniques, land use and living conditions, and try to identify causes of these changes.

While in farmer-led research, the scientists assume that they can never achieve the level of understanding of the local situation which the inhabitants already have or can gain through a process of conscientisation. The scientists act as catalysts; stimulating thoughts and discussion among farmers about their problems and needs, and encouraging farmers' initiatives to improve their situation.

In participatory approach, instead of interviewing, scientists discuss with farmers and encourage discussion between farmers. Instead of imposing their own interpretation of the situation, they remain open to exploring farmers' hypotheses which are not immediately comprehensible to the formally-educated scientific mind but which farmers see as important.

2. Design

From the information (problems and constraints) elicited/ gathered during the diagnostic stage, design stage will follow. This is the process of coming up with potential solutions to the identified problems for testing. The purpose of the design stage is to generate a set of solutions from which farmers can choose those they would like to try. The sources of solutions are firstly the farmers' indigenous experiments/knowledge, and new ideas from findings of research studies at research institutions. From these, selected potential solutions and their interactions with other farming components should be investigated. Thus, with every possible solution there are social, economic and cultural issues to consider. Finally, studies principally examine possible resource constraints and conflicts.

The activities that could be undertaken to come up with alternative solutions to farmers' identified problem include farmers consultation/participation/collaboration; consultation with technical staff; review of existing technologies and/or available solutions related to the specified problems; farmer-researcher interaction; field trips; visit to local training institutes and tapping indigenous resources for information.

Farmers participation and consultation with the technical staff serves as a means for generating an array of possible solutions to the identified problems. This is usually done through meetings and discussions about the problem at hand. With the active involvement of the farmers, possible solutions are evaluated as to their practicability and feasibility. Farmers play a central role in technology development; one as active collaborators, not just as passive observers or receivers.

Review of existing technologies and potential solutions gathered from review of literature may be the easiest way of finding alternative solutions. This is usually done by reviewing what has been practiced by the commercial and progressive farmers in the community. In coming up with potential solutions based on this review, precautions may be taken in terms of farmers' resources and capacity to undertake the alternative solutions themselves.

As a source of insight on practices of farmers in other places, field trips may serve as an effective method of designing solutions. However, this is expensive and participation by farmers may be limited. Considering the vast experiences of farmers, solution to the identified problems can be elicited from the farmers related to the problem which needs to be considered in the design of alternative solutions for testing. Once the information or alternative solutions are identified, there is a need to examine their feasibility considering availability of resources and other important factors. This is needed to narrow down the list of alternatives that would be tested. Eliciting farmers' indigenous solutions can be done through individual interaction with farmers, group discussion and/or consulting key informants.

B. Implementation Phase (On-farm Trial)

This phase in participatory technology development deals with testing solutions by farmers in collaboration with technicians on the farmers' own land, crops or animals. This is usually done by comparing new techniques with farmers' own existing practices. The purpose of this on-farm testing is to find out how potential solutions perform under farm conditions. Usually, performance of the improved technology drops again at the farmer's testing level where the improved technology is in effect being tested for compatibility with the current farming system and managerial know-how of the farmers. The researcher and the farmer usually have some ideas (hypotheses) about how the proposed solution will perform, but seldom are they sure, hence the need for testing.

After the alternative solutions are identified, they are tested using the farmer's fields, crops or animals and following his management style. Farmers' pre-acceptability and understanding of the treatments and objectives of the trial are the determining factors in designing meaningful trials. They should know about the variables considered in testing. Results of the experiment are then compared with the farmers' existing methods.

The design of solution is such that the conduct of the experiment can be done by the farmers themselves. It should consider the highly variable conditions of the farmer's situation, his resources, time available for overall farm and household activities and other responsibilities that he may have to take care of. A simple experiment may involve the existing farmer practice as control against the alternative solution. The farmer-managed research can be modified by the farmer based on his judgment but should not entirely deviate from the broad objectives/goals jointly set by both parties before the conduct of the study.

In designing the trials, the scientists help the farmers plan how to conduct the trials and measure results so that both sides have an objective basis for assessing the innovation. The factors which farmers view as important in testing a new idea are determined by asking farmers what they do with a new crop or variety, observing their informal trials, or using ranking techniques which reveal decision-making criteria.

While in conducting the trials, some external inputs such as new seed, may be provided by the scientists and combined with existing resources according to farmers' criteria. The work is carried out under farmers' control management. Farmers may adjust the trials according to their new ideas or perceptions of the changing conditions. To be able to analyse reasons for differences in farmers' results, scientists must monitor closely what is actually done in the trial plots (eg. Planting densities, additional fertilizer use, grain harvesting dates, harvesting of other plant parts such as leaves). Some records of trial implementation (eg. What was done when and by whom) can also be kept by the farmers themselves, for their own and/ or for scientists' use; even more where literacy is not widespread, pictorial technique could be used. The scientists record the farmers' comments on growth habit, disease susceptibility, yield, marketability of a new variety and others make additional measurements necessary for interpreting the results.

In assessing the results, collaboration in evaluation gives scientists further insight into farmer's value systems and helps in designing subsequent trials. Still more important, it increase farmers' ability to analyse systematically the advantages and disadvantages of innovations and, thus, to make well-founded decisions about changing their farming systems. As PTD is an interactive process, evaluation is not limited to an end stage. It involves constant exchange of ideas and experiences between farmers and scientists during trial implementation. Interim results are discussed jointly by scientists and farmers, who then agree for the next step. The farmers ultimately decide whether to continue applying the innovation and whether to recommend it to other farmers.

The innovations must be assessed in terms of interest to the farmers. For example, farmers facing chronic shortage of cash may be primarily interested in benefit-cost analyses which balance the prices of end-products actually obtained against the costs of purchased inputs. Farmers will be most concerned with yield per unit of limiting production factor e.g., returns to labour during a labour-bottleneck period such as the sowing season, and not necessarily with yield per hectare.

A prime aim of scientists in farmer-led research programme is to strengthen the farmers' research capabilities so that they can adjust more quickly and independently to changing conditions. Here, the important tasks of the scientists are:

(i) To help the farmers decide what to observe and measure so that they can assess their results in a way meaningful to them, and

(ii) To show farmers how they can obtain information from formal R&D services to aid in interpreting their results.

C. Embedding

If farmers have themselves identified the problems, tested potential solutions and evaluated the results, useful techniques thus developed will become part of their farming system. These farmers are likely to become good extensionists, quickly spreading the innovations through traditional communication channels, mainly by word-of-mouth and by passing small amounts of inputs (eg. Seed) to relatives and friends. Participatory R&D programme promotes farmer-to-farmer communication and helps extend it beyond the local community.

However, on account of differences in soil type, climatic variability etc., an eco-farming technique developed within on farming system can rarely be transferred directly to another. Extending eco-farming techniques involve two processes: (1) offering farmers new options which merit testing and modification; (2) promoting infrastructural and institutional development to ensure that the innovation can be embedded in the local farming systems. For eco-farming techniques, the need for external inputs may be low but vital, and increased cash income is likely to be among the small holders' multiple aims. It is therefore important that the rural communities be assisted in creating or attracting local infrastructure needed for both input supply and marketing. Groups are in better position than individuals to exert demands for services and policy support from higher level agencies. Promoting farmer organization and helping force links between different actors in development process (farmers, researchers, extensionists, input suppliers or government officials) are important for embedding not only the innovations but also the very process of generating them.

The Role of Participatory Technology Development in Agricultural Research and Development

A. Necessity for a Participatory Approach

A participatory approach to R&D is necessary in order to develop site-appropriate farming techniques which are both productive and sustainable, to make effective use of research funds in the service of agriculture and to increase smallholders' capacity for self-sustaining development.

Developing Site-appropriate Technologies

Innovations developed on-station are usually for a single cash crop. Those developed by participatory research are more likely to meet the needs of smallholders who produce various commodities and have multiple goals (subsistence, economic / social security, cash income etc). Trials carried out by smallholders mainly with their own resources are more likely to address their most urgent problems than trials planned and financed by resource-rich outsiders.

Scientists can learn more about eco-farming from farmers' techniques, informal trials and adaptations to introduced innovations. Participatory R&D combines farmers' knowledge with formal scientific knowledge of ecological agriculture.

Increasing Efficiency of the Formal R&D System

Tropical environments –referring to local biological, economic, social and political conditions are so heterogeneous that adaptation of new eco-farming techniques to each site would make impossible demands on formal research resources. The demands could be reduced if farmers are enabled to select and adopt technologies to suit their particular environment.

From the point of view of the scientists and planning agencies, participation of local farmers in technology development leads to greater efficiency and precision in identifying the most urgent problems. Formal agricultural research can be better focused and solutions found more quickly.

Empowering Farmers for Self-sustaining Development

A participatory approach to R&D which builds on local knowledge, initiatives and resources strengthen the self-help capabilities of farmers. They gain faith in the value of their own knowledge and how it can be combined with outside knowledge or limited external inputs to solve their current problems. Farmers with this kind of experience will be able to adjust their production systems more quickly to changing conditions and to exert more "demand-pull" on formal R&D institutions for relevant information and services. Knowledge is said to be power. Hence the knowledge gained through participatory R&D can be for the benefit of both the parties:

1. Participatory R&D can empower scientists, who learn from farmers, gain a greater understanding of existing production systems and constraints, and thus can add to the store of knowledge within the formal R&D system;
2. Participatory R&D can empower farmers in that it augments and reinforces their abilities to generate, communicate and use technical knowledge, stimulate greater reliance on their own resources and permit greater influence by farmers on formal R&D.

B. Complementaries between Participatory and Conventional Agricultural R&D

PTD cannot replace conventional research in laboratories on station and in scientists on-farm trials. It involves flexible forms of applied and adaptive research which complement the more rigorous trials according to formal scientific conventions.

What can Participatory R&D Offer to Conventional R&D?

In collaborative and farmer-led trials, farmers may choose to test innovations developed in conventional R&D. The farmers' choices show the scientists which new technical options are consistent with the farmers' value judgments. Farmers' trials give scientists an opportunity to see how innovations actually function within the local farming system and household economy, and so help them to assess where the new technologies could be applied successfully and to redesign promising techniques to reduce risk. Thus PTD not only permits quicker and more accurate focus of formal R&D, it also stimulates ideas among scientists.

Moreover, the conventional R&D system provides a framework for scientific investigation of questions which arise during participatory R&D. Ideally, the formal system should provide service to the farmers. If the trials of the scientists are designed to answer questions arising out of farmers' trials, conventional R&D will be able to provide the information farmers need.

When scientists conduct conventional on-farm trials adjacent to farmers' trials, more frequent or complex measurements can be made than in the latter alone. These data aid in interpreting the results of the farmers' trials. The scientists and farmers involved can observe, compare and discuss each others' results. In eco-farming, R&D scientists controlled-trials play a supportive rather than a leading role, but this support is vital. The trial results must be fed back to the field quickly and in terms which can be readily understood by extensionists and farmers and can specify how the results of conventional trials are applicable to the practical problems of the local farmers.

Initial investigations can be made on-station of innovations which appear to offer potential solution for increasing productivity and sustainability. However, it is important that they be presented to farmers at an early stage as "working models". The response of the farmers, if negative, warns that something is basically wrong with the idea, saving considerable funds which might be spent refining inappropriate technology. For example, during 30 years of refining animal-drawn wheeled tool-carriers on-station, changes brought about by scientists in design increased risk and reduced convenience and flexibility. Substantial research funds and time spent isolated from farmers, produced a technology for which most farmers were not willing to pay (Water-Bayers, 1989). Finally, conventional trials under controlled conditions often remain necessary to convince conventionally-thinking scientists and development planners of the validity of farmer-developed technologies.

PTD's Specific Framework of Activities

For workability purpose, there is a need to specify and describe the five different activities of participatory technology development as an activity to be undertaken by the "outsiders". These are:

1. How to get started;
2. Finding things to try;

3. Trying out;
4. Sharing results; and
5. Sustaining the process.

Items 1 and 2: How to get started and finding things to try comprise the planning stage while number 3 – Trying out, the implementation phase. Sharing results and sustaining the process constitute the embedding phase.

(i) How to Get Started (Diagnostic Phase) : This is the first stage/phase in PTD approach. This phase is carried out by eliciting and gathering information in the community in order to determine the main problem(s) and its causes, and potential solutions, using the RRA techniques. The main objective of this activity is to come up with a list of prioritized problems and their causes as basis for the design of potential solutions. The following are the major activities that would be carried out:

1. Conduct RRA in the community to identify problems limiting production;
2. Identified problems would be ranked according to the degree of importance;
3. The causes that gave rise to these problems should be identified;
4. The relationships between problems and their causes would be analysed; and
5. Begin to consider possible, potential solutions.

(ii) Finding Things to Try : From the information (problems and constraints) gathered during the diagnostic stage, design or finding-thins-to try phase will follow. This is the process of coming up with potential solutions on the identified problems for testing. This could be done by:

1. Identifying potential solutions based on the major problems analysed with the use of problem-cause analysis;

2. Evaluating the potential solutions for the major problem(s);
3. Bringing these potential solutions back to the farmers for verification as to their accurateness and the possibility of adopting these at the farmers' level; and
4. Deciding with farmers what specific solutions to be implemented.

(iii) Trying Out: It is the process of testing/trying out defined solutions on the farmers' farm (on-farm trial). It is an activity wherein the traditional practices of farmers and the new practices (interventions) are compared in terms of their overall farm performance. This is done in order to find out how potential solutions perform under farm conditions for evaluation. Trying out potential solutions should be done on the farmer's field using his crops/animals and employing farmer's managerial techniques. This could be done by:

1. Identifying responsive and research-minded farmers to serve as cooperators of the trials; and securing their willingness to participate;
2. Try the intervention(s) side-by-side with the farmers' practice. Let the farmers manage the trials; and
3. Monitor the performance of the intervention with the farmers.

(iv) Sharing Results/Extension: This is the process of disseminating/ extrapolating the tested and adopted potential solutions to other farmers or places having the same characteristics with that of the recommendation domain.

(v) Sustaining the Process: It is the process of institutionalizing the PTD approach by building institutions among and between farmers/local people. The cooperators have important role to play in sustaining the development process on behalf of the project implementers, they will assume the role of motivating, educating and disseminating appropriate technologies to other farmers so that the approach would become part of the system of the society/community, after the project phases out.

Experiences in Participatory Technology Development

A. The Farming Systems Development Project in Eastern Visayas (FSDP-EV), Region 8, the Philippines

The Farming Systems Development Project in Eastern Visayas (FSDP-EV) was implemented in 1981. It aims at improving the livelihood of the small farmers in selected rainfed areas of Region 8 through increased agricultural production. Its objectives also include the development of appropriate technologies and the establishment of a working mechanism for technology delivery for rainfed areas in the region. The project adhered to the farming systems research and extension or participatory technology development approach which focuses on the technologies adaptable to resource-poor upland farmers.

The project which was a joint effort of the Depart of Agriculture-Region 8 and the Visayas State College of Agriculture (ViSCA) effected its implementation by establishing Site Research Management Units (SRMUs) located at different provinces of Samar, Leyte and Southern Leyte. Each of these SRMUs was considered to be representative of the ecological and socio-economic situation of these provinces at the start of the project, foreign technical assistance was provided by Cornell University while the major source of funding was from USAID.

The SRMUs which were staffed by multi-disciplinary teams were established to serve as pilot sites or "testing" centers of various technologies which were considered to be suitable, if adopted, to that area. This work was done on the sites to evaluate their overall performance for possible dissemination (Bernadas, 1991).

Some Techniques Proven to be Promoting R&E Linkage and Farmer Participation

During the first two years of FSDP-EV, efforts in SRMUs were directed to cropping pattern trials to identify patterns that could increase the income of upland farmers. This was in response to the finding of two one-shot surveys conducted at the sites at the start of the project implementation. The first survey was done by the site leaders who were formerly extension workers of the Department of Agriculture. They were detailed in the project sites to provide leadership in the conduct of site activities. The survey was made using the structured interview technique and a printed questionnaire as a guide. However, farmers' feedback regarding family and farming situations was limited to what was asked in the questionnaire.

When a multidisciplinary team composed of biological and social scientists was organized for each SRMU, one of the initial activities done by the team was to conduct rapid rural appraisal (RRA). The team identified guide topics from which questions during the interviews with key informants and other farmers were formulated.

Results of both surveys concluded that the most pressing problem of farmers was low income due to declining soil fertility. Immediately, the project staff decided to conduct cropping pattern trials in the sites. They organized meetings with farmers to choose the crops to be included in the pattern. They also explained the importance of planting legume after or together with their traditional annual crops. Farmers agreed to provide land, labour, and feedback on the research, the trials on their own farms. Performance of the crops, however, was below expectation of the researchers due to some socio-economic and environmental constrai..ts. Socio-economic constraints were demonstrated in cases where farmers were not able to plant the crop, clean the field etc., because they were paid as labourers by other farmers or they helped harvest rice in the lowland farms. Sometimes, unfavourable weather conditions caused the delay in planting or not being able to plant at all. It was after two years that the project staff realized that introducing new cropping patterns to increase farm income and regain soil fertility which was quite successful in the lowland, was inappropriate in the hillyland areas. The project staff realized that the needs and problems of the farmers are more related to the sustainability of their resource base. This experience led the project staff to involve farmers in deciding what farm intervention to try or technology to develop to increase their income and improve soil fertility. This led to the establishment of informal and highly-focused diagnostic surveys and on-farm trials, discussed below:

(i) ***Informal and Highly-focused Diagnostic Survey:*** In Jaro, one of the SRMUs, for instance where coconut is the main crop, project staff observed that the cropping pattern introduced seemed to contradict the practice followed by the farmers of leaving the land to fallow after several croppings of staple crops (rice and corn) and rootcrops (sweet potato and cassava) in order that the soil regains fertility. So, a series of informal, highly-focused diagnostic and design surveys were conducted by the project staff to get details of the fallow practices of the farmers. Cooperator and non-cooperator farmers of the project site were interviewed using open-ended, interactive, and structured guide questions. These guide questions were related to the key issues on the fallow practices of the farmers. Interviews were conducted in the vernacular. In addition to the surveys, informal conversation and formal group meetings with farmers by the project researchers and extension workers assigned in the area were held to discuss the issue.

Based on this process, the project staff learned that the problems of the farmers associated with the fallow rotation was the growth of cogon (*Imperata cylindrica*) in the fallowed area. Thus, the farmers were asked to suggest a farm intervention that would suppress the growth of cogon. Farmers shared their observation that cogon was shaded out vigorously growing viny plants. They also said that plowing and the use of herbicides were inappropriate solutions for cogon control, because of limited family labour and unavailability of cash.

(ii) ***On-farm Trials:*** In the aforedescribed situation, agreement was reached with the farmers to try several forge legumes: *Centrosema pubescens, Colopogonium muconoides, Pueraria phaseoloides* in monoculture or in mixture. Farmers agreed to provide the labour for plowing thoroughly their fields and collect cuttings of *kudzu (P. phaseoloides)* for the trial establishment. The other legumes were provided by the project. Evaluating the results of the trials, the farmers decided to adopt the *kudzu*. The failure of the *Centosema* and *Colopogonium* to grow aggressively resulted in farmers labeling them "slow". At present, the *kudzu* covercropping to improve the fallow rotation system of farmers is adopted by most farmers in the project site and by some farmers outside the project too.

(iii) ***Organized Visits to Farms of Technology Adopters:*** Organized farmer visits or cross farm visit is not unique to FSR. This mechanism is also popular in other research-extension linkage approaches. In FSDP-EV, organized visit by farmer cooperators to farms of technology adopters was instrumental in the adoption of *ipil-ipil* contour hedgerow.

Together with the cropping pattern trial, contour hedgerow was introduced in one of the SRMUs(in Villaba). Recognizing that the land was a marginal hillyland, the site leader who saw a hillside farming project terraced with ipil-ipil of the Mindanao Baptist Rural Life Centre (MBRLC) in Kinushusan, Bansalan, Davao del Sur, thought of introducing the technology to client farmers in his area. He took special pains to convince farmers of the benefits of the hedgerow technology by showing them pictures of hedgerow establishment and providing farmers with a computation of expected return in terms of increased production. However, the site leader was not successful in convincing the farmers.

At the suggestion of the Director of Agricultural Research Office of the National Department of Agriculture, these farmers were brought to a project site of the World Neighbours – a non-government organization (NGO) in Cebu where the technology was being adopted. They viewed farmers working with different forms of hillyland contouring, especially the *ipil-ipil* hedgerows combined with the local crops. The potential benefits of the technology was effectively conveyed by striking similarities in soil and topographical conditions of this site with those of the FSDP-EV sites and by the farmer-adopters themselves discussing the technology with the visiting farmers. The farmers of the NGO project also taught the visiting farmers the steps/ procedures of adopting the technology. Following the field trip, the farmers noticeably were willing to experiment with *ipil-ipil* on their farms. When the project began to provide them with the planting materials to set up the researcher-managed and farmer-implemented trials, the farmer-cooperators had already decided to establish their own plots of *ipil-ipil* hedgerows with seeds left from the trial plots. In addition, farmers made some modifications or technology consolidation in their trial plots, which suited specific situation. They decided to plant *ipil-ipil* seeds at 1-2 inches deep instead of 5-6 inches as practiced by farmers in the NGO project. The farmers believed that shallower planting would result in a more uniform and higher rate of germination because their soil had more water holding-capacity than the soil where the NGO project was implemented. Pruning was also modified. Instead of cutting the *ipil-ipil* at 50 cm, they pruned at 40 cm.

The farmers experienced that pruning the ipil-ipil at this height was easier because they were still young. They found later, however, that frequent pruning resulted in die-back. So, the use of *Glyricidia sepium* was done to replant missing hills due to the insufficient supply of *ipil-ipil* seeds.

To successfully improve soil fertility over time, periodic pruning of the hedgerows and the incorporation of the leaf matter into the soil is required. But some farmers had an alternative use of the leaf matter. They harvested and dried the leaves and sold the leaf meal in the local market. Therefore, farmers were adopting technologies and trying their own alternatives as necessary and locally appropriate. An important conclusion is that menu of technical alternative based on both "scientific" knowledge and farmer-initiated possibilities are seemingly important and necessary in conducting adaptive research.

B. Participatory Approach to Research and Development in the Low-land and Upland.

The SIRSDP Experience in the Philippines:

I. *Background and Description*

The San Isidro Rural Systems Development Project (SIRSDP) is one of the community-based projects undertaken by the Centre for Social Research in Small Farmer Development, one of the Visayas State College of Agriculture's (VISCA) research and extension centers.

The project began its first year of full operation as a research and development project on July 1, 1984 with funding support from the Land Bank of the Philippines and technical assistance from the Visayas State College of Agriculture. During the year, benchmark surveys were conducted to generate baseline data on animal production, crop production, physical and human resources.

The project covers four *barangays* (villages) located in marginal upland and lowland areas of San Isidro Municipality. The most pressing problems before the start of the project included low farm productivity, lack of employment opportunities, upland degradation, lack of access to agricultural resources, poor health and nutrition, and lack of capital.

During the last five years, the Project has made modest but significant gains in developing the conditions of the beneficiaries in the area. But additional time is needed to institutionalize the reforms that have been started and to provide long-term economic growth and increased productivity sustained by the generation of appropriate technology.

From the start of the project implementation, the project staff have experienced, together with the personnel of the Land Bank of the Philippines and other agencies, a gradually unfolding process of participatory research and development efforts aimed at meeting the objectives of the project.

II. *Project Objectives*

Generally, the project aimed at pilot testing innovative strategies in integrated lowland and upland farming systems development in the municipality of San Isidro and develop the farm households into economically and socially self-reliant social systems. Specifically, the project sought to:

(a) Conduct on-farm research and generate appropriate agricultural technologies suited to the condition of the municipality;

(b) Demonstrate new technologies on lowland and upland crop production in the area;

(c) Increase employment opportunities to farm households through the introduction of appropriate non-traditional and viable crops and development of farm enterprises; and

(d) Provide technical assistance to farm households to increase the capability to manage their own resources and socio-economic affairs.

III. *Project Methodology*

Increasing farm productivity through better cropping systems and improved cultural and management practices was a major goal of the project.

A. *On-farm Research and Field Trials:* The Project continued to develop viable and appropriate technologies from lowland and upland farming systems through on-farm research and field trials established at the own field of Farm and Home Advisers (FHAs). The effort to generate additional technologies continued to look for other crops with appropriate practices which might give farmers better income. Likewise, demonstration farms for non-traditional and high valued crops were established to verify new technologies which may be appropriate to the lowland and upland areas. Special emphasis was also laid on verification and adoptive trials on appropriate cropping and land use patterns in the area. Further, farmers need to diversify their farm production by planting other corps to increase profit and minimize the risk inherent in mono-cropping.

B. *Educational and Training of the Farm and Home Advisers (FHAs) and other Farmers in the Area:* In order to inform, instruct as well as update the farmers with appropriate lowland and upland crop production technologies, continuing education and training on the FHAs were regularly conducted to continue serve as links between the extension workers and the farmers in the community. Likewise, participation of farmers in different forms of training, dialogues and visits in the entire process was encouraged in order to build their capacity to participate in generating appropriate farming systems and production practices.

C. *Technical Assistance:* Technical assistance and educational activities to both farmer-cooperators and non-cooperators in the project area were continuously conducted in order to increase capability of farmers and upgrade their farming and management skills to handle their own resources. Technical assistance, education and training coupled with actual field demonstration and trials as well as field visits were organized to update new crop production technologies found to be appropriate in the lowland and upland area.

D. *Marketing of Farm Products through Farmers Association:* Four farmers associations which were formed into a federation were also existing in the four *barangays* covered by the project. Farm products trading, an activity of the total agri-business project of the associations usually consisted of marketing farmers' produce especially water melon, and other non-traditional crops through the farmers associations. The associations would buy the farmers' produce and market them to retail outlets and consumers, thus freeing the farmers of the worries and risks of marketing losses.

IV. *Clientele's Participation*

A. *Technology Information and Dissemination through Farm and Home Advisers* :The beneficiaries of the project were the farm households of the four *barangays* which constitute 1,125 households with a total of 713 Operation and Land Transfer beneficiaries (OLT). To effectively disseminate the new production technologies and to make sure that the entire farm households in the area are given the necessary technical assistance, the FHAs elected from among the members of a contiguous group of households, farmers to act as depository and source of these new technologies and mobilized and utilized them for this purpose. The FHAs served as effective agents of change among the rural households involved in the project and served as links between the extension worker and the farmers in the community as "barefoot" technicians. Technical assistance was also extended to other farmers in the *barangays* outside the project area.

B. *Participation in Project Planning, Implementation, Evaluation and Management:* Participation of farmers in the different project activities was encouraged, especially in planning and actual implementation of the different on-farm researches, field trials and demonstrations conducted at the farmers' fields. Likewise, participation of farmers in the dissemination of new production technologies to the other farmers within and outside the project area was also encouraged. Further, field visits and home visits were organized to expose the farmers to actual field research and demonstrations and to encourage them to discuss and share experiences in the implementation of various farm practices and thrash out some problems encountered.

V. *Lessons Learned from the Project*

The successes and setbacks provided several great learning opportunities and direction both for the staff involved and the clientele they served. The following discussion summarizes the major lessons learned form the project:

A. *Goals/Terms of the project should be clear to the clientele:* To elicit information in participatory project, the clientele must have clear understanding of the nature of the project e.g. goals, duration, roles of the project staff and of the clientele, benefits of the project etc. In the project, the farmers were clearly informed of the project's philosophy of "helping people to help themselves" which means that they cannot expect dole-outs from the project, except in the form of expertise from the project staff. Having appraised of this information the farmers had to make their choice whether to reject the project or to accept it, do their part, and get the benefits.

B. *Basic inputs needed to achieve clientele's goals, must be available on loan basis:* The target families were wanting in resources which affluent rural families have. For instance, after the series of dialogues and discussions on alternatives to increase their produce and having seen the demonstrations, the farmers were convinced that planting of high yielding crop varieties was one feasible answer. They were eager to plant the new varieties but they lacked seeds, fertilizers, chemical pesticides, and had also no extra fund to pay for them. They discussed their problem with the project staff and with the farmers association but because the project did not promote giving of dole-outs, they proposed a system of repayment for the inputs they got from the project or from the farmers associations. To speed up collection of loan payment it was channeled through the farmers associations.

C. *Farmers adopt a technology with sure profitability:* The project had considerable influence on increasing the level of productivity of the farms and the income of the farmers.

The greatest impact was the commercialization of water melons. This factor attracted many farmers to join the farmers associations. The farmer-cooperators and the neighbouring farmers realized that there was money in water melon farming. In the summer of 1986 there was a tremendous increase in the number of water melon growers. The numbers of growers and correspondingly, the area, increased further in the summer of 1987. A net profit ranging from P.190.85 to P.18, 000.00 per farmer was earned from watermelon planted in rice fields which the farmers used to leave idle during the summer months.

One important lesson learned in water melon production was that farmers who normally did not spend for inputs for traditional crops like rice and corn were willing to take risks and invested on expensive inputs like fertilizers and insecticides because they were sure of the profitability of the crop.

D. *Factual knowledge about the clientele or their environment is a pre-requisite to participation:* Besides the low educational attainment of the beneficiaries, most were not exposed to more advanced communities other than their own home town; thus their visions and perceptions of certain aspects of their lives or their environments were limited. During the initial dialogues with the farmers the only problem they identified were inadequate food and low income; none mentioned the health and sanitation problems in their villages such as dirty surroundings and periodic outbreaks in the area of typhoid fever, cholera or dysentery. However, after they heard from the ViSCA physician in the lectures on parasites, their life-cycle and their effect on the people who were infected, their eyes were opened to the sanitation problem of the community.

E. *Periodic evaluation must be done by the clientele on their performance based on their goals to make them aware of the level of their progress:* The farmers must be constantly made aware of their level of progress based on the goals they had set for themselves. For instance, in crop production activity, each farmer sets specific goals on crops to plant, what cropping and land use pattern to follow, and when to plant them. With these, they should be made aware with regards to the level of achievement they obtained/ gained so that they could adjust and make some modifications, if necessary, to attain their goals.

REFERENCES

Alcober, D.L., "Farming Systems Research (FSR) as a Mechanism for Research and Extension Linkage – ViSCA's Experience in FSDP-EV; FSDP-EV & FARMI Terminal Report No.87" Philippines, 1990.

Bernadas, C.N.Jr., "Lessons in Upland Farmer Participation: The case of Enriched Fallow Technology in Jaro, Leyte" the Philippines (mimeograph), 1991.

Bernadas, C.N.Jr., "Orientation Training and Workshop in FSRE; FSDP-EV and FARMI Terminal Report No.87", Philippines, 1990.

ILEIA, *Proceedings: Participatory Technology Development in Sustainable Agriculture,* 1989.

Tull, K. et al., *Experiences in Success: Case Studies in Growing Enough Food through Regenerative Agriculture,* Rodale International, 1987.

Waters-Bayers, A., *PTD: Some Approaches and Tools,* ODI, 1989.

10

TRAINING AS A PRINCIPAL FACTOR OF HRD INITIATIVE

Training of personnel in all fields of development activities has, in the recent past, gained considerable importance. It is a necessary human input for development. The diverse categories of adults who are trained constitute a different audience from that of a school or university. The success of any training programme depends importantly on five factors: the participant (learner), the trainer (teacher), the sponsoring organizations of the participants and the training institute and the training technology employed. Training essentially is an interaction between the participant and the trainer. Learning very much depends on the climate that is created by the five factors mentioned above.

Training is an essential human resource development activity. It is an investment on people since people are primary in all endeavours in life in making things better. Training is for action, accomplishment, improved performance, managing men and material. It is behaviour to be taught and learnt. The very existence and progress in life in all spheres of life is based on informal and formal training. Training is to meet one's needs and contribute to development. It is well nigh impossible to imagine how life would be minus training. Man is born with genetically transmitted potential. We may call this as nature and nurturing this biological endowment that takes place right from the infancy upto adulthood and beyond the adult stage is the process of training the individual to fit him to meet his needs and work towards the progress of the community. In development administration, training has become an indispensable necessity with increasing innovations and new ways of accomplishing needs and expectations of people. It is to bring about an extended self in the individual with a concern for the amelioration of all segments of people in the society. Training attempts to bring about an attitudinal change to work towards 'Unto The Last'. We may speak at length about various dimensions of training but it is enough to say that minus training it would be groping in the dark. Training is light that leads you towards continuous betterment of life. Even in the epic period, for instance, in the *Mahabharatha*, the Pandava and Kaurava princes were trained in archery. We cannot imagine a soldier or a general in the army without having undergone training in knowledge and skills related to warfare. They are trained especially in discipline, commitment and determination to serve their country. Training, principally, focuses on three areas: knowledge, skills and attitude. For any effective management, the above three components are essential. One can imagine what happens and the consequences of any performance short of or want of one of the three elements. One may have knowledge in a particular area, but lacks skills to use that knowledge and also inclination to use it (attitude). In another case, one has skill but lacks the needed knowledge and proper attitude. Still in another case, one is positively inclined ready to perform but lacks knowledge and skills. They are to be in the proper functional composition and balance meeting the needs of administration and development. The whole operation in life is learnt behaviour. Training may be called as neo-socialization creating an environment to acquire needed new knowledge, develop requisite skills and also to learn conducive interpersonal behaviour in managing people in getting things done.

Training makes you realize where you are and where you should go and what you should do. It gives you an idea that still miles to go by. Sometimes, training throws some glimmering light on future. Training opens new vistas of knowledge. It makes you feel humble and modest in the area of intellectual exposure. Training is an opportunity for the participant to compare his ideas, views, convictions and knowledge. Training provides means for reflections. Training of personnel assumes greater significance and importance when it comes to development administration. We may think of several analogies likened to the import of training. Training is a kind of intellectual refreshment. Training is just like irrigating a crop periodically. It is reminding and helping people what they are expected to do and how to do. Training invigorates the spirit of commitment. It is drawing strength from each other. Training is sometimes a fine soothing breeze. Sometimes, it opens your eyes, kindles and injects your imagination. It is something like dawn from darkness. Training provides intellectual, social and cultural contacts among the participants and faculty. Training generates flow of new ideas. It is a testing ground for the experience of the participants. Training is going into the open and receiving the sunlight. Learning in groups provides a comparative perspective. It is an opportunity for the personnel to tune with changing times and demands. It tells you that there is something better to learn and apply that learning and make things better. The factors or the elements that contribute and enhance human resources are of diverse type. It may be in terms of salaries, promotion, increments, allowances and congenial environment in the work situation, the kind of leadership provided in the department, the way in which the employees at every level are motivated. When an individual joins an organization, he comes with a background: academic qualification, sometimes with some experience in the work field. After the individual joins the organization the measures taken by the employing organization are expected to contribute to the development of the individual employee. We cannot say that every positive attempt made by the organization to improve the performance of the employees will always have a positive effect. HRD is a two-way function. One is interest, inclination, perseverance and ambition on the part of the employee to grow and develop and on the other hand, it is the measures adopted by the organization which are complimentary to the aspirations of the employees in the organization. HRD is to enhance capabilities on the part of the employees not in a vacuum but directed towards accomplishing the tasks of the organization. The concept of HRD is a complex one. It is not simply providing monetary incentive but it has multiple implications. One major means is providing appropriate training to the employees at various stages of their career in the organization.

While looking into the initiatives in the field of HRD taken by the Government of Andhra Pradesh, a brief conceptual analysis of HRD as well as HRM seems relevant. In the following chapter, we briefly look into human resource development as the principle factor of success in organization.

> "In the ultimate analysis the wealth of a nation is its people".
>
> —Arnold Toynbee.

> "The Management to make substantial capital investment on human resources to develop human beings in the organization through training organizing and developing the people at work so that they will be able to make the business productive with the help of the best contribution of the people at work".
>
> —Peter Drucker, The Father of Management

The organizations earlier reflected the type of the political system, social structure and cultural values with predominantly authoritarian management reinforced by bureaucratic style of functioning. In such a climate the individual employee was viewed and used as a human raw material, a worker, ignoring his personal feelings, ideas, views and his job related and life related needs and his career development. The management in the past to a large extent expected the unquestioning behaviour and obedience on the part of the employees and surprisingly, the employees too accepted it as a norm and what was expected of them. But, today, the conditions are changed and changing with the gradual increase of education, communication, endowment of rights and privileges to the employees, diffusion and wider spread of knowledge, skills and technology that mattered in a variety of organizations, emergence of trade unions and increased prominence gained by industrial relations. Human resources in any organization became a precious material which is to be respected, nurtured, motivated and promoted for the good and advancement of the individual, his organization and the larger society.

The simplest definition of Human Resources Development is organized learning experience provided by employers within a specified period of time to bring about the possibilities of performance improvement and on personal growth. The number of activity areas in HRD are the following:

1. Training - Learning focused on the present job of the learner.
2. Education - Learning focused on a future job of the learner.
3. Development - Not job focused.

Nature of HRM/HRD

Human Resources Management (HRM) is concerned with the human beings in an organization. It reflects a new philosophy, a new outlook, approach, and strategy, which views an organization's manpower as its resources and assets, and not as liabilities or mere hands.

Resources are the means which can be drawn on. They are collective means for production, support and defence, as well as a source of strength and aid. Human resources are human wealth or means that can be drawn on. Human capital or manpower resources of an organization can be treated as its human resources. It can otherwise be understood as the resourcefulness of the human beings or people available for an organization.

It is interesting to note that natural resources that a country is endowed with does not automatically make it rich. But it is the human resources that harness and wisely utilize the natural resources towards material affluence and richness of life. The following examples show the paradox in respect to natural and human resources where in it is the human resources that account for the rich or poor state of a country.

RESOURCE RICH	:	RICH
		USA, CANADA, BRAZIL
RESOURCE RICH	:	POOR
		MANY OF THE AFRICAN AND LATIN AMERICAN COUNTRIES AND IN A SENSE INDIA TOO.
RESOURCE POOR	:	RICH
		JAPAN , ISRAEL
RESOURCE POOR	:	POOR
		NEPAL, BANGLADESH

The same paradox applies to some of the states in India.

In generic terms, human resources can be defined as the total knowledge, skills, creative abilities, talents and aptitudes of an organization's workforce, as well as the values, attitudes, approaches and beliefs of the individuals involved in the affairs of the organization. It is the sum total or aggregate of inherent abilities, acquired knowledge and skills represented by the talents and aptitudes of the employed persons in an organization.

Human resources approach takes into consideration the potentiality and vitality of the people available for the organization. Even in an age of automation as of today, manpower is the most essential and indispensable resource of any organization. Resourcefulness of various categories of people say: managers, scientific and research people, executives, supervisors, workers (skilled, unskilled) and all such people available for the organization to be drawn on, can be treated as human resources. In fact, without appropriate human resources, no business or organization can exist and grow. This is, perhaps, the reason why human resources management has become the focus of attention of progressive organizations of today.

Human resources management is the process of managing the people of an organization with a humane approach. Human resources approach to manpower enables the manager to view his people as an important, if not the most important, resource. It is a benevolent approach to develop and effectively utilize the manpower not only for the benefit of the organization but for the growth, development and self satisfaction of the concerned people. Thus, human resources management is a system that focuses on human resources development, on the one hand, and effective management of people on the other.

As a result of the fundamental changes in attitudes, approaches, outlook, philosophy, perspective and practices emerged in the personnel area in the form of human resources management (HRM) strategy, it has become necessary for every organization to develop skills, talents, potentialities, capabilities and attitudes of company's own people to meet the emerging challenges. Hence, HRD (human resources development) policies have been adopted by many organizations. It is now-a-days spreading to many others. HRD strategies are supposed to bring forth necessary changes in skills, capabilities and attitudes of people who are required to cope with the emerging changes. Thus, HRD has become an integral part of human resources management.

The new HRD approach, that stresses the need for developing the organization's own people to suit the updated technology, modernization of machinery and equipments and the changing trends in attitudes and approaches, necessitates to develop individual employee in accordance with his aspirations and potentialities on the one hand, and the organization's requirement on the other. This is what the HRD does. Quite often Organization Development (OD) programmes are effectively integrated with the HRD programmes. Of course, OD programmes are the programmes which the OD interventionists prescribe for the effectiveness of the organization. It need not be what the individual members of the organization seek. HRD interventionists primarily seek to know what the individuals seek to have, and then try to match it with the organizational needs. Training and development programmes form part of OD, while training and development are the most decisive aspects of HRD too.

Firstly, development of leadership (developing leaders capable of working in multicultural environments both within their organizations and across national boundaries). Challenges facing management of people are monumental in the contemporary business and development world. Factors like changes in the world economic and political system, technological aspects and human values, tension over protecting jobs with national boundaries versus looking offshore for cheaper labour costs so as to remain world competitive, fresh economic policy issues stemming from the transformation of economies and job structures, increase of high technology jobs, all such factors necessitate to develop leadership vital for effective actuation.

Secondly, development of a new organizational culture. A revolutionary cultural change triggered by globalisation of business and the resultant demand for strong operational managers necessitate a greater reinforcement in the human resources system. Human resources development to cope with the corporate cultural change is the need of the hour. "It is important to make the implicit explicit: to continually examine the culture through a variety of feedback mechanisms, mapping out the culture, assessing where the organization is, where it wants to go, carefully identifying strategies for change which constantly deal with the cultural gaps, and working the organization culture in relationship to the particular national culture in which it is embedded".

Thirdly, human resources development must focus on new organizational forms. Human resource planning and development strategy must be rightly coupled to business strategies to the extent that the whole organization may take the shape of a viable global organization. New concepts regarding what is work and how to redistribute tasks, redefine roles, authority relationships, and sources of power must be based on the new models emerging globally. Recruiting, selecting, developing, rotating, and managing human resources must aid such a global organization with a new form and perspective.

Human resource development must be able to develop overall capability of individual employees of an organization, and discover and exploit their own potentials for the common goals of the organizations to which they belong, for the betterment of themselves and their families, and for the country as a whole. For this purpose appropriate job design and succession plan must be integrated with any human resource development programme. In fact, HRD approach may take into account the principle of "form-storm-norm-perform".

Six dimensions of human resource development, may be mentioned here. These six dimensions are: (a). Performance appraisal; (b) Potential appraisal; (c) Employee counseling; (d) Career development and planning; (e) Training; and (f) Organizational development. In general any human resource development programme must enable the organization's people to acquire and sharpen their capabilities to perform well on their respective jobs, develop and stimulate their potentialities, and to help them make their best contribution to develop an organization culture of team spirit, cordial relationship, human values and oneness of the management and its people. From this view point, HRD enables an executive to gain a job that provides variety and challenge to one's ability and competence, opportunity to learn and develop skills and competence, social support and recognition at work place, opportunity to relate what an individual performs and produce to his social life, and feeling that work would lead to a desirable future.

Thus, HRD is a continuous process, which matches organizational needs for human resources and the individual needs for a career development. It enables the individuals to gain their best human potential by attaining a total all-round development. It promotes dignity of employment of every employee of an organization, and provides opportunities for team work, personal development and career development. Hence a well-planned HRD system must be a part of human resource management of every organization. Such a human resource development system may have the following elements:

(i) Development of leadership and organizational commitment;

(ii) Career planning and development;

(iii) Performance Appraisal;

(iv) An adequate reward system;

(v) Potential Appraisal;

(vi) Effective counseling;

(vii) Well formulated Human Resource Information System (HRIS);

(viii) An effective grievance handling;

(ix) Management development;

(x) Technical development;

(xi) Supervisory development;

(xii) Organization development;

(xiii) Training and educating;

(xiv) Succession planning;

(xv) Employee welfare; and

(xvi) Feedback.

These elements are presented in the following figure (Fig.1)

Every organization needs to develop leadership and sincere organizational commitment of its people. Hence, it is proper if the HRD starts with developing leadership and people with organizational commitment. As the organization needs its people to have sincere organizational commitment, every employee has his or her own aspirations to have a good career. Hence, career planning and development for every employee in the

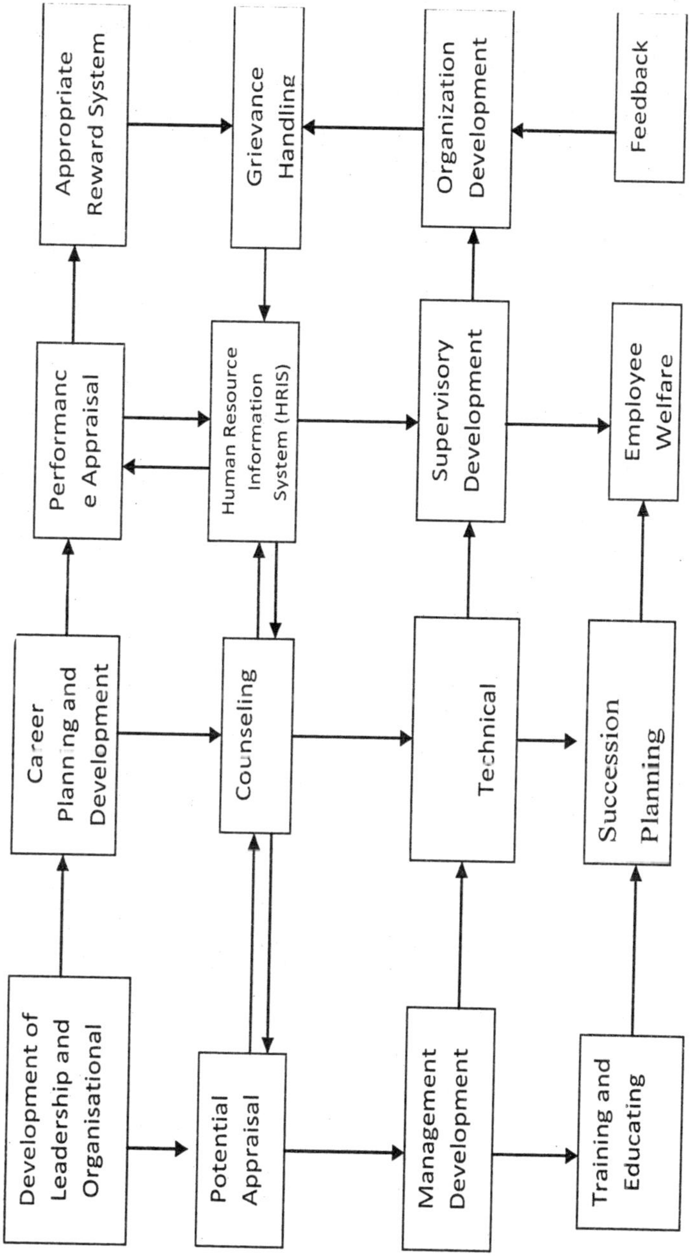

Fig.1: A Model for Human Resource Development

organization should go hand in hand with leadership development.

Career planning and development must be followed by performance appraisal and reward system which should motivate the employees to make their best contribution to the organizational goals and objectives. Leadership development must also be followed by potential appraisal which enable the HRM to determine the potentiality of every individual employee to hold critical positions and tackle critical situations. Counseling, which includes career counseling, motivation counseling and problem solving counseling, facilitates career planning and development, while a human resources information system must function at the center of HRD system. Effective and timely grievance handling must be a part of every HRD system, since no effort for human resource development can bear real fruit without timely grievance handling.

Developing managers to handle organizational resources including human resources and activities effectively is the need of every organization, particularly in the context of rapidly changing business environment. It must be followed by technological and technical development. Updating the organization's technology, modernization of the plant and automation need appropriate people for which human development programmes are required. The actual operation takes place at the supervisory level, and hence supervisory development is the crux of HRD. Developing the workforce development is included in the supervisory development function. All such development programmes must result in organization development. Obviously OD becomes a part of HRD.

Training and educating make an important method of human development in an organization, which enables an organization to prepare its people for various positions. Hence, succession planning goes with human development. Employee welfare has a long way to go in motivating the people of every organization making the HRD intervention effective. Hence, employee welfare is integrated with the HRD model presented here. Feedback also makes a part of this model just like any other management model. Effective feedback goes with every developed organization. Proper grievance handling is, at the same time necessary for the feedback system to function effectively. Some of the steps of HRD model are examined below separately.

Development of Leadership and Organizational Commitment

Every organization of today needs effective leaders. In fact, bosses are replaced by leaders since leadership role is invaluable in the contemporary organizations of knowledge workers and technocrats. Leadership styles and traits coupled with leadership roles go a long way in team building which is an essential aspect of today's managerial effectiveness. This is the reason why leadership development is considered to be an integral part of human resource development.

A good manager-leader provides not only leadership to his subordinates, but he makes leaders from his subordinates. He is not the one who rushes with an answer to every question or a right answer for a wrong question, and its right solution. Rather he is the one who identifies correct alternative solutions and then choosing the best option from among the alternatives. It is he who gets the best solution implemented through his followers or subordinates. HRD must be able to create such leaders in the organization.

Such leaders are assets to the organization. While they will have organizational commitment in themselves, they generate and stimulate organizational commitment in their subordinates and followers. HRD programmes must, therefore, make special efforts to inculcate organizational commitment in every employee, particularly in executives and managers.

Organizational Commitment

Organizational commitment is an important variable of employee behaviour toward his organization. It is employees' identification with the organization and its goals, objectives, methods, values and philosophy. When an individual executive or worker fosters organizational commitment, he identifies himself with the value systems of the organization. It may also mean that the individual's value systems are either identical to the organization's value systems or the individual makes adjustments in his value system in such a way that he commits himself to the organizational goals and objectives, compromising his ideas and values with the organizational values, ideas, standards, objectives, patterns, methods and views. Organizational commitment goes a long way in motivation, morale, job satisfaction and productivity since the employee maintains oneness with the organization.

Factors like job satisfaction, growth prospects, facilities for development, compensation package and other perks, possibility for satisfaction of various needs, organization's attitudes and approaches to its people, corporate image, grievance handling methods, security and safety of employment, group cohesiveness, welfare facilities, and so on may substantially influence the organizational commitment of people. Organizational culture and work culture may also influence the organizational commitment of people. In addition to all such factors, employee values have tremendous impact on organizational commitment, and hence HRD programmes must aim at establishing and developing conducive employee values as well.

Professional Values Replace Societal Values

Professionalization of management, and an increasing desire to foster and uphold professional prejudices, pride, and a professional career among managers and employees have established a new work culture. People have become more self-centred and selfish. Employees are more concerned about their own profession, for the development of which they strive hard day and night. In the process, they use many methods like strikes, direct agitations, gheraos, intimidations, work stoppages, and so on for the sake of their own interests in countries like India. They reveal no concern for the interests of the customers, prospects or the society. They even neglect social values, interests of the society, and their own social integration.

Traditionally strong social bondages give way for social disintegration resulting in a sort of social reorganization. People increasingly turn to liqueur, drugs and other intoxicants. Even a liqueur-based corporate culture begin to be widely accepted. For the sake of professional growth some people sacrifice even human values or family relations, norms and values. Executive stresses increase, and many broken families emerge. In the process, the organizational commitment of people disappear. HRD responsibility backed by counseling is a Herculean task here.

Behaviour Modification

Organizational commitment is a specific employee's behaviour towards his organization, its values, objectives and methods. On account of various reasons or difference in values, there is possibility for certain individuals to reveal behaviour inappropriate for organizational commitment. In such situations human resource development programmes must go a long way to attain behaviour modification of employees.

The assumption is that behaviour is a function of its consequences. The proposition, therefore, is that a behaviour modification is possible by modifying the consequences. It means that behaviour can be improved, changed, suppressed or modified by what may happen as a result of behaviour.

Every behaviour produces consequences. Hence, the nature of these consequences determines or modifies the behaviour. The behaviour that yields positive outcomes is strengthened, and that which results in negative outcomes tends to be avoided. Then actions, which produce positive results, are repeated, and those which result in negative results are abandoned. If the consequences produced by a particular behaviour can be controlled in some manner, the behaviour can be shaped or altered. It is assumed that the tendency of people to perform certain action increases when they are provided with positive reinforcers for engaging in such actions. On the other hand negative reinforcers prevent people from doing certain things.

When these reinforcers, or principles based on these assumptions shape, mould, change or modify behaviour, it is known as behaviour modification. Thus, the basic premise of the behaviour modification theory is that behaviour is controlled or modified by its immediate consequences. Important determinants of behaviour modification are positive reinforcement, punishment, negative reinforcement, extinction and schedule of reinforcement, which substantially help in modifying overt actions or behaviour.

Career Planning and Development

No human resource development can be acceptable to the people of any organization, if it fails to provide opportunities for individual employees to have bright career prospects. It is for this purpose that human resource development integrates career planning and career development with it. Career planning is closely linked with both human resource planning and human resource development. HRD must therefore, incorporate career development too.

Proper career planning also leads to career development. It develops the career of every individual executive, which results in adequate growth of the career of every employee. Hence, succession planning is closely linked with career planning and development.

Performance Appraisal

Performance appraisal is an indispensable aspect of human resource development, which enables the management to understand where their people stand, what is expected of them, what they actually do, where they lack, how can they be updated, and so on.

As a part of appraisal, many organizations follow a

confidential report system. The confidential information and the remarks of the reporting and reviewing officers are kept secret. Such confidential reports are not communicated to the concerned individuals, but used as the basis for decisions concerning them. This is not a policy conducive to the HRD policy.

Appraisal system must, on the contrary, be in-built as a sub-system of the whole HRD system. Appraisal must be a normal aspect of human resources management, and appraisal interview must be held at regular intervals, not to find faults of the employees, but to understand the strengths, weaknesses, needs for further development, potential, performance, contribution to the organizational goals, capabilities, organizational commitment, knowledge levels, expectations, aspirations, drawbacks, needs as a human being, abilities, and so on. Both positive and negative aspects concerning each individual must be communicated to the respective person confidentially; and the individual's weaknesses and drawbacks must never be given publicity. Programmes must be planned for developing every individual in terms of his capabilities, updating technical, human and behavioural capabilities, overcoming weaknesses, improving productivity of his strengths, and so on. It is the appraisal that determines the worth of every employee. One who is capable to take up challenges and responsibilities can be given greater responsibility. One who has the potentials to accept challenges and responsibilities can be trained to be effective. Thus, effective delegation must be based on proper appraisal.

A general weakness of the appraisal practices in many organizations is that a subordinate is evaluated by his superior by virtue of his position, though he does not possess the necessary capability and expertise for the same. There is possibility for bias in such appraisals. Hence, an appraisal system, consisting of the appraisal by the immediate boss on the one hand, and a periodical appraisal by an expert appraisers' group established for the specific purpose of conducting evaluation and appraisal on the other would be more effective.

The ability of an employee to accomplish the targets must be given priority in evaluation, though other aspects are not unimportant.

Similarly, any adverse entry in an individual's appraisal record must be neutralized when the individual improves himself through training and further behaviour, attitudes and actions. This motivates every individual to improve himself, and he gets an opportunity to improve and make behaviour modification. Every appraisal system must include a potential appraisal too, so that the organization can identify talents for tomorrow's operations today. Appraisal must be followed by appropriate compensation and reward system.

Human Resource Information System (HRIS)

A well-formulated information system must form part of any human resource development system. All the necessary information about all employees and executives of the organization backed by a data bank must be included in such a system. Basic information about each and every employee, including training needs, training programmes attended, potential appraisal records, performance records, records of accomplishments and rewards, all such information should be updated and stored. Such information can be retrieved whenever required for training and development purposes, career development needs, promotions, rewards or punishments, special projects, and so on. Who can be developed for what job can be decided upon with the help of HRIS. Hence, human resource development must be backed by human resources information system.

In the context of the recent developments in business, particularly dynamic technological development, human resources information system has a special significance. In large organizations Computerized Human Resources Information System (CHRIS) can play a very vital role. It not only stores and retrieves information regarding training and development needs, but training details and information about those who undergo the various types of training which would be helpful both in potential appraisal and performance appraisal.

Effective communication is an essential aspect of human resources management. Human resources information system helps the communication process in an organization. CHRIS is, thus an effective tool in the tool kit of human resource managers for HRD in particular and HRM in general.

Grievance Handling

Individuals, who form the organization, may have grievances against the organization. Certain needs or demands of organization's own members, which they feel legitimate to be satisfied by the organization, but not provided for by the organization, become their grievances. It may lead to discontentment and grudge on the part of the respective individual. In order to gain cooperation of organization's own people their grievances are required to be settled. Moreover, without settlement of the grievances, HRD programmes may not be effective. Hence, a proper grievance handling machinery should be established in conjunction with the HRD intervention. While genuine grievances must be settled and redressed judiciously, unrealistic and false grievances can be tackled with the help of effective counseling. Covert grievances breed disappointment, a feeling of grudge and problem emotions, resulting in low morale, low organizational commitment, and even weak temperament. A person, who is subjected to such weak emotions, may not be able to positively react to the efforts made by his organization for human resource development. Hence, an organization's HRD system must have a grievance handling machinery with it.

Training Efforts for HRD

Managers, over the years, have relied on training the people as a part of developing their organizations. In recent times Management by Objectives, Management Grid, Transaction Analysis, Quality Circles And Quality Of Work Life programmes have found favour with many organizations. Both professional and traditional managers now harp on fads of one of these names profusely for portraying the progressive nature of their organizations. For an effective human resource development, there must be a constant effort on the part of management to develop their people. The use of these methods and techniques is also not ruled out.

Training is an instrument of developing the employees or workforce by enriching the skills and improving the human behaviour, which result in organization development adequate enough for the accomplishment of objectives from time to time. It helps organizations and individuals to develop themselves in consonance with the changing needs of the environment in which they survive, operate and progress. Training in technology, profession, organizational behaviour, and management development are common. Both on-the –job and off-the-job training are important.

In systematically operating a training system in an organization, the human resource manager may formulate a systematic pattern. It may include:

(1) Assessment of training needs;

(2) Determination of gaps;

(3) Designing training programmes;

(4) Identifying resource persons;

(5) Preparation of training budgets;

(6) Preparation of training materials;

(7) Organization of training programmes;

(8) Evaluation of training effectiveness; and

(9) Revising training pattern or training modules wherever necessary.

Conclusion

Manpower is indisputably the basic resource. It is the indispensable means of converting other resources for the use and benefit of mankind. In the words of the late President

Kennedy. "It is not mere possession of natural resources that makes a nation strong and viable, it is fundamentally the employment of these resources that is significant".

Management is not simply a key that helps in unlocking the magic doors of growth, it is a way of looking at contemporary problems of social and economic change as they are reflected in industry, government and business. For this, men with managerial skills become necessary. One has not only to modernize as best as possible the apparatus of production but also to introduce a change in the attitude of people and in their innovating skills.

Whether it is a government department, a public enterprise or a private organization, it is needless to stress that people are the organization and they could be compared to numeral one and rest of things could be zeros or any numbers. If we place zeros after one, it carries weight, if it were to be placing one after zero it means nothing. There is a great need for any organization to play the role of a MOTHER and see how a mother prepares, fosters, nurtures, educates, and trains her children. The MOTHER is to be a model to any organization. The mother role is to be adopted by all organizations vis-à-vis the employees and create a sense of belonging and a sense of pride among the employees, that they identify themselves with the organization in toto. This could be achieved not only through incentives and training and career planning and development but to a great extent it depends on the attitude on the part of the management towards the employees and the way in which they are communicated with and treated. Every employee irrespective of his role and status in the organization is to be treated as an important contributing human component for the activity and success of the organization.

11

STRATEGIES FOR DEVELOPING ENTREPRENEURSHIP AMONG PEOPLE

When we speak of developing entrepreneurship among women, we cannot think of this effort and programme in isolation. One can think of developing entrepreneurship among women only through creating an environment which would motivate and facilitate women coming forward to take to certain enterprises. This necessitates developing entrepreneurship in rural areas. The present chapter focuses on developing entrepreneurship towards rural industrialization. Such a measure will pave the way and create conditions which will help the women folk from different ethnic segments and economic background to gradually move and shoulder up industrial activity by themselves or with their family members.

As we have pointed out earlier, promoting and developing small-scale and cottage industries inclusive of handicrafts and artisan enterprises in rural areas is not for their own sake, nor is it simply a political strategy to appease the low-income groups in the community, but it is an indispensable measure, whatever be the approaches and methods employed towards the use of the material and human resources at the disposal of the rural communities. So long you have the choice to ignore rural industrialization and that you have better alternatives to it, you are free to pursue such a course of development. But such alternatives are few in view of the enormity of population in some countries, literacy and technological levels out-weighed by material and human resources that could be gradually harnessed and utilized to meet the minimum needs of the people.

We can safely say, irrespective of certain limitation in respect of the whole class of small-scale and cottage industries in terms of productivity, quality of products, profits and poor management of these enterprises, that there is no argument against rural industrialization and development of small-scale and cottage industries.

Promotion and development of small industries will involve, both directly and indirectly, the development of entrepreneurship. The approach and strategies for achieving industrial development may vary from those for entrepreneurship development. Perhaps, the strategies vary accordingly as emphasis is placed on either of the two. Needless to say that industrial development cannot be achieved without entrepreneurship development. Depending upon the emphasis, one becomes the by-product of the other. They are indeed two facets of the same activity.

The inadequacy of entrepreneurship is an inhibiting factor to accelerate the process of industrialization in the newly developing communities. Although there is no such thing as a zero level of entrepreneurship, the absence of an appropriate industrial and entrepreneurial climate and an industrial base, coupled with lack of access to relevant technology, has acted as a handicap for such communities, to achieve rapid industrial development. The inadequate availability of entrepreneurial talent particularly affects the development of modern small manufacturing and processing enterprises for, while large industries can be set up with expatriate capital and entrepreneurship, small industries need to have a domestic entrepreneurial base. The development of indigenous entrepreneurship especially among the rural-tribal populations is, therefore, a key issue and an imperative need on the part of the countries embarking on small industry development programmes.

Our focus in this discussion is on entrepreneurial development in rural communities. Development here means a basic, partial or total transformation, a socio-cultural change in the client community. Entrepreneur in this context is defined as one who would start an industry or take to a new enterprise which is a deviation from his traditional family occupation or profession. Further, entrepreneurship may be defined as a creative activity, the entrepreneur being an innovator who introduces something new into the economy: a method of production not yet tested by experience in the branch of manufacture concerned, a product with which the consumers are not familiar, a new source of raw material, or of a new market hitherto unexploited and other similar innovations.

The approach suggested here is field approach which may be defined s a holistic approach to development comprising the study of the social structure and socio-cultural processes that operate in a given client community. It envisages a thorough understanding of the target community in all its aspects and attempts entrepreneurial development in it, manipulating simultaneously all the key elements in the total system such as physical and human resources, institutions, infrastructure and the entrepreneur himself.

Prior to the advent of entrepreneurial development agencies, entrepreneurship grew as a spontaneous economic activity among certain traditionally entrepreneurial communities wherein this activity was institutionalized. Besides, there has been sporadic emergence of entrepreneurship among other groups based on needs and wants of people, natural resources, innovativeness, managerial and risk-taking abilities on the part of individual entrepreneurs. The rate and volume of spontaneous emergence of entrepreneurship is far behind the desired national, social and economic objectives of entrepreneurial development. Attempts during the past few years have been towards induced entrepreneurship. This was restricted to selective, sporadic and isolated approaches and the results have not been commensurate with the time and money spent on these programmes. It is relevant here to look into some sociological aspects of entrepreneurship citing India as an example.

Sociological Aspects

Entrepreneurship as an economic activity emerges and functions in a sociological and cultural setting. It could be conceived of as an individual's free choice activity or a social group's occupation or profession. In the Indian context, the supply of entrepreneurship in the past was mostly from some functionally designated communities or individual families. The ancient Hindu Varna order and its later ramifications called the caste system were partly based on the division of functions in the Hindu society. Thus we had and have the Brahmin, Kshatriya, Vysya and Sudra with innumerable sub-castes and sects in the first three and hundreds of castes or endogamous groups among the Sudra. Of the four Varnas traditionally, it was the Vysya community that was assigned the entrepreneurial activity comprising farming, trade, commerce and industry. Over the years, trade and commerce became characteristic of them. Further, the caste system, which was the later complex social stratification of the Varna order, was predominantly associated with diverse occupations and professions in a given territorial community. This stratification of Hindu society resulted in the birth of a new institution called the Hindu Jajmani system. It is a service relationship between the service or goods receiver (Jajmani) and the service and goods supplier (Kamin). The rendering of service or supply of goods on the part of a caste has become over centuries hereditary and closely associated with the caste system. The Jajmani system is a complex network of socio-economic relationship and still prevails all over rural India. Thus we had the functional groups such as priests, carpenters, blacksmiths, goldsmiths, potters, dairymen, washer-men, gardeners, water bearers, cobblers, barbers, sweepers, scavengers, oil-mongers, vegetable growers, weavers, traders and scores of others with distinct functions. An occupational or servicing group rendered service or supplied goods as the case may be and received remuneration mostly in kind annually or periodically.

In the jajmani system the farmer was the central figure and other groups served him and served each other. This kind of barter economy and socio-economic relationship streamlined and institutionalized the castes and their distinct functions, as a contrast to the Japanese society where in there has been negligible division of labour or functions. Since it became institutionalized over a period of time, it tended to be rigid, each caste pursuing its traditionally designated or customary function. Thus, as a sequence of the jajmani system, activities relating to industry, trade and commerce and small enterprises such as handicrafts made by artisans and their counterparts elsewhere in the country (Agarwal, Marwari etc.), the smith and artisan groups are examples of those who are predominantly engaged in trade, commerce and small enterprises, manufacturing, processing, the supply of entrepreneurs was sociologically and culturally limited to the traditional entrepreneurial groups. That is, only certain caste groups forced by the value system and tradition entered the field of entrepreneurship. Alongside the traditional entrepreneurial caste groups, in a sporadic way, a few individual pioneers and innovators drawn from the non-traditional entrepreneurial groups have taken to entrepreneurship.

During the past two-three decades in the context of India and other developing countries in Asia, as a consequence of a combination of factors such as increase in education, forces working against the institution of caste (in India), democracy as an ideal and value, territorial mobility, urbanization, increase in population, new impetus in science and technology, the state's intervention and emphasis on industrialization, new economic policy and diversification of occupations, a climate is being created inducing and encouraging development of entrepreneurship both among traditional and non-traditional groups.

Assumptions

In our approach to the problem of developing entrepreneurship in rural communities, a basic question needs to be answered. Does promotion and development entrepreneurship depend on inherent entrepreneurial ability or quality of individuals in a given community? If the answer is 'yes', and since the inherent factor is a constant in all societies, it ceases to be a significant change-inducing factor. We may grant that entrepreneurial ability as a consequence of social and environmental background is distributed in a given population to a smaller degree. Assuming that, how do we explain and account for the transformation of agrarian societies into industrial societies. Almost the whole western society and Japan are examples of this transformation. In the case of Japan, which lacks most of the natural material resources, it was the human resource, the quality of man and the entrepreneurial climate it has built-up that put it on the map of highly industrialized countries in the world. The kind of transformation that has taken place in once-agrarian countries leads us to make the following assumptions:

1. We assume that agrarian societies could be transformed into industrial societies. The chief element in this change process is 'time', provided that factors such as finance, technology, marketing of the product and organizational machinery – necessary concomitants of industrialization are taken care of.

2. We assume that physical and institutional infrastructure could be provided with comparative ease in developing entrepreneurship.

3. We assume that conditions could be created and talented persons could be trained to become successful entrepreneurs.

We realize that the real problem we encounter in promoting entrepreneurship in the client community is the 'human factor', the individual in society, his network of relationships, his aspirational level, his attitudes and his group norms. This leads us to the study and understanding of the target community wherein we have to locate and develop entrepreneurship. We may call this a field approach or a total systems approach to the development of entrepreneurship.

This approach does not ignore the individual or selective approach by the use of projective tests and other psychological tools. Field approach is employed to see that the potential entrepreneur secures encouragement and support from the local institutions and environment of which he is a constituent. This modus operandi requires an understanding of the clientele community.

Aspects of the Client Community to be Studied

In the field approach, we take the entire community, be it a village, a cluster of villages, a mandal, a block, an occupational or a professional group as a unit of action. We study all aspects of the client system, physical, economic, human resources, cultural patterns, social, political and ecclesiastical structure, local institutions and institutional leadership. The study of the client system precedes the programmes related to entrepreneurial development. The data that are already available in respect to a unit of action (industrial potential surveys, lead bank surveys, techno-economic surveys, monographs, census reports etc.) will be made use of. The gaps in the aspects of the clientele group will have to be studied afresh. The major aspects to be studied of a client group may be described briefly.

Physical Conditions

It includes the physical resources that the area is endowed with, such as rainfall, terrain, quality of soil, the kind of farm activities that are in practice and enterprises that can be undertaken in the locality. This part of the study subsumes the industrial potential survey, as to how the people in the area have interacted with the given resources such as agricultural, horticultural, mineral, forest, marine etc., in the past and the resultant economic and industrial activities of the people and the related skills the people are proficient in. It will give us an idea of the ongoing activities, skills, attitudes, preferences on the part of the people and the kind of entrepreneurial activities that need modernization and innovative enterprises that could be introduced in the area.

Economic Structure of the Community

In the economic field, we study the types of production within the community, the organization of producing units, capital and labour resources, the ratio in which labour and capital resources are used, occupational structure, the functioning of the local marketing system, farm organization and land tenure. In this area, we also study the network of economic relationships the community has with the outside world.

Human Resources

Usually, the industrial potential surveys or techno-economic surveys that are undertaken by different agencies connected with industrial development pay a meagre attention to human resources. The requisite emphasis on human resources has not been there. The focus has been on economic resources and the potential thereof and not on the man and the group behind him. In the field approach, man or the human resource is at the centre. He is the starting point. Under the human resources, we go in for a census enumeration of literate population, skilled workers, technically qualified people, educated unemployed and various native skills available in the community. Another human resource is the leadership in the client group which is to be studied, promoted and utilized for introducing changes in the community. We will further deal with the resources aspect in the following pages.

Women constitute a potential human resource, untapped and underutilized and there is a need to make special efforts to promote entrepreneurship among women.

Cultural Patterns

A community or a social group has history, a value system and tradition in terms of its occupation and or profession and choices or preference for economic activities. Individuals in the group when intend or motivated to take to some entrepreneurial activity look in for sanction and support from within the group. And so, in the field approach we make a historical analysis of the community and the patterns of diffusion and change. We look in for the direction and trend of change taking place in the community. The understanding of the cultural patterns of the group lends us some insight into the group's ethos and it will serve as a lead for further action in the filed of entrepreneurial development.

A study of the cultural patterns of the community takes us to the other intimately associated aspect of it – its social structure. In a general sense, entrepreneurship may be taken as an individual's free choice affair, but when the development of entrepreneurship comes to a rural-tribal community, it ceases to be purely an individual's affair. Here it is the group's choice. And hence the need for understanding the social structure of the group, the network of relationship between various sub-groups and institutions, and the dynamics of the group's influence over the individual and vice-versa.

In social structure of the community, we study the various constituents and the institutions in it. We may begin with the basic constituent of the society – the family, its structure, the decision-making process in the family, functional aspects of the family, and the typology of the families based on occupation and division of functions. Around the family is the kin-group with a set of consanguineous and affinal kin shaping, and influencing the individuals' decision making and behaviour. We study the kin-group in the client community, its structure and functions, intraclan, inter-clan, inter-tribal relationships and the role of certain kin in kinship circles.

Ethnic or tribal councils are significant and viable social institutions. We may say that tribal councils are almost universal among the tribes in the world. Despite the influence of Christianity, western styles of life and new politico-administrative institutions among certain tribal groups at the village-community level, the tribal councils still continue to be significant and functional in the life of a tribe. For instance in India, we find a high incidence of caste councils among the so-called lower castes. These are village or settlement-based and community-based in a region. Though caste councils are sporadic among middle-ranking and higher castes, we come across among some of them formal caste associations at town, district and regional levels. These caste associations (Sanghams) are a kind of foundations to promote the education of the children and other welfare activities of the group. Wherever the caste-tribal councils obtain, whatever may be their strength and influence over the individual and group today, they are to be reckoned with as factors of influence, Positive and negative. Further, ethnic groups in a multi-ethnic community maintain or enjoy certain social balance, a particular group being predominant over the other, a particular group subservient to the other, a group dependent on another for leadership and guidance or a group blocking changes or progress in the other. In the Indian context, in the rural-tribal settings, inter-caste and caste-tribe relationships matter while attempting planned changes among them. This takes us to the study of caste-tribal council, its constitution and functions, the role and influence of the chief of the council, the council's influence over its members, and the degree of their dependence on the council in the matters economic and social. Further, we study the nexus of relationship between tribals and non-tribals.

The traditional village council (non-statutory) is another ancient social institution still in vogue in most of the villages. It chiefly deals with village affairs, celebration of local deities, sundry civil and criminal issues and divorce cases. The office of the chief of the traditional village council is either hereditary or elected. In some cases, the caste/tribal council itself functions as the traditional village council. Despite the advent of statutory village council in some communities, the traditional one, still enjoys status and influence over the local community. It is also to be studied and its relationship utilized for entrepreneurial development.

Besides the traditional institutions referred to above there are the modern associate or feeder organizations viz. Farmers' Forum, Youth Club, Women's Club, and recently organized users committees in the rural areas in Andhra Pradesh etc.

which do matter as sources of influence, guidance and leadership in the entrepreneurial development programmes.

While studying the social structure of the client community we may also take into account the sacred institutions in the community, the temple, church, mosque and the sacred specialists or the religious leaders associated with the sacred institutions. Though their domain is religious/spiritual, they are significant people in the community. The entrepreneurship developer may work through them to clear the way and secure sanction and support for the potential entrepreneur to go about his enterprises.

Further, the schoolteacher also considered a friend, guide and philosopher to the local folk is a force to be reckoned with and he plays the role of a catalyst and his services may be utilized in the programme. Mention may be made of the local medical practitioner and he sometimes as a source of influence for the programmes.

The Political Structure of the Community

Entrepreneurial development or introducing of any change in the client group depends on the political leadership, power structure and the politico-administrative institutions at the village, and district levels. In other words, it has a bearing on the initiative, lead and encouragement given by the local leaders. Under the political structure we study the leadership patterns in the community. At the village level we can think of five different kinds of leaders:

(1) Hereditary leaders such as village level officials (in some cases), Chiefs of Caste-tribal councils and traditional village councils;

(2) Functional leaders who matter in specific areas;

(3) Sectional leaders who represent a class, tribe, a neighbourhood or a locality;

(4) Elected leaders of the statutory council and cooperative; and

(5) Professional leaders who are from outside the community, officials of different developmental agencies operating at the village level.

In the field approach we identify the different kinds of leaders in the community and work through them towards entrepreneurial development. Wherever the existing leadership is inadequate for entrepreneurial promotion, new organizations are to be developed. It may be noted here that a potential entrepreneur in the community may tend to look for some nodding approval and encouragement from the people whom he considers significant in the group. If the potential entrepreneur is convinced of his project or enterprise and if he can venture into action on his own, we need not bother about his environment and referent groups. But the situation in the rural and tribal areas is not so. Even if he is sure of his project and ready to take the risk and thinks that he could manage his enterprise, he has sometimes an obligation to seek the opinion and secure the approval from the significant members in the group. And so, the entrepreneurial developer enters the client system through the local leaders, expose to them the idea and prospects of some entrepreneurial activity, try to convince them so that either they encourage the potential entrepreneurs to go ahead with their ventures or do not stand in their way of movement. There is every likelihood of the local leaders sometimes playing a negative role.

On the institutional side in this field, the elected council at the village level, and village cooperative may be used as sources of information and as levers to influence potential entrepreneurs in the community.

In sum, it may be observed here, that institutions and organizations in the community may or may not have a direct bearing on or a functional relationship to entrepreneurship or economic activity. The tribal council, the caste council, the religious institutions for example, deal mostly with social aspects of the community, but as traditional and deeply rooted institutions, they influence and control the behaviour of people. The change agent tries to make use of these existing institutions and customs to communicate to the people. The leadership in all spheres of communal activity will be utilized to bring about desirable changes in the client community.

Barriers and Stimulants to Change

We may pose here a basic question. What is the supply position of entrepreneurship in developing countries today? The field experience and the rate of growth of entrepreneurship in the area of small-scale industries in most of the developing communities show that the supply of entrepreneurship (the number of entrepreneurs that take up some enterprise) in a given period of time is short of what the Industrial Development Agencies demand or in a position to support and promote. When there is spontaneous emergence or adequate supply of entrepreneurship, then the problem is to meet the new entrepreneurs' needs and providing them with physical and economic infrastructure to help them start and run their enterprises successfully. But unfortunately, the State as the chief promoter of entrepreneurship wants to, within the constraints of scarce resources, promote entrepreneurship. In this process of inducing entrepreneurship among the rural-tribal people we meet with shyness and resistance on the part of individuals and groups to go in for some enterprises. Entrepreneurial development is a basic complex change. It is met with different kinds of resistance and so it leads us to identify the barriers (areas of resistance) and stimulants (promotional factors) to change.

Foster (1973, 82-146) discusses at length the different kinds of barriers and stimulants to change. All societies are constantly in a state of relative tension. Each society can be thought of as a host to two kinds of forces – those that seek to promote change, and those that strive to maintain the status quo. These forces are locked in perpetual combat, the former trying to throw the latter off balance in order to gain ascendancy and the latter trying to prevent this from happening. [1]

It is necessary on the part of the entrepreneurial development agency to identify the areas of resistance and the factors that contribute to change, here the entrepreneurial development.

We can think of three kinds of barriers – cultural, social and psychological. These are interrelated in any community. Here, basically we go in for an understanding of the value system of the client community, the factors that inhibit or promote change. On identifying the barriers, we work toward loosening their grip over the potential changees, simultaneously using the positive factors available from within the client group.

Despite barriers changes do take place in all spheres of life-religious, political, ideological, economic and social. When a group is faced with the prospect of change, there exists a balance of forces. On one side are those forces which are against change, viz., conservatism, apathy, fear and the like; on the other side are the forces for change such as dissatisfaction with the existing conditions, pride of new occupation, profession, new status or economic and social benefits that are anticipated in the new activity. Successful entrepreneurial development consists largely of choosing those enterprises where the balance is almost even and then trying to lighten the forces against change or to increase the factors that promote change.

Some of the positive factors that could be used for inducing change are motivating people to change through education and demonstration of the usefulness of the new activity, working on the desire of clients for economic gain and prestige, making use of a competitive situation obtaining in the client group, using the positive forces of authority and timing and sequencing the programmes in such a way that the total effort and process results in entrepreneurial development.

One crucial factor in working with tribal groups is their value system. The change agent needs to have a knowledge of the dominant values in the culture of the group, and working through these values, gradually bring about desirable changes in the group. The two constants to community wide changes are the tribe's identity and the tribe's moral beliefs. It is important for them to know that they can maintain their identity while making changes in their value system. It may be noted here that an important value of a tribal group is: "what they want to be".

Another important factor that is to be taken into account in our approach to bring about entrepreneurial development among tribal groups is to know what agencies have worked so far with them, what programmes have been attempted, and with what results. This leads us to an understanding of the tribe's perception, attitude and experience of the agencies and developmental programmes. For instance, community development agencies, Christian missionaries and several voluntary organizations have been working with tribal groups for their development for sometime now. An understanding of the tribals' reactions and experiences vis-à-vis the development or change agencies, whatever may be their sphere of activity, will give us an insight into their problem, and help us in avoiding the pit-falls. This will help us formulate our strategy in a manner that will make the process of change smooth and gradual.

Social change relating to entrepreneurial development is a complex phenomenon. It requires an integrated approach, a sustained effort on the part of the organizations that promote industrial development.

Problems

In developing entrepreneurship, we are confronted with several problems. The barriers we referred to earlier relate to the client community which are of general nature, but we may also look into some specific kind of problems in promoting entrepreneurship in rural communities.

The problems of entrepreneurial development are of individual, group and of institutional nature. Ultimately, it is the individual who has to take the initiative to decide on, start and manage his enterprise. He also needs the approval and support of his kin-group or community. The individual and the group constitute the client system. The institutions are to stimulate the client system towards entrepreneurial activity.

The institutions are the various governmental and autonomous agencies that are concerned with entrepreneurial development. They are the source of several commissions and omissions that impede and slow down the process of entrepreneurial development. We may briefly look into some of the problems that centre around the individual, group and the institutions.

Individual

1. Lack of motivation.
2. Shyness and inhibition.
3. Ignorant of opportunities that he can avail himself of.
4. Lack of requisite managerial skills to start and manage his enterprise.
5. Lack of finance for initial investment.
6. Lack of familial and community support for his enterprise.
7. Is scared of the cumbersome and time-consuming process in establishing the enterprise.
8. Even if he starts the enterprise, he is not sure of sustained support from the promotional agencies in terms of timely and adequate credit and marketing of his products.

Group

1. Lack of awareness.
2. Preference for traditional occupations and professions.
3. Don't think of alternative avocations.
4. Apathy, sense of fear and insecurity towards government initiated and sponsored programmes.
5. Ignorant of their own potential: material and human.
6. Economically and politically weak.
7. Lack the freedom to choose and pursue their choices

as a consequence to the power-sway of the local elite or the dominant caste.

8. They are more tradition-bound, and their values are, to continue with their institutionalized familial occupations.
9. They prefer to be what they want to be.

Institutional

1. Vague and unrealistic policies, and policies not supported by action.
2. Lack of teamwork and internal coordination in the agencies.
3. Lack of inter-agency coordination.
4. Bureaucratic style of working.
5. The functions of the personnel are not vested with the requisite power and authority.
6. Overlapping and duplication of functions both at the apex and operational levels.
7. A multiplicity of agencies performing a more or less similar task.
8. The field-level personnel are not supported in their promises and performance by the higher-ups in the organizations.
9. Lack of work motivation and commitment to their task.
10. Lack of relevant training on the part of the EDP personnel.
11. Lack of appreciation of the importance of human factors in development.
12. Lack of knowledge of technical know-how on the part of the personnel.

Other problems of entrepreneurial development are in respect of provision of infrastructural facilities, including finance and marketing.

The problems mentioned above though are stupendous and complex, are not insurmountable, an inter-disciplinary and multi-pronged approach is required to find solutions to these problems.

The problems listed above are not inherent or unchangeable. Through gradual entrepreneurial education, organizational and institutional support provided to the people in terms of motivation, incentives, infrastructural facilities, supply of certain inputs, credit and market support, the neo-entrepreneurs will gain confidence through their experience and success and they would be the factors creating congenial entrepreneurial climate. These problems are interrelated and they are to be looked at by the industrial development agencies and the community leaders. As mentioned above, entrepreneurial education through entrepreneurial activity and training provided to the development personnel and potential entrepreneurs would gradually create conditions favouring a positive change in the problems listed above.

Contributing Factors

In the foregoing discussion of field approach to entrepreneurial development, the focus and emphasis has been on the understanding of the client group and using the physical, economic and social resources. But when we look at the entire gamut of entrepreneurial development in terms of an action programme, we find four factors significantly contributing to entrepreneurial development. They are (1) Resources, (2) Organizations concerned with entrepreneurial development, (3) Infrastructure and (4) The entrepreneur. We may briefly examine them.[2]

Resources

The resources of a client community are of two kinds: material and human. The material side consists of the natural resources, primary (nature given) and secondary (man-made) that the community is endowed with viz., climatic, geographic, agricultural, horticultural, mineral, marine, forest, animal, textile, etc. Here we examine how a given community living in a region has interacted with the resources it is endowed with. What kind of economic and industrial activities and associated skills have been generated as a result of people's interaction with the resources. This will give us an idea of the enterprises that the people in the area carry on with, and which have become a part of their culture. Based on the ongoing economic activities, we can demarcate the enterprises that need modernization and the areas in which innovation can be introduced based on the available resources. Here we move from the familiar (to the people) to the unfamiliar but associated entrepreneurial activities. What is envisaged here is that the entrepreneurship development agency should examine the potentialities of the material resources, in what manner they could be developed making use of the human material available in the target community.

A word here about analyzing resources. A resource is truly a resource in the economic sense only if it can help to produce something which somebody wants at a cost that he is willing to pay. In analyzing the resources of an area from the point of view of the area's suitability for various kinds of enterprises we cannot count among today's resources like timber located in the middle of the jungle or minerals so far underground or so far from transportation that the labour of getting them out-costs more than the materials are worth. The cost factor is all important in appraising the industrial usefulness of an area's resources. The resources need not always be available in the immediate local community and they can be obtained from elsewhere so long the enterprise would be profitable. In fact, successful manufacturing areas rarely have a complete supply of the resources they use.

The existence of certain very evident resources, especially raw materials, within an area does not necessarily mean that enterprises based on these resources will be economical and beneficial in the area. Other resources not quite as evident may even more important than this raw material in determining the total cost of resources that go into the manufactured product, for example, technical labour, supervision and capital equipment. The total cost of all the input items is the important thing on the resource side. Also factors on the marketing side may pull enterprises to a location quite far from the origin of the most conspicuous material.

In the analysis of an area's industrial potential it is necessary to make a systematic inventory of al types of resources in the area that might be usable in some enterprises. The purpose is to determine the presence or absence of specific kinds of resources required in different kinds of enterprises and to ascertain their location, quality, abundance and probable cost. This information, when fitted together with information about the resource requirements of different industries and the market demand for the products of these industries, will enable an intelligent preliminary choice to be made of enterprises most suitable for promotion and development in the area.

The analysis of the resources can be conducted with almost any desired degree of comprehensiveness in detail. It can be merely a quick survey for general orientation based on information available in published materials or readily obtainable through quick surveys. Otherwise, it could be a comprehensive and detailed assessment of potential and usable resources based on industrial potential surveys.

Speaking of natural resources, we may think of a particular natural resource, how it is being utilized in a given area, in how many ways and how the same resource is utilized or processed in another area, or what kind of industries are based on a particular natural resource. Let us take for example, the coconut. It is cultivated in abundance in Assam (India), but it is chiefly used as a food article as it is and for ritual and ceremonial purposes, but whereas the same coconut is used in over a hundred different ways in Kerala. Coconut constitutes a base in Kerala's economy. Similarly bamboo is used in multiple ways for handicrafts in Tripura but its economic or industrial use elsewhere in India is limited to a couple of utilities. Another example is the abundant cultivation of ginger in Mizoram (India) but a total absence of any industry based on this resource in the state.

As we have pointed out earlier, industrial resources are not solely material. In the ultimate analysis it is the area's human and social resources – labour, management and organization are the key to successful industrial development. Japan and Switzerland are the most striking examples wherein the human resources have been the dominant factor in their tremendous advancement in industrial development[3].

It is the human resources that shape and control the material resources in industrial development. Ways can be found to overcome many material deficiencies if the human talents are highly developed and if environment of social, political and economic institutions is favourable. But if the human skills and institutions which make for effective industrial production are not available in an area, then no amount of material resources will bring a successful industrialization. It is the reason all the more to lay emphasis on entrepreneurship development which is the human side of industrial development.

In sum, it is the responsibility of the industrial development agencies to assess the resources available in the area, the possible industrial uses they could be exploited for and the kind of technology and infrastructure required for the newer uses of a resource and thus guide the potential entrepreneur and his group.

Organization

In a basic sense, entrepreneurial/small enterprise development is based on the individual initiative and when it is either lacking or meager, it is to be induced and promoted by the state. The situation in many of the Asian countries demand an induced entrepreneurial development and consequently we find several organizations figuring in the realm of entrepreneurial development. These are governmental, quasi-governmental and some are voluntary organizations. The nomenclatures, structure, functions, area of operation, size and number of such organizations vary from country to country.

For instance, in a medium-sized state in India there are about twenty-five organizations or departments that are in a way connected with industrial development. The kind of their functional responsibilities and the degree of their involvement in industrial promotion vary. Again, India may be taken as an example which largely represents the role responsibilities of development organizations in other Asian countries. Based on the way the organizations are related to entrepreneurial/ industrial development, they may be categorized into three groups.

The first group of organizations have a primary function and a direct responsibility in entrepreneurial development. They are chiefly organizations such as: (i) Directorate of Industries, (at the State level), (ii) District Industries Centres, and (iii) Small Industry Service Institutes (SISIs). These primary small industry development agencies are supposed to carry on both stimulatory and supportive kind of activities in respect to entrepreneurial development. It is the Directorate of Industries and more especially the District Industries Centres (DICs) which are charged with the task of identifying technically feasible and economically viable enterprises and identifying, motivating, selecting and training the small-scale entrepreneurs. They are to do the primary job of bringing in the entrepreneurs to the threshold of entrepreneurship. But in many of the cases, we find that the stimulatory part of their job is lacking and they are more at ease and successful in supportive kind of activities such as financial, infrastructural and technical. Concerted and persevering efforts are necessary in the filed of stimulatory activity in generating an entrepreneurial climate to bring in new entrepreneurs.

The second group of organizations which may be called secondary consisting of different corporations of finance, infrastructure, raw materials and machinery, banking and marketing mostly carry on supportive and sustaining kind of activities. These organizations are partly or distantly related to the primary function of development of entrepreneurship in the small-scale sector.

The basic task of finding an entrepreneur or responding to a potential entrepreneur lies largely on the first category of organizations.

We may call the third group of organizations as tertiary which are mostly governmental development departments or line agencies which are indirectly or remotely connected with industrial-entrepreneurial development. Departments of agriculture, horticulture, sericulture, sylviculture, pisciculture, animal husbandry, mineral, power, irrigation, highways, transport, communications, education, both basic and technical, textile and so on, fall under this category. Though these departments or agencies are not directly connected with industrial-entrepreneurial development, any improvement or expansion in them contributes to industrial development. They are the sources, feeder and support agencies which generate the potential for industrial development and ultimately contribute to its promotion.

The purpose of this brief preceding discussion is not just academic but it is to emphasize that the functions of organizations charged with industrial-entrepreneurial development are to be clearly demarcated and well defined in order to avoid or reduce overlapping or duplication of activities and ensure a synergetic effect on small industry promotion. A periodic examination of the functions of these organizations, their strengths, needs and shortcomings and the coordination among them is necessary. The whole promotional machinery is to be streamlined to deliver the goods, taking into account the institutional problems that have been listed out earlier. In other words, there is an imperative need to build up functional linkages and relative accountability among the three categories of organizations at the State (provincial), and the district levels, which should finally facilitate a rapid entrepreneurial development.

Infrastructure

We mostly relate infrastructure to physical facilities such as land, site, building, power, water, transport and communication facilities for starting an industry or an enterprise. Some of the infrastructural requirements are enterprise specific and some are of general nature and further we may consider the enterprise-specific infrastructural facilities as primary and other facilities such as schools, hospitals, housing and marketing for day-to-day requirements for the entrepreneurs, their families and workers as secondary. But the latter facilities gradually emerge and get established once the enterprises are started. In the induced and planned entrepreneurial-industrial development provision of infrastructural facilities is a necessary primary condition. Some of the facilities may be managed by the entrepreneurs themselves but some such as power, communications, sometimes, land and work-sheds are beyond the capability and affordability on the part of the small-scale entrepreneurs. Such a provision solely rests on the government development agencies.

Usually, infrastructure as pointed out above is mostly taken to be the physical and material facilities, but it constitutes only a part of the infrastructure in a comprehensive sense. We may think of two kinds of infrastructure for industrial-entrepreneurial development. They are: (a) physical and economic infrastructure; and (b) social infrastructure. The first one comprises the items noted above plus finance and marketing facilities. The social infrastructure consists of clear-cut industrial development policies, political commitment, an able and well-trained, motivated and committed industrial development personnel, a well-coordinated institutional support, positive attitudes, values and preferences of people and an entrepreneurial climate for developing entrepreneurship. Another significant social infrastructure is the entrepreneurial leadership in the target community. One could see that the provision of physical and economic infrastructure is in the hands of and under the purview of governmental agencies. Most of these agencies fall under secondary and tertiary organizations, discussed above. The state regulates the provision of these facilities. Again in a relative sense, the physical and economic infrastructure could be provided by the State with comparative ease. But the question arises: whose responsibility is it to educate the community and the potential entrepreneurs and generate an entrepreneurial climate? It falls largely on the primary set of organizations which have the task of creating the entrepreneurial climate in the communities. The role of other agencies in building up or providing the social infrastructure directly for entrepreneurial development is rather marginal and peripheral. However, it may be noted that the presence or provision of any physical infrastructure is a likely inducement to the population in the area to gradually venture into some enterprises. But there is no denial of the fact that physical and economic infrastructure is a necessary condition but not sufficient for entrepreneurial development. The physical and social infrastructure contributes to the growth of one another and they are complementary to each other, but undeniably it is the social infrastructure which is paramount. Once it is strong, once it is generated both on the part of the development agencies and the people, the physical and economic infrastructure would follow. It is here that the primary industrial development agencies are to play a vital role apprising the client community of what its resources and potentials are, in what direction and ways it could harness and develop its material and human resources, what local consumer needs and external market it could respond to, and the ways and the extent to which the agencies could extend their help to the community in entrepreneurial development.

The approach envisages an intimate and continuous dialogue between the clientele group and the development agencies. It is obvious that some of the material resources (finance, power, transport) are scarce and they are to be allocated judiciously for industrial development, but the more scarce material is the entrepreneur himself. How to identify him, how to motivate, encourage and assure him so that he takes the initiative and ventures into some entrepreneurial activity. What may be called the human-end product (the entrepreneur) in entrepreneurship is the function of the social infrastructure or the entrepreneurial climate. This leads us now to the entrepreneur.

In this context, we may briefly look into the concept and characteristics of successful entrepreneurs as defined and interpreted by social scientists.

Characteristics of Entrepreneurs

When we try to conceptualize the term entrepreneur, we note that though it originated in the west, it has undergone many changes from time to time. In the early 16th century, it was used to denote a dealer who bought a thing at a certain price and sold it at an uncertain price making a profit out of it. A sort of social stigma was attached to this concept. Towards 1961, Schumpeter redefined entrepreneur 'as an agent for change'.... an innovator. Subsequently, it took on the meaning of 'an efficient manager'. In the Indian context and in the context of other developing countries, however, a new concept emerged i.e., 'a person who undertakes to organize, own and run an enterprise'.[3]

Various attempts have been made to understand the emergence of entrepreneurship. Sociologists analyze the phenomenon of entrepreneurship in terms of caste, social status, values, migration, family socialization pattern, etc. Psychologists attempt to explain it on the basis of personality traits or characteristics such as, need for achievement, creativity, propensity to take risk, independence and leadership. Economists consider it from the point of view of occupational background, access to capital, technical experience and insight to exploit economic opportunities and attain economic gains. From these different approaches, it becomes evident that a strict compartmentalized approach will not be of any help in understanding the emergence of entrepreneurship. Since entreprêneur is an individual who lives in a society, both individual and social factors have to be taken into consideration. Similarly, when we talk about a woman entrepreneur, she should be regarded, as an individual who takes up a challenging role in which she wants to adjust her personality needs, family life, social life and economic independence. Such an integrated approach may help us visualize this phenomenon more adequately.[4]

Some of the basic or inherent characteristics may be there in the beginning but as the entrepreneur moves forward with expansion and success in promoting his enterprise other kinds of characteristics are born or emerge in the individual. In a sense, it is a learning kind of thing on the part of the entrepreneur. As he moves forward the essential characteristics which stand for success in entrepreneurial activity emerge and grow over a period of time. The entrepreneur learns on the job, through his success and failure in his venture.

A review of the available literature on the factors contributing to successful entrepreneurship supports the contention that certain personality characteristics are associated with successful entrepreneurs.

McClelland and his associates have reported that entrepreneurs are characterized by (1) unusual creativeness (2) propensity of risk-taking and (3) strong need for achievement. They have also reported that persons high on need for achievement have some specific characteristics. While research has established that achievement motive contributes largely to entrepreneurship, it has also been observed that though achievement helps one to become an entrepreneur, it is not the only factor in making him successful. It is also found that an entrepreneurial manager should have a high need for influencing others (need for power), a low need for affiliation and a large capacity to discipline one's self (inhibition). An entrepreneurial manager is also found to possess flexibility in style and displays high psychosocial maturity. Further, it is also to be noted that entrepreneurs decision to start an industrial unit was not influenced by level of education, income differences, risk-taking ability and need for achievement, but rather an ambition, social prestige, social responsibility, economic gain and perception of demand for a particular product.

The most significant characteristics associated with

entrepreneurs are need for achievement, support, independence and leadership. On the basis of the information given by participants of a symposium on Development of Entrepreneurship, the following appear to be the characteristics:

1. Perseverance and hard work
2. Risk-taking ability
3. High aspiration
4. Willingness to learn
5. Dynamic and creative
6. Adoptable
7. Innovative
8. Good Salesmanship
9. Ability to make friends and overcome losses
10. Initiative
11. Self-confidence
12. Will-power
13. Determination to succeed
14. Pleasing personality, composed and tactful
15. High integrity
16. Responsible
17. Excellence in work
18. Perception of time

The research available clearly reveals that an entrepreneur is certainly different from the non-entrepreneur in terms of his psychological and social dispositions. The available evidence only points to some dominant traits in successful entrepreneurs; the optimal combination of characteristics needed for success has not yet been arrived at.

Further, some researchers have come up with another set of characteristics listed below:

1. Drive
2. Self-confidence
3. Long-term involvement
4. Money as a measure
5. Persistent problem-solving
6. Goal setting
7. Moderate risk-taking
8. Dealing with failure
9. Use of feedback
10. Taking initiative and seeking personal responsibility
11. Use of resources
12. Competing against self-imposed standards
13. Internal locus control
14. Tolerance of ambiguity and uncertainty

Further, the following eight (8) aspects are described as entrepreneurial role requirements.

Eight Entrepreneurial Role Requirements

1. Accommodation to venture
2. Total immersion and commitment
3. Creativity and innovation
4. Knowledge of business you want to launch
5. People and team building
6. Economic values
7. Ethics
8. Integrity and reliability

By and large, characteristics that differentiate entrepreneurs from non-entrepreneurs are: confidence, perseverance, determination, hard work, general knowledge, dynamism, risk taking, optimism, technical knowledge, information gathering ability and initiative.

Entrepreneur

The entrepreneur may be likened to the fourth factor in production-organization (the rest being land, labour and capital). He is as significant as 'organization' in production. Interestingly, these two factors – entrepreneur and organization are intimately associated. What happens when you have the required resources, promotional organizations, physical and economic infrastructure and lack the entrepreneur? To a considerable extent, this is the situation in many of the Asian countries. We are looking for the right kind of entrepreneurs. They are not born as such, but they could be made as such.

There are two kinds of entrepreneurs, the ongoing and the potential ones. The ongoing entrepreneurs are those who are in the field already, some who have taken to entrepreneurship on their own in a spontaneous sense and others who have been induced to this activity. The industrial development agencies in their initial enthusiasm and under pressure of targets for putting a certain number of individuals in the field of entrepreneurship, brought in some entrepreneurs and fulfilled their paper targets. But a considerable number of them are left in the lurch. They are at various stages with varying problems struggling to reach the take-off point in respect to their enterprises. Some are struggling to complete the formalities for final registration of their units, some are held up for want of adequate raw material, working capital, or the requisite machinery and equipment, some waiting for power, some finding it difficult to market their products, and some being tossed over for X or Y licence to go about their business. In a word the entrepreneur who is already in the field faces some problems. Unless the industrial development agencies assess the problems of the ongoing entrepreneur and assist him in ameliorating his condition, we cannot go in for a new entrepreneur. Every satisfied and well-served entrepreneur is a positive force in generating a conducive entrepreneurial climate which in turn motivates, induces and encourages a potential entrepreneur to enter the field.

On the other hand a dissatisfied, not-very-much-cared for left-in-the-lurch-entrepreneur is a potential source of demotivation and discouragement to the new entrepreneur. We do not advocate here that the entrepreneur should be spoon-fed and that he should be a protected child. But he needs a prop in the initial stages in his growth and development. It is not wrong to say that a well-attended to and successful entrepreneur is equal to several professional agents of entrepreneurial development when it comes to motivating people to take to some entrepreneurial activity. If we take care of the ongoing entrepreneurs it would be easy for us to bring the new entrepreneurs into the field.

Identifying, selecting, motivating and training the new entrepreneurs constitute a major task for the entrepreneurial development agency. The promotion or development of entrepreneurship may be undertaken in five phases and we may briefly look into each phase.

Phase I

The first phase relates to the basic physico-psycho-socio-cultural and economic study and understanding of the area where the programme is to be implemented as detailed earlier. Industrial potential survey focusing both on material and human resources of the area will be the basis, based on which feasibility studies are to be prepared for each viable candidate industry covering technical, economic, financial, demand and marketing aspects of the enterprise. Such a study will serve the purposes of developing an action – programme for identifying viable enterprises either resource-based, demand-based or footloose and potential entrepreneurs.

Here the emphasis is to be laid on starting small-scale enterprises where the people are living now, cheap enough so that they can be created in large numbers without calling for an unattainable level of capital formation and imports, with relatively simple production methods, so that the demands for high skills are minimized not only in the production process itself but also in matters of organization, raw material supply, financing, marketing, and the production mainly based on local materials and for local use. With such a purpose, initially to make use of the local resources and the local consumer demands, we are not to look for highly talented, sophisticated entrepreneurs, but people with some interest, with some investment capacity, who are partially unemployed or totally unemployed, people who are looking for some avenues to increase their income, people who are likely to take certain amount of risk in venturing into some entrepreneurial activity. Highly achievement-oriented individuals seek opportunities, create conditions, need less propping and venture into industrial activity. Such people can take care of themselves with minimal support from the development agencies. But our task is to gradually shape the common man into an entrepreneur. Against this objective, potential entrepreneurs in the client community may be drawn from the following segments: (a) artisan groups, (b) high school dropouts, (c) educated unemployed, (d) merchant-trading groups, (e) farmers who are in the process of or likely to partly shift to some enterprise, (f) farm-labourers who are likely to take some small business or enterprise and (g) woman entrepreneurs.

In the first phase as a constructive approach and strategy, the entire client community is to be exposed to the idea of entrepreneurship development. No segment in the community should feel it is isolated or ignored and the programmes are meant only for certain sections. The general exposure of the entire client community to the idea and prospects of entrepreneurship will create awareness, interest among them which will gradually motivate the potential entrepreneurs to move into action.

The creating of awareness, preparing the community, motivating and facilitating some individuals in the community to take decisions, secure the sanction of their families and opinion leaders, that is cutting through the socio-cultural barriers may be done through entrepreneurship-extension education through individual and group methods and through the mass media, always reinforced by personal contacts and counseling. One of the foremost things in the process is raising the aspiration level of the people. They have to be told convincingly of the social and economic advantage inherent in industrial activity. The rise in their standard of living as a result of successfully running an enterprise has to be projected and brought home to them. These ends can be achieved through what is called 'intensive campaign' technique. It is a package of activities comprising an industrial potential survey, publication of the survey findings, holding of small group meetings explaining to people in the community, the kind of enterprises that are feasible in the area, the requirements for starting the recommended enterprises, who can undertake them, the kind of assistance they can expect from the various industrial development agencies and in such a type of campaign, the industrial development personnel and the selected local and political leaders will be involved. The inclusion of influential local and district leadership would build and reinforce confidence and morale on the part of the potential entrepreneurs in the local community.

It may be in order to mention here the steps that may be taken in identifying the viable enterprises and potential entrepreneurs in the client community.

The Steps

1. Identification of the natural resources the community is endowed with.
2. Listing out the ongoing economic and industrial activities carried on by the community based on the resources at its command.
3. Listing out the associated skills available with the members of the community (or the target population).
4. Listing out the kind of new enterprises technically feasible and economically viable that could be promoted based on the available resources and skills.

5. Listing out the existing and required infrastructural facilities in view of the new enterprises suggested.

6. Appraising the client system of:
   - the kind of new enterprises they could take to;
   - the financial, managerial, technical and marketing requirements in respect to each enterprise;
   - the kind of people who can take up the suggested enterprises;
   - specifying in general the qualifications, personal aptitude and abilities and investment capacity on the part of the prospective entrepreneurs.

7. Appraising the client system of:
   - the kind of help the multiplicity of agencies connected with entrepreneurial development can extend to the prospective entrepreneurs, which may cover questions like What? When? To what extent? How often? To what purpose? etc.

8. Final identification of potential entrepreneurs and matching their interest with the enterprises.

A word on identification of potential entrepreneurs. Depending on the extent of response, the level of candidates, the potential and the capabilities that are sought among the candidates, the optimum number that the resources and schemes could support and sustain, one may go in for psychological tests such as: (a) Achievement Motivation, (b) Risk Taking, (c) Value Orientation, (d) Adoption Propensity, (e) Level of Aspiration, etc. These projective or psychological instruments are rather complementary to the information provided on the application that the candidate fills in, concerning his family background, his educational attainment, work experience, his choice of enterprise, his experience if any in entrepreneurial activity, his investment capacity and his socio-cultural affiliations.

Importantly, the means employed for identification are the

application, interview and if need be, the tests mentioned above. One invaluable resource for identifying potential entrepreneurs is the client community itself.

When it comes to identification and selection of potential entrepreneurs, more often, we ignore the local community. The people in the local community may not be conversant with attributes or traits that are contributive to successful entrepreneurship, may not have any idea and understanding of some of the projective techniques used sometimes to measure the strength of need for achievement, value orientation, risk taking and adoption propensity on the part of the prospective entrepreneurs, but they will have a fairly good understanding of the people in the community as to who would do what and to what extent one would fair well and who is innovative and who would manage an activity effectively. This kind of knowledge of individuals is based on the day-to-day observations irrespective of an individual's profession or occupation. And so, one can, to a large extent depend upon and make use of the local community, the small groups in the community for identifying and selecting potential entrepreneurs. As we have pointed out earlier, once the viable enterprises have been identified based on industrial potential survey, one may list out the personal requirements that one is looking for or in other words the kind of people who can answer these requirements in order to respond to the recommended enterprises. Once this information is communicated to the community through individual contact and small group meetings, it is possible for the local community to indicate the names of individuals who are likely to be successful as small entrepreneurs. This could be in addition to individuals themselves coming forward to take to some entrepreneurial activity. The stress here is that the local community could well serve as a source and guide in selecting potential entrepreneurs.

Phase II

It consists of training various categories of personnel who will be involved in locating and developing entrepreneurship in the area under question. A general but comprehensive course of three to four weeks is to be prepared keeping in view the earlier work-experience of the personnel. The participants will be familiarized with the prospects and problems of entrepreneurial development in the area of operation. Further, the programme will include inputs on feasibility studies, techno-economic surveys, preparation of industrial profiles, entrepreneurial development, marketing, etc. (See Appendix for a model training programme). Representatives of financial institutions in the area may be associated with the training programmes. By the end of the second phase, the agency will be in readiness with the knowledge of the area of operation, and also trained personnel to select and train entrepreneurs.

Phase III

It consists of selection and training of potential entrepreneurs in the client community by the agency. The training of the entrepreneurs will be arranged at district or sub-district headquarters. The personnel of the development agency who have already undergone training will conduct the training programme. The duration of this training may range from two to six weeks. It depends on funds and the category of candidates trained. In some cases, inclusive of in-plant studies, the courses are run for 14-20 weeks. The training inputs will include elements that would enable the entrepreneur-trainees acquire basic knowledge, skills and motivation to establish their units and manage them successfully. The training will be both theoretical and practical. Towards the end of their training, the candidates will go back to their villages and make a mini-market survey concerning their enterprises, or prepare project reports. They bring back the field data, and work these into project proposals for securing funds from financial institutions.

Phase IV

It consists of the agency collaborating with other functionally associated agencies to guide and help the trained entrepreneurs in establishing their enterprises, either individually, in small groups or through industrial cooperatives.

Phase V

In the final phase, which will be taken up after a lapse of six months after the training of entrepreneurs, the training programme will be evaluated. The objective of the evaluation is to find out as to how many of the trained entrepreneurs were able to establish their enterprises and the problems they faced in setting up their ventures. In the light of this experience the training programme for other batches of entrepreneurs will be restructured if necessary.

Support for Marketing of Products

More often, the entire success of small enterprise promotion in rural-tribal communities hinges on marketing of products of the neo-entrepreneurs. In the initial stages and also, in some cases on the sustained basis, the promotional agencies should help in marketing of the products. The induced and emerging entrepreneurs may be too weak to organize the marketing of their products on their own. The promotional agencies may go in for internal or external export of the indigenous handicrafts and products through a network of marketing channels. Such a support would sustain the ongoing entrepreneurs and also motivate the potential entrepreneurs to ventures into the field.

In sum, we may say that the women constitute a significant segment in the population. Till now, they have not been the focus of entrepreneurial development. The need today to develop entrepreneurship among them is imperative, the development of entrepreneurship among men and women being simultaneous. The question of EDP among women is a question of choice, priority and organization.

REFERENCES

1. Somsak Tambunlertchai and Utis Kaothien, "Thailand's Industrial Transformation and Regional development: Situational Review

and Policy Evaluation" (Paper presented at the International Conference on Industrial Transformation and Regional Development in an Age of Global Interdependence, 18-21 September, 1989, Nagoya and Tokyo), p.1.

2. United Nations Economic and Social Commission for Asia and the Pacific (UN/ESCAP), *Entrepreneurship Development for Small and Medium-Scale Industries in Selected Developing Countries* (New York, 1989), pp.2-3.

3. Dr. Asghari Mohiuddin, *Entrepreneurship Development Among Women – Retrospects and Prospects*, SEDME, Hyderabad, Volume X, Number-1, March, 1983.

4. Medhi Krongkaew, 'The Development of Small and Medium Scale Industries in Thailand" in *Asian Development Review*, Vol.6, No.2, (Manila: ADB, 1988), p.90.

12

EXTENSION EDUCATION IN AID OF AGRICULTURAL MARKETING

Extension which may be called as an applied social science though began with agriculture, the very concept and the methods are applicable to several fields and especially to the field of small scale industrial development. One of the major problems that governs small-scale and cottage industries is marketing of goods and services. The chapter though here deals with agricultural marketing, the principles and the methodology are equally relevant and applicable to industrial extension.

It is paradoxical that agricultural extension tries to help the farmers with a package of improved farm practices to improve and increase farm production and productivity, but unfortunately, it stops with the production function only. Negligible attention is paid by the extension agency in helping the farmer in the marketing of the produce. There is a need for a new kind of extension education especially in helping the farmers in securing remunerative prices for their hard earned produce.

Before we look into extension education in aid of agricultural marketing let us briefly look into the concept and other dimensions of extension education.

(1) The Concept

i) Helping people by means of education to put useful

knowledge to work for them, is the essence of extension education.

ii) The process of selling across new ideas and new techniques based on the knowledge of recent advances in science and technology to people who need to use it most is generally called "Extension" and the method is "Education".

iii) It is working with people for their betterment.

iv) It is a two-way communication.

v) It is an applied education.

vi) It aims at change in the ways of life of people through education.

(2) Activity-wise it consists of

i) Imparting of new knowledge

ii) Imparting of new skills

iii) Change of outlook/attitude

iv) Supplies

v) Services

(3) It is based on the triple tenets of faith

i) Faith in the individual

ii) Faith in democracy

iii) Faith in science and technology

(4) As an applied education it comprises

i) Research findings

ii) Accumulated field experiences

iii) A judicious dose of appropriate technology

iv) A body of philosophy, principles and methods based on behavioural sciences.

(5)Philosophy of Extension

i) Extension has a philosophy of democracy.

ii) Extension has a philosophy of co-operating with agencies that are interested in the common welfare of the people.

iii) The basic philosophy of extension is centred around the welfare of the individuals and their families.

iv) The great principles underlying the philosophy and extension are:

- The individual is supreme in democracy.
- The home is a fundamental unit in civilization.
- The family is the first training ground of the human race.

v) Extension has a philosophy of working out problems by group action, based upon the needs of the people and developed by the people.

vi) Extension has a philosophy of education for all.

vii) Extension has a philosophy covering teaching.

In the words of Seaman A Knapp *"What we hear we may doubt. What we see we may possibly doubt but what we do we cannot doubt"*.

viii) Extension has a philosophy of truth and seeking for truth.

ix) Extension has a philosophy of culture, it recognizes the customs, manners, conventions, norms, habits and behavior of the people.

x) Extension has a philosophy of leadership (working with local leaders – developing new leadership)

xi) Extension has a philosophy of the dignity of the individual.

xii) Extension has a philosophy of local responsibility (people's participation)

(6) Principles of Extension

i) Extension work must be educational.

ii) Extension must work through understanding the traditions, customs, manners, and cultural values of the people so that it is in harmony with the culture of the people.

iii) Extension work must be started where the people are, at their economic, educational, social, physical and cultural level. The technical knowledge, education, intelligence, capacity of understanding and group and physical standard should be considered.

iv) Extension programmes should be based on the interests and needs of the people, which are determined by general acceptance and full support of those for whom they are chalked out. They should not have undue support from the government, except that of technical guidance and essential finances, the government acting as a catalyst.

v) Extension should use democratic methods.

vi) The implementation of an extension programme must be done by the people through their local leaders, the govt. agency giving proper guidance at the appropriate time.

vii) As extension is a two-way channel, the extension worker should not hesitate to learn from the people while he helps them solve their problems.

viii) The extension programme should be started first with those problems which appear simple yet, are very important and urgent in nature.

ix) Extension programme must be flexible. It should permit adjustments to local needs.

x) Extension work must always be educational. It should be persuasive and convincing but never coercive.

xi) Extension must be a continuous and an on-going process.

xii) It should evaluate and re-adjust or modify according to need.

xiii) Extension programme must suit young and old, men and women. Extension work should be challenging and satisfying.

xiv) Extension should work with all classes of people irrespective of race, creed, caste or community.

xv) Extension work must not be combined with regulatory functions.

xvi) Extension work must develop programmes gradually.

xvii) Extension must promote the fuller utilization of local resources, both physical and human.

xviii) Extension must keep in view the national policies and programmes.

xix) Extension must use the community approach.

xx) Extension work should be supported by technical expertise, services and supplies.

The proper recognition of the philosophy underlying extension work and applying the principles are bound to bring in the desirable changes among people to reach the ultimate objective of:

- Developing finer families
- Living in better homes
- On more productive farms
- In more progressive communities

(7) Main Components of Extension

(a) Programme planning

(b) Programme implementation

(c) Programme evaluation

- The entire process of planning for agricultural marketing development implies a need for change.
- The question then arises; change from what, to what, by whom, where, by what methods?

"If we could but know where we are now, and where ought to go, we could better judge what to do, and how to do it" – Abraham Lincoln.

(a) Programme Planning focuses on

1. Needs
2. Resources
3. Obstacles
4. Processes - Steps
5. Methods
6. Evaluation

(b) Programme Implementation implies

i) Organizing wide publicity to the programme

ii) Drawing up a plan of action

iii) Evaluating the programme during and after its execution

iv) Four pillars of implementation

- Research
- Service
- Supplies
- Credit

(c) Programme Evaluation

Evaluation is an integral part of extension cycle. The following steps illustrate the place and importance of extension evaluation in the entire extension cycle.

1. Analyse situation
2. Identify objectives
3. Determine objectives
4. Plan programme
5. Decide on subject – matter or methods
6. Make changes as needed
7. Plan evaluation
8. Collect information
9. Summarize and report findings
10. Interpret and use findings

(8) Extension Methods in Aid of Agricultural Marketing

i) Farm and home visits

ii) General meetings

iii) Group contacts

iv) Campaigns

v) Working with voluntary and local leaders

vi) Exhibits and models

vii) Tours and excursions

viii) Literature-leaflets, folders, circular letters and newspapers on prices and prospects of remunerative marketing agri-products.

ix) Farmers' calls.

x) Radio/TV programmes.

Prior to helping the farmer in marketing his produce there is a greater need to help him produce more at an economical cost. This leads us to a closer view of the farmers' culture and psychology.

Farmers share a village agricultural point of view. It is characterized by:

- ***A Holistic Outlook***: Agriculture is a central activity, but it is only part of a whole, a connected way of life. For example, things which can be contributed to farm work like money and labour are constantly required to meet other family needs as well. The village family allocates these resources by looking at the whole.
- ***Environmental Sensitivity***: All farmers have to be extremely sensitive to their environments in order to survive. They sense from collective and individual observation what elements of the environment are critical to their success as farmers. They are particularly sensitive to cyclical things like rainfall and storm patterns. More than any one else, they know the mini-environments of their individual farms intimately.
- ***Local Focus***: Small-scale farmers especially know a lot about local things and much less about regional, national or global things. Most of these farmers' *interests* are local as well.
- ***Self-Interest***: Each small-scale farmer has a list of priorities that helps him make decisions. This list defines a farmer's self-interest, which is a central part of his worldview.
- ***Farmer's bias***: A farmer's view of things is colored by the physical and economic realities of farm work. These practical preoccupations are uppermost in a farmer's mind.
- ***Tradition, fatalism and adaptability to change:*** Carrying out the tradition of farming is a normal and reliable habit of mind. This unchanging habit of mind is negatively reinforced by adverse outside opinions about village people like small-scale farmers. It has also been reinforced by the inability of tradition to contend with the new problems brought on by accelerated change. As a result, one of the extremes of a small-scale farmers' point of view is a kind of fatalism and feeling of impotence amid rapid change.

> The other end of the spectrum is a real, though often talent openness and adaptability to change, for farming is a constant process of successful adaptation. Like other people, small-scale farmers are ambivalent towards change.

For small-scale farmers with all the above characteristics, change is not worthwhile unless it is:

- Culturally appropriate
- In agreement with self-interest
- Respectful of tradition
- Clearly beneficial
- Not economically risky.

Elaborating on economic risk, John Guy Smith offered this description in 1970:

"Farming is subject to numerous risks from weather, pests, diseases, price fluctuations and other uncertainties. For the small-scale farmer, these risks are accentuated by his precarious economic condition. Much of a small-scale farmer's supposed conservatism is really a very shrewd attempt to avoid or minimize risk".

For example, Yigi Kamara grows rice in Sierra Leone. Every year, he grows his crop during May to September, the rainy season. In August and September, while waiting for the harvest, the stores from the previous year dwindle, and there is a "hungry season". Yigi plants millet and cassava on a hillside in March and April to deal with this. In order to grow rice year round and perhaps even grow a surplus, Yigi is thinking of building gravity-fed ditches and dikes in a swamp near his hill farm. The work will take four months, from January to May. Is it worth the effort? If he doesn't plant millet or cassava, will there be enough food this "hungry season"? Can he afford a shovel? Will his family be able to harvest, thresh, store and grind all the expected new rice? Can he sell some to make it worthwhile? What will his neighbours say?

What about the old stores about the dangers of working in the swamp?

Small-scale farmers like Yigi change as individual cultural beings, as practical farmers, and as economic producers. They have considerable resources which they bring to bear on the problems of agricultural production and livelihood in developing countries:

- Expertise in local technologies and a variety of practical skills (eg. – masonry, carpentry, etc.)
- Expertise regarding local conditions affecting farming
- Status as independent economic unit
- Experience as farmers (traditions)
- A practical, critical viewpoint
- Adaptability
- Openness to producing a usable surplus
- Their limitations include:
- Lack of capital beyond family supply
- Habit of not investing in or using credit or outside inputs
- Interests and roles which compete with agriculture
- Little access to outside agricultural support services
- Reluctance to take risks

Along with these, however, there are factors from beyond the village which also limit the small-scale farmer's ability to deal with change. Most directed technological change, like the promoting of new practices, is based on the priorities and interests of development planners and leaders. This may exclude small-scale farmers or be irrelevant to their needs. Governments, development agencies and private business promote change this way. Example may be mechanization or mono-cropping which benefit large-scale farmers and foreign markets more than small-scale farmers.

Understanding People

Self-interest is the basis for all that a farmer does. The source of a farmer's motivation, whatever it may be in a given case, can be quite obscure to the extension worker. A farmer who seems to be strong, intelligent, financially secure, and aware enough to be successful, may still cling to his timeworn practices rather than opt for something new that he perceives to be against his interest. Neither repeated contact with an extension agent nor weighty scientific evidence will change his mind. The farmer's personal concerns – his religion, his desire for material possessions that he feels can be more quickly had by other means – are foremost in his mind. As such they are of primary concern to extension workers.

An extension agent needs to learn what the people he lives with value and consider important. This understanding is at the heart of the two-way communication process. Without it, the extensionist can gain no perspective on the appropriateness of the change he promotes. Nor can he determine what training methods are most suitable to local people's needs. Finally, and perhaps most importantly, the agent will be unable to emphasize or even communicate effectively with his friends and neighbours.

To learn anything about a person's self-interest requires time and shared experience. It takes hours sweating over plow blades, eating from the same bowl and walking together in sadness in a funeral procession. The "methods" used are informal, but the information gleaned is of crucial importance. The farming aspect of a villager's life, is connected with all other aspects. Labour resources for farm work are also labour resources required by virtue of kinship and money for improved livestock strains can just as easily become money for a niece's school fees. As an extension worker enters a community, and begins to make initial social contacts, he should take note of the various special interests people display in order to better understand how to go about his work.

Administering Credit

Farmers can exercise certain options only when they have

the financial resources to do so. Accumulating these resources (sometimes called "capital") is a necessary first step toward innovation and change. Farmers can accumulate resource by saving surplus income or borrowing resources from other sources. To the small-scale farmer saving presents a major problem because even the diligent application of customary farm practices does not often yield much surplus beyond home needs. One of the major catalysts of potential farmer innovation in developing countries is therefore the provision of credit.

There are many kinds of credit: informal sharing of a plough and family communal labour, village-level borrowing at the money lender's bank loans or input-credit schemes. Beyond the village level, credit is both a powerful tool and a potential cause of dependence. Cooperative ventures and capital-sharing are better ways to help small scale-farmers gain access to the resources for change.

Farmers themselves have various motives for using credit:

Consumer Credit

- ***Survival*** – when a crop failure or family illness causes the normal balance of home needs and harvest to go out of balance
- ***Family and Social Obligations*** – when a wedding, funeral or other family obligation requires money or resources not at hand
- ***Consumption*** – when something the farm family wants is beyond normal means
- ***Investment in the Home or Cottage Industry*** – when the farm family wants to buy a labour-saving device *(corn grinder)*, set up cottage industry *(sewing machine and cloth)* or repair/expand a house.

Agricultural Credit

- ***Survival of Farm Enterprise*** – *(e.g. securing seed or using a cultivator)* securing resources necessary to keep the farm going

- ***Paying for Seasonal Labour*** – Extra labour beyond the family may be needed to plant, weed or harvest when there is no surplus to provide wages
- ***Acquiring Inputs*** – purchasing new tools, fertilizer or equipment to carry out a new package of practices
- ***Increasing Efficiency*** – sometimes farmers wish to substitute animal or machine power for human power for land preparation, for example, but need to borrow to employ it before realizing profits.
- ***Marketing*** – while waiting for a good price for their produce farmers may need to borrow to survive
- ***Expanding the Scale of Farm Business*** – to acquire additional land, to finance farm improvements *(clearing land, building storage facilities, constructing irrigation works, etc.)* to increase herd size.

It is important for the extension worker and farmers to understand why and how credit is extended to farmers. Credit being a form of dependence on resources beyond the farmer's control, it should be carefully and cautiously used. When the motivation of the lender is different than the farmer's motivation, there is much less opportunity for informality, for leeway with regard to the repayment of loan, and generally for sympathy for the farmer's precarious position. It is of prime importance that the extension worker and farmer seeking credit be aware of the motives of lenders.

Locally, credit can be extended as a social obligation or an aspect of friendship or family responsibility. However, credit is most often proffered in order to earn interest on the loan. This is the basis of commercial lending in and out of the village. Beyond earning interest, credit is loaned to facilitate sales, to assure the delivery of farm products or as public service through development projects. These motives are important to consider in seeking credit with farmers.

Most of the cost of a commercial loan is interest. Interest is calculated in a variety of ways, each resulting in a different amount of credit and a different costs. A common form of interest for small-scale farmers is the advance sale of crops, in which the lender is promised crops at current prices even though the price will be higher at harvest time. The different in price constitutes a loss to the farmer which is a form of interest, or credit cost.

"Credit terms" are all the conditions, including credit costs, that are part of an agreement between lender and borrower. The usefulness of credit is a measure of the costs and terms versus the returns or results or credit use. Cost/benefit is calculated in monetary terms for most commercial credit, although timeliness, social appropriateness and other considerations also must be weighed. Most especially, the extension worker must help a farmer weigh the value of credit against the danger of dependency on factors beyond the farmer's control. This must always be part of the calculation of credit cost/benefit.

Because most commercial credit is extended for profit, it is rarely extended to the small-scale farmer. What with the uncertainties of weather, pests and diseases, the limited money-making ability of the small-scale farm, and the inconvenience of the administering credit to a far-flung clientele in rural areas, the small-scale farmer is often not considered a good "risk".

Other forms of institutional credit (through development project or agro product distributors), where these exist, are more readily available to small-scale farmers, but do not allow freedom to use the loan for any purpose. The loan must go to producing a certain crop or buying certain inputs. Thus, it is not easy to help small-scale farmers gain access to credit.

The process of acquiring credit involves, first, surveying a farmers' needs and clarifying with him the specific need to borrow capital. Secondly, the farmer and extensionist must inventory local credit sources. Next, extensionist and farmer must calculate the costs of credit and estimate the returns to the credit to determine the cost/benefit of employing the credit opportunities identified. This would include clarifying the terms of credit. Finally, the extensionist must help the farmer honor the terms of the loan and re-pay it when due.

One facilitating means for the farmer to secure credit is the village cooperative society. It can not only serve his credit needs but it can also be used effectively in marketing his farm produce at a reasonably better price at the appropriate time to the benefit of the farmer.

Providing Storage

Storage facilities constitute a significant factor in agricultural marketing.

Approximately thirty per cent of grain in storage all over the world is lost because of insects, rodents and moulds. For the small-scale farmers with whom extensionists work, this is a major problem of every day life. In villages, protection from such pests and moulds is lacking. Since this is a vital area in which to help the farmer, attention may be focused on the following topics:

- The Grain Storage Problems
- Grain Is a Living Thing
- Grain, Moisture and Air
- Preparing Grain for Storage
- Grain Dryer Models
- Enemies of Grain
- Storage Methods.

Extension workers must focus some of their attention on issues beyond the production of agricultural products. By helping a farmer double his grain or vegetable yield, an extensionist may cause a major storage problem. Where does the new grain go? How does the farmer protect it from pests, moisture, thieves? The technical information necessary to solve storage problems is to be provided to the farmers. An extensionist can help by encouraging farmers to plan their storage strategies. Also, farmers can determine the most appropriate storage facilities and strategies with the extension worker's help. Finally, adequate storage is the most practical marketing tool a farmer has. He or she can hold onto a crop until prices become favourable if storage is adequate. The importance of storage facilities cannot be over emphasized.

Besides storage, pooling of grain by the farmers at the village level and also of grading of grain or agri-products are conducive to fetching better prices. These could be done through the local cooperative or Farmers' Association.

Marketing Agricultural Products

The extensionist is often in a good position to help farmers understand and participate more successfully in the marketing system. One of the largest and most uninviting areas the small-scale farmer enters by virtue of change is the market place. In it, he is subject to the forces of supply, demand, big business and government policies and regulations. Here, if anywhere, the farmer needs the direct assistance an extensionist can provide.

There are two main ways in which extensionists can help small-scale farmers successfully approach the market system: by organizing large-scale cooperative groups aimed at gaining local or regional price advantages, or by securing favourable prices through timely marketing, and or through cooperative marketing.

The process of helping farmers secure price advantages through timely marketing involves four steps:

I. Establish who controls the crop/animals at harvest and under what conditions:

  (a) Advance sales: farmers may receive payment in advance for a crop thereby obligating it to a buyer.

  (b) Contracted sales: farmers may contact to sell a crop to buyer at a certain price for certain quality and quantity.

(c) Loan or credit restrictions on sale: farmers may have to sell a harvest when a loan payment is due.

(d) Tenancy or rent restrictions on sale: farmers may have to sell or give part of a harvest to a landowner or local leader due to tenancy terms, rent due or local customs.

II. Estimate the costs of holding products off the market.

(a) Estimate the average length of the "holding period" between the middle of the period of average high price and average low prices.

(b) Estimate roughly the cost of holding each product *(rice or any product)* off the market. *(eg.–storage facility cost or depreciation; storage losses; handling costs, etc.).*

(c) Estimate the profit or loss to the farmer by holding a crop out of the market. (This depends on the difference between the cost of holding out and the anticipated seasonal price rise).

Net Benefit

Estimate Price rise – Estimated holding cost = Net Benefit (per unit of crop)

III. Decide to hold crop or sell

Before a farmer can contemplate marketing strategies, his crop must be free at harvest of any restricting arrangements. If the crop is free at harvest, and if the net benefit of holding the crop out of the market place is significant (more than 25 per cent), then the extensionist can advise the farmer to hold his crop out until the price rises to the seasonal average high price.

There are other strategies for successfully participating in the market system. They are listed as one of the *TOOLS*, "interventions by Farmers in the Market System". This tool also serves to illustrate the points raised in this section.

Illustration

THE FARMER HAS A VESTED	BECAUSE IT DETERMINES	AND HE PROBABLY INTEREST IN RELATED TO	BUT HE PROBABLY KNOWS IT'S DOES NOT KNOW IT IS RELATED TO
MARKET	Which commodities he can produce	Transport facilities, quotas, "monopoly" control	Effects of government policies
MARKETING STANDARDS (WEIGHTS, GRADES)	How he prepares his crop for market	Local customs. Buyers' preferences	Legislation. Legislation. preferences.
THE AVAILABILITY AND QUALITY OF DIRECT MARKETING SERVICES (weighing, timeliness of payment credit, others	His choice of buyers for his crop	His personal relationship with buyers. The buyers' honesty. The buyer's resources.	Buyer's management ability How much it costs the buyer to perform marketing functions.
OVERALL MARKETING EFFICIENCY	Marketing margins and the price he receives.	How efficiently the transport and assembly functions are performed.	Management and technical skills. Productivity of labour. Many and varied costs. The less visible market functions.
COMPETI-TIVENESS OF THE SYSTEM	Marketing margins and the price he receives. His choice buyers.	Number of potential buyers, and alternative markets. The buyers' financial and political power.	Control of financing. National policies. The subtler forms of influence.
THE MARKET EQUATING SUPPLY AND DEMAND (price	More than any other factor determines the prices he receives for	Orderly marketing. Seasonal factors. The size of the	National policies. How much of the consumer price is absorbed by the

determination)	his products, planting and harvesting schedules, and his farm enterprise mix.	total crop. Distant demand factors beyond his control.	market process. Internal supply and demand. Costs of holding the crop.

TOOL

Checklist for Collecting Price Data

SOURCE OF DATA (Current)

- Actual sales
  - reported by farmers
  - reported by local people
  - reported by handlers of products
- Reports by ministries, market publications, etc. (Historical)
- Recent memory
  - as above
- Official reports and studies as above.

ANALYZING DATA

- Collect data from sources
- Convert all data to common units of value.
- Check prices to eliminate abnormally high or low prices.
- Make sure information on prices is relevant to the community in which farmers/clients live.
- Establish average prices by observing them over a regular period of time (2 or 3 weeks).

TOOL

Interventions Farmers Can Make in the Market System

Farmers can influence four factors which affect the prices of their products over a short period of time:

- Time of sale
- Choice of buyer
- Collective or individual marketing
- Condition of the product

Farmers can learn about their options concerning these four factors with extension workers. Often the price of a product is lower near normal harvest time, so holding the product in storage is often a way to gain a higher price. Storage depends on perishability, facilities, farmer's ability to wait for income, etc. The choice of buyers is often limited for small-scale farmers, due to transportation costs. Collective marketing is advantageous when costly transportation is a means to a higher price. Collective marketing involves thorough planning of harvest, handling and storage as well as price and profit-sharing agreements. The extension worker can help point out the need for these considerations and can facilitate the process of dealing with them.

It may not be out of place here to briefly look into the marketing of rural industries products. In a larger sense they are allied to agri-products.

Marketing Rural Industries Products

Rural Industries Products

The problem of marketing rural industries products stems from the poor socio-economic background of the artisans, competition from the better-equipped factory sector, lack of sufficient infrastructural facilities in producing raw materials, products not changing rapidly enough with consumer tastes and preferences, labour-intensive technology, inadequate storage facilities and the non-availability of distribution channels.

S. Vanaja Rao (*Economic Times*, Jan.10, 1984) observes that few organizations serve as a link between village industry producers and the market and makes out a case for a district-level organization for procuring raw material and finding markets for the finished products.

To assist the marketing of rural industries products she suggests:

- The KVIC *(Khadi & Village Industries Commission)* open more bhandars and bhavans (emporia) at the block and district level.
- The KVIC renovate existing bhandars and bhavans and set up a big emporium at each state headquarters, supported by a number of bhandars.
- A separate marketing organization to be set up for each village industry for raw material supply and procuring finished products for sale to bhandars and bhavans.
- Action should be taken against government departments which do not purchase reserved items from the KVIC/ Small Scale Sector.
- The KVIC and other organizations engaged in marketing V&CI products should take the assistance of the public distribution systems and the marketing outlets of corporate public sector organizations.
- Sale of some products can be made on a contractual basis while for others, intensive sales drives can be encouraged.
- Commercial banks should come in a big way to provide assistance to entrepreneurs who take up marketing and distribution of these products.
- The government controlled media should publicize these products on a preferential basis.
- The quality of products be improved.
- The KVIC should supply suitable machinery and spares that will enable production of improved products.
- The staff or managers of the KVIC and retail

organizations should be better compensated to attract suitable persons to man sales depots *(incentives)*.

Mass Media

Vehicles of information normally classed under the heading of "mass media" – television, radio, newspapers, magazines, and newsletters – can be used by extension agents. Usually, extensionists involved in mass communication efforts adopt other training methods to a larger audience size. Role-plays and dramas are shifted from verandah and village clearings to stages where a hundred or more people can view them simultaneously. Poster designs originally intended only for local use can prove successful enough at calling attention to some new aspect of agriculture to warrant mass production and distribution through Ministry channels over a much wider area.

Media within the realm of possibility for extension work include periodicals, fairs, and radio. Periodicals can be used as discussion starters in farmer meetings where at least a portion of those present are literate. Agricultural fairs are conducted in many developing countries to encourage agriculture development. Volunteers can make use of these fairs by encouraging some of the farmers in certain areas to compete for prizes in farm produce competitions. Such prizes can be valuable form of reward and recognition for a farmer's achievements. Radio provides the most exciting opportunity of any of the standard mass communication devices. This medium can be put to use as a simple information vehicle – to relay announcements of upcoming farmer meetings in an area, for example, or it can be employed in more creative ways. Extensionists with experience in radio broadcasting and production may be able to work within Ministry channels to produce simple and yet highly effective advertisements on the radio for new techniques. Serialized skits, songs and humorous stories are very popular in countries where national radio stations, receive widespread attention.

Radio and TV in local languages would be an effective media for disseminating marketing information.

Conclusion

At the field level there is a greater need to carry out marketing extension education by the village level extension functionaries, village panchayats, youth clubs, farmers' forums, mahila mandals. Though some of the above mentioned people's organizations have their own unique functions as people's institutions, they can be used as an effective means and media to disseminate market information to the farmers. There is a greater need to have a synergetic effect of personal field extension and mass media such as, Radio, TV and newspapers. The extension functionaries to be effective as agri-marketing specialists may have to acquaint themselves with the ongoing agri-marketing practices and the problems and bottlenecks in respect to transportation, communication, storage facility, staying capacity and credit requirements on the part of the farmers. The agricultural marketing extension agents are to be aware of the existing system of agri-marketing and the better prospects available outside the system and also create better prospects in respect to profitable marketing of agricultural produce.

There is a need for continuous concerted efforts on the part of the farmers themselves, farm leaders, local institutions, extension agents to really help the farmers not only produce more but also to have better price for their products.

13

EACH VILLAGE AS A UNIT OF RURAL DEVELOPMENT

The process of organizing rural communities for their participation in development involves working and interacting with the people in the communities. The prerequisite for effective interaction with the people in the rural communities is a knowledge of the characteristics of the rural communities, their way of life, the value systems, traditions and customs, the network or relationships and the kind of changes taking place among them. In the clinical approach, there is a need to consider each village as a unit of development. In order to do this we should have a comprehensive and detailed data pertaining to the village. This will help us identify the historical background of the settlement, its natural resources, the kind of avocations people are engaged in, the kind of infrastructure, the topographical details and the human resources the community is endowed with. Further, we may also look into the community common needs and in some cases individual needs also. Treating each village community as a unit of development is a necessity in carrying out gradual sustained development activities in each village. In this context, we may briefly look into the characteristics of the rural communities as a kind of background to understand the general nature of rural communities in India.

Rural communities are not identical in every respect. There is a considerable diversity among them. They could be ranged along a continuum. At one end, we have the sacred-folk societies and at the other end the secular ones, varying in terms of simplicity and complexity. In folk-sacred societies, established practices and ideas are taken for granted. There are few contacts with persons outside of the local geographic areas. Kinship relations are dominant. There is little formalized education; teaching is by means of family training, conversation, preaching and ceremonial. Occupations are learned by apprenticeship. The older men, who have lived longest and whose experiences and memories reach back farthest, are respected and relied upon for advice and guidance. Such societies are relatively changeless; they, in fact, quite generally resist change.

In a highly secular society, means and methods of communication and transportation are ample and ready. Persons are highly mobile both physically and mentally. Formal education is universal occupations and professions are learned as technical sciences. Most social relations are impersonal. Even kinship relations are loose in terms of duties and obligations. Changes of all kinds are prevalent, rapid, and generally welcome. Individuals are members of many groups and live by a number of different value systems.

To be completely bound by folk customs and traditions would mean stagnation. To be completely secular would be inhuman or non-social. No present day society is completely either of them. Those which are nearer the folk end of this continuum are working, some rapidly, toward the secular end of the continuum. The results of too rapid a movement in this direction have been discovered by the study of the most mobile part of the people who live in large cities. The results of little or no movement in this direction are illustrated in a number of countries where a thin layer of wealthy, educated, elite at the top of the social and political structure purposely sabotage change in the large folk segments of their society.

Concept of Communities

Territorial boundary and the sentimental bindings are the essential factors in a community. The group of people that live within a geographic region have the uniformity or similarity in many customs and habits, such as food, clothing, occupation etc. These matters depend upon the availability of material, climatic conditions, nature of soil, etc. The above factors bind the people together.

Another factor, which is the outcome of face-to-face, intensive functional interaction, is the community sentiment. This sentiment, that makes them feel that they are one, or the "we" feeling is the life of the community. The sentiment gives rise to responsibility, makes the members of the communities conscious of their rights and duties. Rights and obligations implicate inter-dependence of the members.

A community then means a group of people living in a given area with common interests, bound by a sense of and common mode of living. A village satisfies the requisite to form a community. It gives the inhabitants a common area of land, common past that brings about a sharing of experience and standard of behaviour and attitudes. They share some degree of common activities or some degree of common life, irrespective of their social and religious differences. It is not confined to any of the various restricted fields of community life on the basis of religion, caste, race, language or profession but one that envelops the whole life of the total community. Whatever affects the villages, affects the whole population. A community may be settled or an unsettled one. It may be migratory having come from another area in search of livelihood or it may belong to the new village where they live for centuries, or they might be newcomers.

Some of the distinguishing features of rural community are:

1. Occupation is mainly agriculture and/ or allied professions.
2. People live closer together and closer to the natural environment. This makes their life and attitude simpler and unaffected.
3. Smallness of the size of the community brings the

members closer together in everyday life. This and the common occupational interest make the people know each other better than the urban people do.

4. Lesser density of population is caused by the nature of occupation. People in the rural areas can move more freely.
5. There is greater homogeneity of life than in urban areas; because the people are bound not only by common occupation, but also are bound by common traditions, customs and common heritage.
6. Relatively, there is very little social mobility in the community. They live in the same land generation after generation, by the same occupation, follow the same old customs and habits and maintain the purity of their ethnic identity by avoiding inter-caste and communal marriage or any other type of social intercourse.

Hundreds of local communities in folk societies have been studied by anthropologists. Based on these studies, the characteristics of communities of folk societies can be broadly generalized as follows:

1. Each community is something approximating a complete society in terms of both geography and people.
2. No external forces other than the physical environment enter the community. Few strangers ever come to the community.
3. Each community is composed of families and other kinship groups, the systematic relations between which constitute the social structure of the community.
4. The rights and duties of these groups are passed down from generation to generation and maintained by a value system which consists of the mores of the community. They are accepted by everyone.
5. There are no written constitutions or contracts.

Relations between groups are monitored and even enforced by the elders of the group.

6. The community perpetuates itself by teaching each on-coming generations its old way of doing and thinking. Apprenticeship in occupations and initiation into each age group by various types of ceremonial guarantees that each new generation shall know and do as the old generation did.
7. The natural resources with which the people used to sustain their economic life are generally owned by the whole community. Each family sustains itself economically by participating in the development and utilization of these resources, and participates in the economic returns from the resources.
8. The economic relations of the community are the accepted division of labour between groups rather than by trade or even by barter. The economic and social security of all is, therefore, a total community responsibility.
9. There is thus less possibility of change in the status of groups, much less of individuals in the community.

To the degree that simple communities manifest these characteristics, they are whole societies, in terms not only of social, economic and political structures, but in terms of value systems. Each person growing up in one of these communities believes and practices these values, plays his assigned roles without questioning, and as a person is pretty much a complete reflection of the community as a whole.

In the present societies some new types of behaviour develop, but by no means do all the old characteristics of folk society disappear. The total or relative social and cultural isolation of the peasant communities is on the decline. The outside world has moved in on them. Due to multiple factors of influence such as, planned and guided community development efforts on the part of the government, increase in transport and communication, the gradual process of urbanization and industrialization, the emergence of new political and economic institutions, the rural communities in general are in the process of change and the situation in the past few decades may be summarized as follows:

1. The first thing was that trade and commerce entered the village.
2. As contact with trade centers, either with merchants located in the village or with trade towns, developed, at least on the part of a few of the village people there, a knowledge of the outside world in terms of activities about which they had previously known very little. What they learned naturally became matters of gossip within the village and, therefore, some understanding of marketing , prices, and things of that kind developed on the part of all village people.
3. Government had entered all of these villages many years back, but modern government of the type which brings services and assistance to villagers was fairly new in all of the villages. Agents of the government had come in and promoted development and welfare activities. When this once began there was a new basis for forming new parties, and often new factions developed.
4. Government servants, located in or serving the village were seldom local villagers themselves, therefore, new persons, generally persons with more education and receiving higher incomes than the villagers, introduced a new type of person and, in some ways, tended to introduce new social status among the other statuses of the village.
5. Government made incursions in all cases, sooner or later, in terms of establishing and helping to maintain schools. School teachers were new citizens of the community and in some cases, played quite different roles than any outsider ever played in the village.

6. As some youth of the village received considerable education, they became capable of making contacts and did make contact outside the village and thus became a channel of cultural traffic in and out of the village.
7. In a few cases, persons with a degree of education took up new occupations different from those which they had traditionally followed, and moved away from the village. This has led to occupational and territorial mobility.
8. As the price and market economy entered the village, some persons began making more money. Those who had made more money or had better contacts with outside agencies became money-lenders. Some of them began purchasing land previously owned by peasants who now lost the ownership of their land. Thus a whole new elite developed in the village, sometimes quite a powerful group.
9. In the case of contacts with the market town or with outside sources of income, some of the villages began to attend picture shows and other recreational events outside the village.
10. A new kind of formal and informal leaders emerged. The youth or the younger generation began influencing the developmental activities in the village. In some cases, government servants began to be looked up to rather than feared.
11. In most villages a degree of individualism developed. Some persons were paid special attention by the development agencies. They gained new importance and they tended to form a group which protected the group against the large owners.
12. In most villages, the lower classes, that is, the lower income people, were paid special attention by the development agencies. They gained new importance and they tended to form a group which protected the

group against the large owners.

13. It may be stated here, that the same old reverence for elders, and for the set class structure, and even for the villagers' values, had been considerably diluted.

The rural communities are, however, far from having lost all their old folk characteristics. The following such characteristics, though somewhat modified, are still maintained, (Taylor).

(a) The elders, while they no longer constitute the village government, are highly respected and are still counselors in many types of issue.

(b) The village community's organization is perpetuated by each new generation tending to follow the family occupations of previous generations.

(c) There is in all of the villages some division of labour between the families, this division being fixed by the traditions of the community.

(d) Families, generally extended families, are more integral social groups than are the villages as a whole.

(e) Sentiment for the land, pride and tenacity in the ownership of the land, is still very strong.

(f) There is relatively little tolerance for new ways of thinking and doing. If the people were asked to choose between tradition and progress, tradition would perhaps be their instinctive choice although a second choice might induce them to take a few hesitating steps in the direction of change.

REFERENCE

Taylor,Carl (n.d), *Community Mobilization for Group Formulation*

Note:- Please see Appendix for 'Study of Rural Community – Aspects to be covered'.

14

GUIDELINES FOR SECTORAL DEVELOPMENT

For the Panchayat Samithi and the Village Panchayats to be effective in helping the people find solutions to their problems, all programmes taken up by the Block Samithi and the Village Panchayats must be related to solving problems which the people themselves have participated in identifying and have expressed a desire to work together to solve. This being true, there are no alternatives to having the Panchayat Samithi each year assist each village panchayat systematically: (1) identify their village problems; (2) understand what cause the problems; (3) know what steps are required to solve the problems; (4) be concerned and eager to solve the problems; and finally (5) to decide which of the specific problems they wish to tackle for the coming year. For each village panchayat to take all its village people through these steps each year will make it possible for each village panchayat to have before it a realistic village development programme. Only as each village panchayat completes this kind of systematic analysis will it be possible for the Panchayat Samithi to put together a Block programme. Until there is a Block programme which is a composite of these village programmes, the Samithi cannot intelligently allocate staff and financial resources to the village panchayats. It will be absolutely imperative for the panchayat Samithi to have such a realistic programme if the Block staff is to be effective in carrying out an extension educational programme in each village as a sponsored specific panchayat programme.

A prerequisite to the Block staff's effective working relationship with village people through the panchayat Samithi and the village panchayat, the cooperative and other village institutions and organizations is that they themselves be clear about the village problems. Each member of the Block staff– the gram sevak, the technical specialist and the Block Development Officer – should be able to help village people identify their key problems. While it should be the responsibility of each subject-matter technical specialist to guide the staff in an analysis of the village problems which fall within their respective fields, all members of the Block staff should know the most important things that cause the problem, and the basic action steps each specialist recommends if village people are to solve their problems themselves.

Village life is lived first in integrated families and second in a complex set of village relations. Only as each member of the Block development staff assumes that he is, first, a generalized development and extension officer, and second, a staff member with a specialized function to perform, will he be able to make his maximum contribution to helping the village people in solving their many problems largely through their own efforts, utilizing to the fullest any and all technical help which can be interpreted to them in meaningful and understanding terms. This means, for example, that before the animal husbandry technical specialist can make a significant contribution to improving the cattle, goats, sheep, swine and poultry, he must know the important place each has in the lives of the families. He must know the nature and depth of family and village attitudes and practices with respect to the animals and poultry. He must know which members of the family are responsible for carrying out each individual practice. He must know, in relationship to the many village problems, the relative importance villagers will place on improving their livestock and poultry in contrast to improving their crops. He must know the religious significance the village places on the livestock and what may be involved and implied if he makes specific recommendations about how to improve the livestock and poultry. He must know the place village families assign to livestock in their total village economy. As a basis for finalizing his recommendations he should know why the villagers follow their current practices and what other practices they have followed over the years.

The Block development staff must, as a development team, forever accept the principle that the emphasis for development in each village must be centred on the problems the village panchayats are at that moment ready to recognize and to give a position of prominence in terms of devoting time and effort to their solution. To accept this position does not mean a de-emphasis on educating the village people to the existence of problems which the Block staff may feel to be of urgent importance. What it does mean, however, is that programmes for correction or for the solution of village problems must wait until the staff can, through education, demonstration, and persuasion, bring the village people working, their Panchayat to be concerned enough about the problems to want to accept technical help and guidance in their solution. Any other approach is more-or-less wasted effort, in that it takes up a lot of staff time without enlisting village action.

A wise Block development staff will learn the priorities each village panchayat places on its many problems, and will at first concentrate its own limited resources on helping the village panchayat solve the problems it has concluded to be important at the moment. A wise staff will also know, however, that one of its basic continuing functions is to educate the village panchayat to the existence of problems it may not at the moment consider important.

This chapter devotes lengthy treatment of village problems so as to guide the Block development staff in its working relationships with panchayat Samithi and the village panchayats within the Block. For each significant village problem listed, there follows first a list of generalized conditions which cause the problem, and second, a list of generalized steps which, if taken, would contribute toward the solution of the problem. Each Block staff will need to prepare a similar list for its respective Block, if it is a wise staff and is to make the maximum contribution toward helping village panchayats identify, become concerned about, and take steps to solve, village problems. This generalized list of problems for the Block should then be broken down and developed for each village. Each village list must be refined with experience and understanding.

A valuable educational experience for each village panchayat would be for the panchayat to develop a large poster on which they would list their problems as they became recognized as significant and meaningful. This would become especially valuable as the panchayats learned to associate with a problem the things which contribute to it, and as they came to know what steps should be taken to solve the problem. The village-by-village definition of problems, the detailing of the things that cause the problems, and step-by-step recommendations should in the first instance be developed jointly by the respective technical specialist, the Gram Sevak, and the panchayat.

Diagnosing and prescribing for village problems requires three steps. First, the many individual village problems must be identified; second, the thing which causes village problems must be known; third, action steps should be recommended to solve each village problem. This is an essential process of getting the village people through their panchayats to look searchingly at themselves, and is the only basis on which the village Panchayat can take intelligent decisions as to what they want to do, when they want to do it, how they want to do it, and who is to take the initiative.

This process of village-by-village definition of problems and agreement on action steps is also essential for the Block staff as a team, if it is to have a purposeful working relationship with each village panchayat. With this kind of village-by-village analysis and planning, all members of the Block staff can and should take an interest in all phases of village activity as they visit the villages to work systematically with the gram sevaks there, they were originally called Village Level Workers, later as Village Development Officers and recently they are redesignated as Panchayat Secretaries in Andhra Pradesh

Without this individual problem analysis and later putting together of a village's diagnosis of its many problems and suggested action steps, the gram sevak and extension specialist cannot possibly be effective. The gram sevak must always see the village as a whole, as well as seeing and understanding its many individual problems. Only with this kind of analysis and village planning can the gram sevak make the maximum use of his individual village visits.

One and all should understand that, as the Rural Development staff gains experience and as Village people respond and themselves change with the changes they bring about in the villages, the village problems will be defined and the priorities panchayats give to taking action steps will change. This simply means that the definition of village problems, the detailing of the causes of the problems, and the outlining of action steps should be a more or less continuous process. As a minimum these village-by-village analyses should be updated once a year.

We come now to a detailing of the generalized village problems. For each problem a generalized analysis is given of the things which cause the problem and the recommended action steps to correct the problem.

I. *Low Crop Yields* is a village problem.

Low crop yields are caused by some or all the following conditions:

1. Following traditional farming methods and using primitive tools.
2. Lack of knowledge about superior yields possible from improved seeds, use of commercial fertilizers, improved agricultural implements and better tillage practices.
3. Lack of understanding about importance of making compost manure and of proper application of compost manure.

4. Lack of enough sure water and improper use of available water.
5. Lack of understanding about the importance of soil testing as a basis for determining the kind and amount of commercial fertilizer to use.
6. Lack of knowledge about the need for growing and ploughing under green manure crops.
7. Fragmented land-holding works against better use of water and use of improved tillage practices.
8. Lack of desirable tenure arrangements, providing security of tenure and appropriate redistribution of land holdings.
9. Lack of credit, at reasonable interest and available as needed, prevents many cultivators from being able to purchase improved seed, improved implements, better bullocks, and fertilizer.
10. Lack of adequate power to quickly prepare the soil, plant the crops, and harvest them.
11. Insufficient plant protection measures against insects, rodents, and other pests.
12. Shortage of pure seed.
13. While increasing number of village cultivators are taking up one or more improved agricultural methods, the need is for more and more of the cultivators to apply as many as possible of the improved practices as a "package".
14. Inadequate supply of electricity for farm operations.
15. Unremunerative prices for agri-produce.
16. Increase in cost of cultivation.

Crop yields can without much extra expense be substantially increased as the Block staff, working through the village panchayats, succeeds in getting village cultivators to recognize that their yields are low; to understand the things which contribute to low yield; to want to increase their yields; to know the specific things they as cultivators can do to increase their yields; and as the cultivators are helped through demonstrations and educational guidance in gaining successful experience with the new practices and methods.

Action Steps for Increasing Agricultural Yields

1. The village extension worker with the advice of the Block extension staff should, working through the panchayat, keep all village cultivators informed about improved agricultural practices for all the major agricultural crops grown in the village.

For each of the major crops, the practices recommended to the village should be a package and cover all phases of the crops life cycle, e.g., cultural practices, improved seeds, fertilizers – kind and application, insecticides – kind and application, agricultural implements, water use, etc.

2. Under village conditions test, through well organized result demonstrations, a package of technical recommendations made by the gram sevaks. Once these improved agricultural practices and methods have been adequately tested under village conditions, then and only then should the recommendations be made on a village and Block-wide basis and intense educational programmes be organized to get widespread acceptance of the proven recommendations.

3. If the village people are to follow through and themselves adopt the improved practices and methods which have through village demonstrations proven to be superior to the traditional practices, the Block staff must then turn to the cooperatives and help the cooperatives become effective in making available the needed supplies (seed, fertilizers, implements, insecticides, etc.). The cooperatives and also the Government must assure that these supplies will be available when they are needed, in sufficient quantity and in close proximity to all villages, and at prices the villagers can afford. If the villagers are to

purchase these supplies credit must through the cooperative be readily available on terms and conditions appropriate to all classes of cultivators.

4. Assuming the population base is adequate to organize a cooperative in sufficient size to provide volume and quality service and support competent business management, the Block staff should educate the village people to understand how a well-run cooperative could assist them in at least three important ways:

   (a) The cooperative must provide the credit required for villagers to be able to purchase the recommended improved seed, the improved implements, required bullocks, tractors, power tillers needed fertilizer and insecticides.

   (b) The cooperative must be the distributing organization for stocking and selling to the cultivators the required and recommended improved seed and implements, fertilizers and insecticides. Private commercial agencies also may do the job.

   (c) The cooperative and the Government must assist the villagers in the marketing of their products – essential if the cultivators are to realize the maximum net return on the products sold.

5. While the actual improved agricultural practices can only be carried out by the individual cultivators, the village panchayat can and must take the leadership in assisting the village community to do many things together. It is the combination activity by the individual cultivator and the village community which will be necessary to step up crop yields.

6. There should be adequate supply of power for cultivation.

7. The farmers should be guided and assisted in conserving and judicious use of rainwater both for agricultural and domestic purposes.

II. *Fragmentized Land holdings* is a village problem.

Fragmentized land holdings in the villages is primarily associated with population pressure on the land. This along with limited out migration, decay in handicraft economy, and limited employment opportunities in village industries has forced village families to follow the practice of sub-division of land holdings as the only means of providing economic opportunity, though meager, to the oncoming generations.

Since India's immediate need is substantial increased agricultural production, it is imperative for the panchayats and Block staff to give the highest priority to village programmes which will result in increased agricultural production. It is a well-known fact that the present scattered, small and unevenly shaped fragments of land holding prevent cultivators from adopting many of the improved agricultural practices essential for agricultural development. Putting first things first means the panchayats should under the guidance of the Panchayat Samithi develop soon far-reaching programmes to bring the present fragmented land holdings into rectangular consolidated holdings and do so within the shortest possible period of time. To be effective, this programme of consolidation should be taken up and sponsored by the District Zilla Parishad and the Block Panchayat Samithi.

Action Steps for Consolidation

1. Experience with land consolidation in many States clearly indicates that village people are themselves concerned about their fragmentized land holdings and will with the intelligent guidance of the Zilla Parishad and the Panchayat Samithi give full cooperation in working up village consolidation programmes. The Government may come up with a policy on land consolidation.
2. Facts about how other villages have gone about and benefited from consolidating their land holdings should be presented to village people, through the panchayats.
3. Individual villagers – panchayat members and others – who are interested in land consolidation might be taken

to villages where land consolidation has been completed so they can make first-hand observations about the programme.

4. As a means of developing villager interest and guiding the village through a land consolidation programme, the village panchayat should be encouraged to establish a land consolidation committee to deal with this specific problem.

5. As a village panchayat's interest is aroused in the problem of fragmentized land holding, steps can and should be taken to prepare an up-to-date map giving precise measurements of all land holdings.

6. When the majority of villagers are ready to cooperate in a village-wide land consolidation programme, a plan should be agreed to for determining the land classification values of each strip of land. These land classification values may be based on any one of the following:

   (a) Valuation on the basis of market value.

   (b) Valuation on the basis of productivity.

   (c) Valuation on the basis of rental value.

The finalized programme for land consolidation should give to each landholder a rectangular piece of land having the total value of his various strips.

7. In finalizing the village land consolidation the Panchayat should be encouraged to integrate this programme with all round village development. This means in the final land consolidation plan particular attention should be paid to the following:

   (a) Setting aside appropriate land for village roads, drainage, irrigation, etc.

   (b) Providing land for such community purposes as pasture lands, fuel plantations, schools, panchayat ghars, play grounds, etc.

   (c) Valuation on the basis of rental value of village site or a new piece of land so the entire village lay out may be modernized to permit wide, drained streets, adequate space for houses with latrines, etc.

(d) Setting aside a part of the land for cultivation through the village community, the income from such land being utilized to augment the village panchayat funds.

(e) Development of schemes for more intensive cultivation by improvement of land, adoption of improved techniques and conservation of soil.

III. *Limited Employment Opportunities* is a village problem.

Limited employment opportunities are the result of at least the following conditions:

1. The population is increasing faster than production resources and new work opportunities are presently being organized.
2. Lack of planned cottage and village industries keyed to market demand, available raw materials and technical resources.
3. Lack of financial help for small industries –
   (a) to modernize existing industries,
   (b) to procure raw materials,
   (c) to market products,
   (d) to organize new industries.
4. Lack of adequate technical research and training programmes to help cottage and village industries keep up-to-date on scientific and industrial development.
5. Lack of organized village initiative for improving existing cottage and village industries and establishing new ones.
6. Since many village industry products are of inferior quality and not keyed to market demand, they are not able to successfully compete with similar products produced by larger, more modern industries.

7. Educational institutions are not providing adequate technical training to prepare village boys for useful service in cottage and village industries.
8. Arable land for new workers in agriculture is definitely limited.
9. Too much village emphasis is currently placed on crops which required limited labour – thus definitely limiting the motivations to push up production of commercial crops which may require more labour and investment, but are more profitable.
10. Because of lack of emphasis on water use much land is only partially used and therefore, has limited labour requirements.
11. Until recently little has been done to frame a systematic plan to counteract the growing unemployment in the villages.

As the agricultural segment of the village economy begins to respond, pushing up production and income, and the village people become alert to their new opportunities and express new needs, there will develop in the villages new market demand which can be met through locally produced and marked products. To meet these rising expectations of village people, the Panchayat Samithi should develop as a priority programme the provision of educational guidance and technical assistance to the present and potential cottage and village industries within the Block.

Action Steps for Increasing the Employment Opportunities of Village People

Following are the more important and feasible action steps which, if taken jointly by the cottage and village industrialists and the Panchayat Samithi, should increase employment opportunities in the Rural Development Blocks.

1. Collect data about existing whole-time, part-time and subsidiary occupations.

2. Conduct industrial and marketing surveys of the Block to determine the present and potential market demands and to give guidance about what types of industries have a good chance of succeeding in the area.

3. Through education and demonstrations, help the village artisans and village industrialists realize the need for assistance and recognize that through the Rural Development Block programme, technical service programmes will be organized to assist them in at least the following ways:

   (a) Determine consumer needs, including design and quality preference.

   (b) Establish working contacts with agencies set up for helping the development of rural industries, including the village and small industries technical-research-training-service institute or their branches to help village artisans keep current on processing methods.

   (c) Obtain required low-cost financing.

   (d) Secure essential good-quality raw materials at a reasonable price.

   (e) Move their products into marketing channels.

4. Wherever feasible, modest industrial estates should be organized in selected villages – to provide power, improved working conditions, and better concentration of technical services.

5. Careful study should be made of the slack work seasons to determine the types of cottage and village industries which best lend themselves to spare-time work.

6. The village industries should be actively assisted to reach the minimum strength required for establishment of sound cooperatives and bank financial assistance with full-time competent business management. The organization of such bank facilities and cooperatives should be encouraged to take over a three-fold service:

(a) Provide the required credit.

(b) Assist in the procurement of raw materials, machines and tools.

(c) Assist in marketing products.

7. Programmes for the re-building of villages offer great scope for increased employment. Building materials can be produced by cooperatives which in turn can provide employment.

8. Public works programmes should be organized to take up economic producing programmes such as digging irrigation and drainage channels, leveling of land, contour bunding, planting of trees, and the construction of farm—to-market roads.

Phases to Promote Entrepreneurship

Identifying, selecting, motivating and training the new entrepreneurs constitute a major task for the entrepreneurial development agency. The promotion or development of entrepreneurship may be undertaken in five phases and we may briefly look into each phase.

Phase - I

The first phase relates to the basic physico-psycho-socio-cultural and economic study and understanding of the area where the programme is to be implemented as detailed earlier. Industrial potential survey focusing both on material and human resources of the area will be the basis, based on which feasibility studies are to be prepared for each viable candidate industry covering technical, economic, financial, demand and marketing aspects of the enterprise. Such a study will serve the purposes of developing an action – programme for identifying viable enterprises either resource-based, demand-based or footloose and potential entrepreneurs.

Here the emphasis is to be laid on starting small-scale enterprises where the people are living now, cheap enough so that they can be created in large numbers without calling for an unattainable level of capital formation and imports, with relatively simple production methods, so that the demands for high skills are minimized not only in the production process itself but also in matters of organization, raw material supply, financing, marketing, and the production mainly based on local materials and for local use. With such a purpose, initially to make use of the local resources and the local consumer demands, we are not to look for highly talented, sophisticated entrepreneurs, but people with some interest, with some investment capacity, who are partially unemployed or totally unemployed, people who are looking for some avenues to increase their income, people who are likely to take certain amount of risk in venturing into some entrepreneurial activity. Highly achievement-oriented individuals seek opportunities, create conditions, need less propping and venture into industrial activity.

Such people can take care of themselves with minimal support from the development agencies. But our task is to gradually shape the common man into an entrepreneur.

Against this objective, potential entrepreneurs in the client community may be drawn from the following segments: (a) artisan groups, (b) high school dropouts, (c) educated unemployed, (d) merchant-trading groups, (e) farmers who are in the process of or likely to partly shift to some enterprise, (f) farm-labourers who are likely to take some small business or enterprise and (g) woman entrepreneurs.

Remarkably the first phase as a constructive approach and strategy, the entire client community is to be exposed to the idea of entrepreneurship development. No segment in the community should feel it is isolated or ignored and the programmes are meant only for certain sections. The general exposure of the entire client community to the idea and prospects of entrepreneurship will create awareness, interest among them which will gradually motivate the potential entrepreneurs to move into action.

The creating of awareness, preparing the community, motivating and facilitating some individuals in the community to take decisions, secure the sanction of their families and opinion leaders, that is cutting through the socio-cultural barriers may be done through entrepreneurship-extension education through individual and group methods and through the mass media, always reinforced by personal contacts and counselling.

One of the foremost things in the process is raising the aspiration level of the people. They have to be told convincingly of the social and economic advantage inherent in industrial activity. The rise in their standard of living as a result of successfully running an enterprise has to be projected and brought home to them. These ends can be achieved through what is called 'intensive campaign' technique. It is a package of activities comprising an industrial potential survey, publication of the survey findings, holding of small group meetings explaining to people in the community, the kind of enterprises that are feasible in the area, the requirements for starting the recommended enterprises, who can undertake them, the kind of assistance they can expect from the various industrial development agencies and in such a type of campaign, the industrial development personnel and the selected local and political leaders will be involved.

The inclusion of influential local and district leadership would build and reinforce confidence and morale on the part of the potential entrepreneurs in the local community.

It may be in order to mention here the steps that may be taken in identifying the viable enterprises and potential entrepreneurs in the client community.

The Steps

1. Identification of the natural resources the community is endowed with.
2. Listing out the ongoing economic and industrial activities carried on by the community based on the resources at its command.

3. Listing out the associated skills available with the members of the community (or the target population).
4. Listing out the kind of new enterprises technically feasible and economically viable that could be promoted based on the available resources and skills.
5. Listing out the existing and required infrastructural facilities in view of the new enterprises suggested.
6. Appraising the client system of:
   - the kind of new enterprises they could take to;
   - the financial, managerial, technical and marketing requirements in respect to each enterprise;
   - the kind of people who can take up the suggested enterprises;
   - specifying in general the qualifications, personal aptitude and abilities and investment capacity on the part of the prospective entrepreneurs.
7. Appraising the client system of:
   - the kind of help the multiplicity of agencies connected with entrepreneurial development can extend to the prospective entrepreneurs, which may cover questions like What? When? To what extent? How often? To what purpose? etc.
8. Final identification of potential entrepreneurs and matching their interest with the enterprises.

A word on identification of potential entrepreneurs. Depending on the extent of response, the level of candidates, the potential and the capabilities that are sought among the candidates, the optimum number that the resources and schemes could support and sustain, one may go in for psychological tests such as: (a) Achievement Motivation, (b) Risk Taking, (c) Value Orientation, (d) Adoption Propensity, (e) Level of Aspiration, etc. These projective or psychological instruments are rather complementary to the information provided on the application that the candidate fills in, concerning his family background, his educational attainment, work experience, his choice of enterprise, his experience if any in entrepreneurial activity, his investment capacity and his socio-cultural affiliations.

Importantly, the means employed for identification are the application, interview and if need be, the tests mentioned above. One invaluable resource for identifying potential entrepreneurs is the client community itself.

When it comes to identification and selection of potential entrepreneurs, more often, we ignore the local community. The people in the local community may not be conversant with attributes or traits that are contributive to successful entrepreneurship, may not have any idea and understanding of some of the projective techniques used sometimes to measure the strength of need for achievement, value orientation, risk taking and adoption propensity on the part of the prospective entrepreneurs, but they will have a fairly good understanding of the people in the community as to who would do what and to what extent one would fair well and who is innovative and who would manage an activity effectively. This kind of knowledge of individuals is based on the day-to-day observations irrespective of an individual's profession or occupation. And so, one can, to a large extent depend upon and make use of the local community, the small groups in the community for identifying and selecting potential entrepreneurs. As we have pointed out earlier, once the viable enterprises have been identified based on industrial potential survey, one may list out the personal requirements that one is looking for or in other words the kind of people who can answer these requirements in order to respond to the recommended enterprises. Once this information is communicated to the community through individual contact and small group meetings, it is possible for the local community to indicate the names of individuals who are likely to be successful as small entrepreneurs. This could be in addition to individuals themselves coming forward to take to some entrepreneurial activity. The stress here is that the local community could well serve as a source and guide in selecting potential entrepreneurs.

Phase II

It consists of training various categories of personnel who will be involved in locating and developing entrepreneurship in the area under question. A general but comprehensive course of three to four weeks is to be prepared keeping in view the earlier work-experience of the personnel. The participants will be familiarized with the prospects and problems of entrepreneurial development in the area of operation. Further, the programme will include inputs on feasibility studies, techno-economic surveys, preparation of industrial profiles, entrepreneurial development, marketing, etc. Representatives of financial institutions in the area may be associated with the training programmes. By the end of the second phase, the agency will be in readiness with the knowledge of the area of operation, and also trained personnel to select and train entrepreneurs.

Phase III

It consists of selection and training of potential entrepreneurs in the client community by the agency. The training of the entrepreneurs will be arranged at district or sub-district headquarters. The personnel of the development agency who have already undergone training will conduct the training programme. The duration of this training may range from two to six weeks. It depends on funds and the category of candidates trained. In some cases, inclusive of in-plant studies, the courses are run for 14-20 weeks. The training inputs will include elements that would enable the entrepreneur-trainees acquire basic knowledge, skills and motivation to establish their units and manage them successfully. The training will be both theoretical and practical. Towards the end of their training, the candidates will go back to their villages and make a mini-market survey concerning their enterprises, or prepare project reports. They bring back the field data, and work these into project proposals for securing funds from financial institutions.

Phase IV

It consists of the agency collaborating with other functionally associated agencies to guide and help the trained entrepreneurs in establishing their enterprises, either individually, in small groups or through industrial cooperatives.

Phase V

In the final phase, which will be taken up after a lapse of six months after the training of entrepreneurs, the training programme will be evaluated. The objective of the evaluation is to find out as to how many of the trained entrepreneurs were able to establish their enterprises and the problems they faced in setting up their ventures. In the light of this experience the training programme for other batches of entrepreneurs will be restructured if necessary.

Marketing of Products

Generally it is seen, the entire success of small enterprise promotion in rural-tribal communities hinges on marketing of products of the neo-entrepreneurs. In the initial stages and also, in some cases on the sustained basis, the promotional agencies should help in marketing of the products. The induced and emerging entrepreneurs may be too weak to organize the marketing of their products on their own. The promotional agencies may go in for internal or external export of the indigenous handicrafts and products through a network of marketing channels. Such a support would sustain the ongoing entrepreneurs and also motivate the potential entrepreneurs to ventures into the field.

In sum, we may say that the women constitute a significant segment in the population. Till now, they have not been the focus of entrepreneurial development. The need today to develop entrepreneurship among them is imperative, the development of entrepreneurship among men and women being simultaneous. The question of EDP among women is a question of choice, priority and organization.

IV. *Lack of village schools,* poorly trained and inadequately paid teachers, a school programme unrelated to village life and development, and high illiteracy among teen-age youth and adults, constitute major educational problems for the villages of India.

Some of the more important things which have contributed, and still do contribute, to the educational problems of the villages are listed as follows:

1. Because of the economic pressures on the village families to earn and produce the base essentials for survival, some of the children have of necessity had to remain out of school and go to work.
2. Much as they value education for their children, the villagers look at their past experience and conclude, with some at least of the actual facts on their side, that the youth who have gone to school have become dissatisfied with village life and have moved on to the larger towns and cities.
3. The village school, the village teacher, and the school programme are not effectively related to village within the village and to earn an effective living either as a cultivator, artisan, or village industrialist.
4. Many villages are without schools.
5. Many villages are without teachers.
6. Because, the villages of India pay such low salaries to teachers and have such limited facilities for their effective living, including meager recreation and health services, the better trained teachers who have other opportunities avoid going to the villages where they are so sorely needed.
7. Until we gained independence and new opportunities arose for all to contribute to the nation's development and to their own personal economic and social advancement, being

literate held no particular attraction for the masses of village people, for it could not convincingly demonstrate that to be literate would result in their advancement.

8. Now that it can be demonstrated that being literate is essential if all are to fully profit from independence and are to make their maximum contribution to the building of New India, there are limited facilities and too few teachers trained in the modern techniques of literacy education.

9. There is a great scarcity, of good reading material, readily available at a reasonable price for the neo-literate.

One has only to exercise his mind to understand that, in the building of New India through the process of re-building each of our 558,000 villages as significant cultural units, effective education for all is essential. The study of world history and of the rise and fall of great civilizations supports the conclusion that a nation's greatness is dependent upon the importance the nation places on education, and upon the effectiveness of the educational institutions in training people with creative, reflective minds capable of guiding the nation's growth and sustaining a great and significant culture. It is, therefore, of great importance that the Panchayat Samithi and village panchayats accept the challenge which is theirs to help all villages in the process of rural development tackle the village educational problems, bringing to this task the forthright leadership the people deserve and must receive if India is to again grow into a great nation.

Action Steps for Improving the Status, Services and Facilities of Education in the Villages

1. Through various educational media, demonstrate to the people the importance of all being literate in order to take advantage of the benefits of science and technology and all children having an opportunity to attend a school taught by a competent, well-trained teacher adequately paid.

2. As the village grows in its interest in having a village school, help the village organize itself to contribute its labor and as much material as possible toward the construction of a school.

3. Assist the village in organizing literacy classes. Whenever literate local people are available, they should be trained and assisted in conducting the literacy classes. When local literacy instructors are not available plans should be worked out for outside instructors systematically to visit the village to conduct the literacy classes.

4. To assist in the socio-economic upgrading of the village teacher and thus in enabling the village to secure and keep a competent teacher, the panchayats should be encouraged to see the importance of the village providing the teacher with a house and an adequate vegetable garden. Panchayats should also be encouraged to develop plans for self-taxation to contribute towards increasing the salary of the village teacher.

5. So that the village school can increasingly become an effective village institution and the teacher can play a more prominent role in village development, the Panchayat Samithi should in the first instance organize a ten-day training camp for all the village teachers in the Block. The purpose of this training should be to train the village teacher to serve as a village leader, assisting in stimulating the entire village to be interested in all-round development. Following the first camp, yearly refresher camps of a week should be organized.

6. Continue to emphasize to the village people that, while in the past they have survived with limited or no education, in the future education will become more and more important for success as a cultivator, artisan or industrialist, and for participation in village and

state affairs. Point out that, whereas in the past survival was based on familiarity with traditional methods, the future will require familiarity with and understanding of the application of science.

7. School and the Community-Drawing Strength from Each Other

School availing facilities in the neighbourhood communities and the community making use of the facilities at the school, playground, library, etc. The school periodically organizing some extension lectures for the farmers. These lectures will relate to any useful information, namely health and sanitation, importance of adult literacy, augmenting the creation of awareness on important local and national issues. School will play as a forum for dissemination of information relevant to the community. The kind of relation between the school and the communities depends on the location of the school, whether it is of rural setting, urban setting or in a metropolitan area. Because, the environment such as farming, industry, service, do matter in respect to the children learning from their environment and the communities making use of the facilities at the school. Interaction between the teachers and the community members especially the teachers interacting with newly emerging rural leadership such as self-help groups (SHGs). The schools inviting people who are known for their expertise in certain fields to address the pupils at the school. The children also may be placed in the rural communities to learn something as to what goes on in terms of activities that are carried on in the rural areas related to farming, and sometimes the children may also benefit from the way in which the segments in the community and the community mobilize the resources to resolve their disputes. It is bringing the school closer to the community and drawing the community closer to the school. That will enthuse both the parents and their children. The teachers may also become part of the community. The result of such an interaction between the school and the community will create healthy relationship and establish emotional bonds which would enthuse both the school and the community. And when we come down to the elementary school, for example, we find the teachers having intimate to moderate contact with the community where the school is located. The children apart from their learning through the stipulated curricula would learn more about the dynamics of the community life. You may call this as extra curricular education. The school children will also at their earliest age may come to know the newly instituted Village Panchayats, mandals/ development blocks and so on. Some times, the school may also invite some of the functionaries of several departments operating at the village and mandal/development block level to address the student community sharing the kind of programmes/activities they do in rural communities. Depending on the resources of the school, they may have a mini or a modest extension centre wherein they may organize seminars, workshops, extension lectures, and permanent exhibits. Sometimes, depending on the interest, with the capability on the part of the schoolteachers, they may take-up some of the issues, problems and needs confronting the community and carry on research on those aspects which would be a kind of further education. The Community-School approach to rural development was initiated as a model in the Philippines. A toilet, kitchen garden and planting of trees and sanitation may first be introduced at the school, so that the children get used to such facilities and they will be the promotional agents of such things in their families and the communities. Involvement of the children in environmental sanitation. The school may interact with the newly emerging community level associations such as DWCRA, Vana Samraksha Samithis, and Neeru-Meeru Programme.

V. *Poor Health* is a major village problem.

Some of the more important things which contribute to poor health in the villages are listed as follows:

1. The villages have all too few medical services and facilities.
2. Lack of family planning, spacing of children, contributes to poor health of the mother and children and intensifies the problem of inadequate food.

3. Village people have deep-seated religious and traditional attitudes and biases in favour of traditional remedies and health practices.

4. The following types of poor environmental sanitation contribute to poor health:

(a) contaminated drinking water,

(b) pollution of tanks, soil and surroundings with night soil and animal dung,

(c) smoke-filled and poorly ventilated houses,

(d) inadequately cleaned and drained village streets.

5. Insect and rodent are carriers of diseases – flies, mosquitoes, flees, rats, etc. – contribute directly to poor village health.

6. Lack of adequate and nutritious diet contributes to poor health.

7. Lack of protection from certain preventable disease through immunization causes poor health.

Regardless of what programmes the Panchayat Samithi may feel demand priority attention, developmental experience all over the world supports the conclusion that the response of village people and their participation in sustained development is closely related to their physical and mental health. Because this is so, it does not follow that the Block staff should be expected to impose a health programme on the people before they are ready to accept such a programme and to provide the required leadership to make good health a village goal. The implication and strong recommendation, however, is that the Block staff should early and continuously use all effective media for educating and guiding the Panchayat Samithi and the village panchayats toward improvement of all phases of village health.

Action Steps for Improving Village Health

Following are some of the more important action steps involving both the Panchayat Samithi and the village panchayats in improving village health –

1. Because village people have for so many years learned to live with poor health, the Block staff should devote its best efforts to a village-by-village health education programme that will awaken the village people to want better health, and will aid them in understanding

2. Minimum adequate health service and facilities should be provided for each Block, and continuous health education programmes should be carried on to guide the village people to make appropriate use of the newly provided services and facilities.

3. Each village panchayat should be encouraged to want and should be helped to provide and protect a safe drinking water supply for the village. Arrangements should be made for maintaining the pump and keeping the area near the well drained and clean.

4. Special attention should be concentrated on educating the people to construct and use suitable latrines. Villagers should be told that the diarrhoea and dysenteries which kill about twenty lakhs of persons every year in India and make about five crore ill are due to improper disposal of human excreta.

5. Educate the villagers to see the relationship between many of the common diseases and insects and rodents, and then assist the village panchayats in organizing programmes to eliminate these disease-carrying insects and rodents.

6. Through education, assist the village people to understand the relation between the food they eat and their health, and then assist them in raising more varieties of vegetables and fruits to broaden their diet, and in following methods of food preparation which will give them a more nutritious diet.

7. Educate villagers to see that many of the deaths in the village could have been prevented if all were protected by immunization against certain diseases common to the village such as smallpox, cholera, typhoid, tetanus, and diphtheria. Encourage those who want protection from

these diseases to get their inoculations regularly at the health centre.

8. As the village health programme takes shape, the panchayat should be encouraged to involve the village school in order to assure that all phases of the village health programme are taught and practiced in the school programme.

9. Educate villagers to understand that a village house which is fully protected against rain and cold, and which permits entrance of sunlight and fresh air, is a healthier house for the family. As village people express interest in ventilation, guide them in installing protective windows and smokeless chulhas.

10. Through education, continue to impress on the village people that is much easier to prevent disease by following protective health programmes than it is to cure disease.

11. The Block staff should know the religious and traditional village attitudes toward present and recommended health practices. The staff should seek guidance as to appropriate approaches directed toward changing these religious and traditional attitudes.

12. Get the village panchayat to understand that a village with clean, well-drained, paved streets will also be a healthier village.

13. Through educational programmes, village panchayats should awaken the village people to the importance of family planning in relation to the health of the mother and the children and the social and economic well-being of the family. The Block health centre should be the distribution point for information on the recommended family planning methods and their application.

14. The village extension workers and the entire Block staff should set an example by their own housing, sanitary facilities and health practices.

(Note:- Please see Chapters 14 & 15 for more details.)

VI. *Poor Family Living* is a universal problem of all villages.

Poor family living is caused by some or all of the following conditions:

1. Until Independence and the organization of the Community Development Programme, village families had generally neither the means nor the incentives to live better, thus producing attitudes of indifference toward all aspects of family living conditions.
2. Throughout the villages most families do not always fully appreciate the full importance of –
   (a) Personal body cleanliness and clean clothing;
   (b) Clean food;
   (c) Clean, attractive, ventilated homes;
   (d) Clean, drained streets;
   (e) Clean courtyards;
   (f) Destruction of pests;
   (g) Beauty in their surroundings;
   (h) Using a sanitary latrine;
   (i) Having pure water to drink;
   (j) Sheltering cattle away from the house;
   (k) All members of the family knowing how to read and write.
3. Village people live as they do partly because they lack knowledge of the following things:
   (a) The importance of growing and eating fruit and vegetables essential for a nutritionally healthy diet;
   (b) How to make such simple improvements in their homes as building smokeless chulha;
   (c) How to care for children;
   (d) How to get family planning information about appropriate methods of spacing the children born in the family;

(e) How to make and mend clothing;

(f) How to preserve fruits and vegetables;

(g) How to store and care for clothing and bedding;

(h) How to provide more recreation.

The building of New India must start by kindling within the families of village India a desire for a better way of life. Through the Rural Development Blocks, programmes will be organized to make possible a gradual and sustained rise in the level of family and village living. If the programmes which the Block emphasizes and the various services available are to make their maximum contribution, *it is essential for all having a responsibility for the programme to understand that the manner in which the services will be used, and the ultimate success of the entire programme, will rest upon the rising expectations of the families for a higher standard of living and upon the motivations from within these families to achieve and sustain such a higher standard.*

Those who plan administer and serve the Rural Development Block programmes must understand that broadly defined village problems and needs take on significance only as they find expression within the family. As a problem takes on significance to the family the motivation for its solution also takes new shape. To illustrate – as the family builds up a desire for better family living expressed in a desire for better housing, clothing, health, education, food and recreation, the motivation for increasing agricultural production becomes a family motivation and therefore, a purposeful one commanding sustained family effort.

In using the terms levels and standards of living the reader should understand that *level of living* is used to mean the things village people now have and the way now live and *standard of living* is used to mean the things the people express as new wants and the way they wish they could live, and are willing to strive to attain.

Some Suggested Action Steps for Improving Family Living

1. The first essential step in improving family living is, through education, to create an earnest desire on the part of the families for attaining a standard of living, i.e., more and better food, clothing, shelter, health, education, recreation – which is higher than their present level of living – i.e., the things they now have and the way they now live.
2. Three new values which should, through education, become important family and village values are orderliness, cleanliness and beauty. These can best be developed by the Block staff taking an active interest in encouraging village after village in the Block to plan new village, providing for straight, wide, drained and paved streets, space between houses, sanitary latrines, a village park, flower-beds, a school, a community-cum-panchayat hall, and attractive well-ventilated village houses.
3. As the interest of village women is developed, they should be given training and guidance in the following activities and programmes —

   (a) Sewing, knitting, embroidery and care of clothing and bedding;

   (b) Women taking to mini-entrepreneurial activities, small business;

   (c) Learning the nutritional importance of different foods;

   (d) Learning how to prepare, cook and serve food in ways that will preserve the maximum nutritional value and ensure clean handling of the food;

   (e) Understanding the importance of more milk in the family diet;

   (f) Learning how to plan, plant and care for a family vegetable garden;

   (g) Learning how to preserve fruits and vegetables;

   (h) Learning how to store food.

4. Encourage interest in and use of recommended family planning methods.
5. Using carefully selected, influential families demonstrate how to build and use the smokeless chulha, showing how it saves fuel and removes smoke from the house. Then encourage all families to construct and learn the proper use of a smokeless chulha.
6. Demonstrate the importance of providing appropriate storage space for utensils, and the simple construction necessary for this.
7. Demonstrate the desirability of each family having a sanitary place to wash dishes and utensils, and aid in developing simple plans for this.
8. Create interest in and organize group programme to train women in better care of children.
9. Develop family plans for construction of a sanitary latrine adapted to the village, and demonstrate in family group meetings how to build a latrine. Through education, build up village social pressure for each family to have and use a sanitary latrine.
10. Develop village plans for housing the animals away from the family living quarters. These plans may be either for housing the animals in a separate shed in the compound, or for the villagers working together to construct a village cattle shed near the edge of the village, in which each villager would have his unit of stalls.
11. Encourage families who would be expected to have a good following in the village to clean up their courtyards and keep them clean, and to plant shrubs, trees, and flowers. Encourage the entire village to adopt "clean attractive courtyards" as a village programme.
12. Demonstrate plans for getting more sunlight and fresh air into the homes.
13. Create an interest in and get the village panchayats to

organize campaigns for continuous destruction of flies, mosquitoes, rodents, etc.

14. Create an interest in the family having and using pure water for all household purposes.
15. Provide and demonstrate improved plans for family grain storage.
16. Demonstrate and create an interest in washing clothes often and properly and in storing them properly.
17. Create a desire on the part of all members of the family to learn to read and write – pointing out through case illustrations how families have profited and been aided in their business transactions by being literate. Great emphasis should be placed on the fact that the Community programmes are family and village programmes, and on the fact that those who are literate can both participate and contribute to the maximum.

VII. *Dirty, Cluttered Villages and Poor Housing* are village problems

Dirty, cluttered villages and poor housing are the results of some or all of the following conditions:

1. Poorly planned villages with narrow, crooked, and inadequately drained streets.
2. Lack of appreciation of importance of cleanliness or orderliness.
3. Acceptance of present conditions.
4. Failure to see the need for better houses.
5. Designs for better homes using indigenous materials not available.
6. Lack of community planning.
7. Simple, inexpensive improvements in homes have not been demonstrated.
8. Local readily available building materials have not been used effectively.

9. Better construction methods have not been demonstrated.
10. Needed rural credit for home improvement is not available.
11. There are too many houses on too little land.
12. Animals are housed under the same roof with the family.
13. Grain is stored in the same space the family lives in.
14. Space for family and village latrines is lacking.

In the building of New India village people must be educated to have a new outlook and assisted in achieving a higher level of living. They must see themselves as self-respecting citizens, capable of planning for their future, and must learn through experience that they possess within themselves the resources to solve most of their problems. They must, through education and extension education programmes, develop new values and new attitudes which motivate them to want a better standard of living. They must through experience learn that only as they apply themselves and take full advantage of science and technology in improving their agriculture, industries and cooperatives can they achieve their new desires for better living, expressed in improved house, improved water supply, improved sanitation, better schools, and recreational facilities.

Today village people live in crowded, dirty villages which in and of themselves produce a "cow-dung psychology".

What is needed is a Panchayat Samithi programme, underpinned by village panchayat plans to rebuild the villages. Such a programme will go a long way towards creating the "New –village" outlook that is so essential in making village development a continuous dynamic force. In this new outlook which can flow from the physical rebuilding of our villages, two new values – *Orderliness and Cleanliness* – can be expected to emerge.

Furthermore, village families will become concerned about wanting to live better. As they move into new and improved houses in new villages with wide, paved streets; with drains; with houses spaced to permit sanitary latrines and planting of flowers and shrubs; with playgrounds, village schools and community buildings; and with pure water – as they learn to want to live better – they will be motivated to exert greater effort toward learning how to improve their agricultural and industrial production, which will provide them the additional resources required to meet their growing demands for better living. As the villagers' desires and needs multiply, the basis for an expanding village industries programme can be fostered through the creation of community workshops.

Such an approach would stimulate at one end and at the same time an increasing demand for goods and an increasing capacity to produce the wanted goods. The growing village market for bricks, tiles, simple home furnishings, locks, hinges, window-frames, and soon would make it much more feasible than otherwise to foster new village industries.

A Block programme for the planning and physical rebuilding of our villages need not be approached as requiring large expenditure of funds. The immediate need is for an educational approach to the village panchayats to awaken in them the desire to rebuild their village, either by expanding the present site or on an adjoining piece of land. Once the interest is created the village panchayats will require help in laying out a new village, including land allocation for each type of building, location of wells, playgrounds, community hall, latrines, schools and a modest village community workshop. There will also be a need for help in learning about improved building plans.

Perhaps the greater need will be to help the village panchayat develop a village plan for the building of new houses or the rebuilding of existing ones, development of streets, wells, schools, and community halls and community workshops. It is here that village cooperatives can play a significant part. A cooperative brick kiln may be appropriate, likewise cooperatives to provide other building materials, such as a carpenter shop to produce doors and windows and a pottery to provide tiles for the roofs. A cooperative to manage a community workshop should have a prominent place. By working together the villagers can on a five to ten-year programme basis build for themselves new villages – without requiring much outside capital.

Once new village plans have been laid out in Rural Development Blocks, under the sponsorship of the panchayat Samithis, the resources allocated for wells, paving of streets, and building of schools, should be applied to the new village as an added incentive for the villagers to take up the building of new houses.

In arousing the villagers' interest in moving the village to a nearby site, a search should first be made to find a piece of land. Wherever possible an effort should be made to have the new site contributed through Bhoodan. Where a land gift is not possible then plans for the panchayat to purchase a new site should be worked out. In some cases government grants will be required for the purchase of a new village site.

Action Steps for Planning and Rebuilding our Villages

1. Stimulate the panchayats to take up the rebuilding of their village, either by expanding acreage of present site or moving to a new site.
2. Create panchayat interest in wanting the village to be clean and orderly.
3. Develop panchayat interest in desirable sanitary practices essential for better health.
4. Take influential villagers to adjoining areas to see how villagers have worked together in rebuilding or improving their village.
5. Demonstrate:
    - the advantages of improved housing design;
    - the better use of local and inexpensive building material;
    - improved construction methods;
    - various types of latrines.
6. Emphasize simple improvements:

- smokeless chulha;
- sanitary place for washing utensils;
- adequate, well-ventilated space for family members;
- storage for clothing, bedding and cooking utensils.

7. Recommended:
   - village and family latrine areas;
   - animal shelters away from family living area;
   - safe storage space;
   - courtyards with gardens;
   - planting of trees, flowers and shrubs;
   - paving of village streets;
   - drains for village streets;
   - sanitary bathing areas;
   - windows for home to permit sunlight and fresh air.

VIII. *Too Many Poor Cattle* is village problem.

Some of the causes of too many poor cattle are the following:

1. Limited area for grazing.
2. Limited fodder for feeding.
3. Poor breeding practices.
4. Restraints against killing useless cattle.
5. Diseased cattle left unattended.
6. Scrub bulls allowed to run free in the villages.
7. Prejudice against artificial insemination.
8. Limited veterinary services.

Common sense dictates that village people cannot and must not continue their current practice of keeping a large number of unproductive and useless cattle which compete heavily with village people for the all-too limited food and fibre.

Action Steps for Improving Village Cattle

1. Through soil and water conservation practices increase grass yields from grazing area.
2. Encourage practice of tying cattle and cutting and feeding forage and fodder.
3. Intensify education and services of artificial insemination centers.
4. Encourage panchayats to sponsor programmes for castration of all bull calves not planned for later use in artificial insemination centre.
5. Discourage practice of allowing stray cattle free movement in village area.
6. Educate people to the importance of fewer but better cattle for both milk and work.

IX. *Poor Roads* is village problem.

Poor village roads are caused by the following:

1. Failure to see that village panchayats have a responsibility for constructing and maintaining good roads.
2. Roads are frequently made without information on proper construction and drainage methods.
3. Monsoons are heavy destroyers of roads.
4. Failure to appreciate the need for multi-purpose roads.
5. Failure to see the importance of clean, well-drained village streets.

If our village people are to remove themselves from their traditional isolation and participate effectively in purchasing essential supplies and in marketing their products they must have approach roads which are kept in good repair all year round.

Action Steps for Improving Village Roads

Following are some of the important things which can be

done to assist panchayats to provide for and maintain improved roads.

1. Demonstrate the importance of good roads:
   - easier and faster procurement of supplies and marketing goods;
   - easier and faster communication with other areas.
2. Showing well constructed and maintained roads:
   - well drained;
   - usable in all seasons;
   - adequate for village-to-market use.
3. Encourage the panchayat to organize a "better road" committee that will:
   - help village people understand the importance of good roads;
   - obtain the advice of a good road engineer;
   - stimulate the village people to build roads with their own labour;
   - encourage village people to work together to maintain roads.
4. Impress on the village people the importance of clean, well-drained village streets.
5. As a means of providing employment for those either partially or entirely unemployed and to assure the construction and maintenance of needed good farm-to-market roads, the panchayat Samithi should organize and have each village panchayat participate in carrying out a public works programmes for the construction of roads.

X. Lack of Recreation Programmes and Facilities is a village problem

Following are some of the more important reasons why our village people have little recreation life: *(Please see chapter: Role of Youth in Rural Development for more details)*

1. Failure to understand the importance of recreation.
2. Limited experience in assuming initiative for organizing recreational programmes.
3. Training on recreational leadership is lacking.
4. Facilities for recreation are lacking.
5. Youth's energy and enthusiasm are not channeled into healthy and constructive activities.
6. Cultural folk art is being forgotten.

The villagers must through the Panchayat's leadership be awakened from their slumber and put to work making village life attractive and stimulating. A full recreation programme for all age groups, both men and women, and all classes of village life will do much to bring new satisfaction and create a healthy atmosphere for village cooperation in all phases of development.

Action Steps for Improving Recreational Programmes and Facilities

1. Creating a desire for a well-planned village recreation programme.
2. Encouraging the panchayat to organize a village committee responsible for a recreation programme, and assisting villagers in:
   - planning for recreational activities;
   - finding and training recreational leaders and recreational talent;
   - establishing places for recreational activities;
   - obtaining recreational equipment.
3. Encouraging village people to keep alive the best of their folk art in:
   - dramas;
   - songs;
   - poetry;

- puppet shows;
- dances;
- bhajans.

4. Encouraging the panchayat to take the leadership in organizing youth clubs for both boys and girls.

XI. Lack of Youth Participation in all Phases of Village Life is a village problem.

Some of the explanations for limited youth participation are the following:

1. Village traditions have in the past ruled out consideration of youth's:
   - ideas;
   - enthusiasm and energy;
   - cooperative spirit;
   - sincerity and readiness to participate in development programmes.

2. Lack of youth organizations.

It is as certain as night follows day that the youth of today will be the men and women of tomorrow. The surest way to guarantee that the village of tomorrow will be better than the village of today is to start today working with and training the youth in effective citizenship by providing them with a variety of opportunities to participate in youth programmes and activities.

Action Steps to Improve Youth's Participation in Village Life

Following are some of the action steps for improving youth's participation in village life:

1. Through education change traditional village attitudes to make it possible for youth to assist in decisions in regard to family, village, and national problems. This can best be done by having the panchayats sponsor youth clubs.

2. Helping panchayats secure better teachers and provide schools for girls and boys.
3. Helping all village youth become literate.
4. Promoting better health.
5. providing wholesome recreation programmes and activities.
6. Demonstrating home improvements to make the home more livable and attractive.
7. Encourage village panchayats to early bring young people into village panchayats.
8. Through youth clubs encourage youth to take the lead in demonstrating new agricultural practices.
9. Training youth leaders.
10. Encourage village elders to give youth greater leadership responsibilities. (Please see Chapter 8 for further details)

XII. Lack of Voluntary Village Organizations is a village problem

Some of the more important factors which contribute to the lack of voluntary village organizations are the following:

1. Traditional dependency on outside agencies for both aid and decisions.
2. Organizations for self-help village work only recently encouraged.
3. Cooperative organizations have in the past tended to be operated organizations and not people's cooperatives which have come up from the people's understanding, interest and leadership.
4. Few people trained in-group organization to guide and encourage village people in setting up their own organizations.
5. Caste prejudice divides people.
6. Group factions tend to be interested in the welfare of limited groups only.

7. Village people tend to shy away from formal organizations.
8. Conflicts persist between present elected panchayats and village-organized informal panchayats of the past.

To assure the full, effective and sustained participation of village people in making the community programme a people's programme, intense effort must be given to encouraging a wide variety of voluntary non-government organizations and institutions.

Following are some suggested action steps for encouraging and nurturing the growth of voluntary village organizations:

1. Panchayats must play an effective role in all round village development.
2. Encourage the organization of people's cooperatives which have their roots deep in the villages.
3. Encourage present leaders to expand their scope and help new leaders develop.
4. Develop self-help activities for the entire community.
5. Encourage panchayats to sponsor the organization of:
   - farmers' forums and associations;
   - women's clubs;
   - youth clubs;
   - boys' clubs;
   - girls' clubs;
   - recreation clubs.
6. Train leaders in-group methods.

Once the village panchayats have, with the active assistance of the Block staff, completed the village by village diagnosis of their problems, and decided on the programmes they wish to emphasize, the next step will be for the panchayat Samithi to consolidate these village plans into a Panchayat Samithi programme. When this is completed, the sarpanches and the village extension workers will have common objectives in stimulating village panchayat activities and the Block technical staff will have clearly defined objectives and work assignments as they move into the villages.

Note:- Partially adopted from Dr. Douglas Ensminger's " *A Guide to Community Development* (Revised) 1962, Ministry of Community Development & Cooperation, Government of India.

15

APPLICATION OF TECHNOLOGIES APPROPRIATE TO RURAL AREAS

When new ideas, procedures, systems and technology are introduced in a community, normally the responses will be either acceptance or rejection. When people are used to a particular way of life the tendency is to continue with the same. People at the time of introducing a change may not be in the need of or aware of the benefits of new things that are being introduced. In order to make people accept the benefit of the changes they are to be guided, educated and motivated, so that they will accept and become familiar with the new elements of change and adopt them for better in their life. You cannot think of blindly introducing any technology in a traditional type of community. As it is obvious to everybody, one is to be wary in introducing changes and preparing the people to accept changes. In this context, we may briefly refer to introducing new technologies in a rural community.

One of the objectives of rural development is to develop, transfer and popularize technologies in the rural areas in the fields of agriculture, small and agro based enterprises. Such a scheme for rural development necessitates a plan of action to take into account:

a) An understanding of existing technologies in the specific areas of development;

b) Identification of appropriate technologies available within the country and elsewhere for a specific process or operation in farm and non-farm activities;

c) Identification of gaps in technology; and

d) Prioritizing, selecting and concentrating on a few technologies for dissemination to begin with.

The above background information, the state of the situation, the gaps in technology, the technological problems faced by the farmers in their several farm operations and the small-scale entrepreneurs in terms of increasing production and productivity, reducing cost of input and labour, saving time and the overall enhancement of their earnings is necessary. Such knowledge on the part of the project personnel would facilitate the development, adoption, modification and extension of technology to the users.

Concentration on Select Items

It is suggested that a list of priorities with a broad time frame may be made and work on a few selected items which may meet the following criteria:

a) The immediate problem it would alleviate

b) The drudgery it would reduce

c) The time it would save

d) The economic gains it would provide

e) The potential population it would be relevant and useful to

f) The cost of the technology

g) How soon could it be made available to the clients.

Personnel and Expertise

In order to develop, strengthen, motivate, familiarize and keep abreast of the technology development in the targeted fields, the technical / research staff may visit or keep in touch with technology research and dissemination institutions in the country. This would facilitate coordination of efforts and reduce or eliminate duplication and overlapping of work.

Establishing Functional-Operational Linkages

Development and transfer of appropriate technology towards rural development cannot be a sporadic and scattered effort. As a technological input towards rural economic and social transformation, it is of utmost national importance. There is a need to mobilize, integrate and channel the efforts of institutions engaged in some or several aspects of development and transfer of appropriate technology for rural development. The project may establish informal and formal functional and operational linkages with development, academic and research institutions in the country such as:

a) Relevant government institutions/organizations.

b) Technical universities/institutions

c) Farmers associations

d) Small Industrialists

e) Manufacturers

f) Traders

g) Non-Government Organizations (NGOs).

For instance, when a prototype technology has been tested at the lab and the field and found to be useful, the concerned department may invite some small-scale industrialists or manufacturers to appraise the technology recommended and encourage or support them or support them to produce the machine or the tool on a commercial basis. The manufacturers and traders are the effective and quick means of technology transfer.

Further, technologies at different stages of development, testing and application may be grouped under different development heads, viz., agriculture, small-scale / cottage industries, handicrafts, domestic appliances, etc., and establish linkages with the relevant agencies for popularizing these technologies through their on-going extension machinery.

Profiles of Technology

There is a need for preparing a detailed profile of each technology on hand. These profiles will be useful for publicity and help the extension personnel a great deal. The profiles may also be sent to some of the prospective entrepreneur-manufacturers, and other agencies of publicity.

The profiles may cover the following aspects:

1. Name of technology
2. Whether original, innovative, prototype (adopted or modified)
3. Its technical components, design and physical properties
4. The stage at which its development is.
5. Its uses.
6. Its advantages
7. Its limitations if any.
8. Its production capacity, efficiency.
9. Does it replace any existing technology?
10. Is it a substitution?
11. As a substitute, how better it is?
12. The cost of production of a unit
13. Cost of a unit when mass produced
14. Energy used
15. Who will be the potential users?
16. The attempts made thus far to disseminate the technology
17. The response to the technology transfer
18. the channels and methods employed in technology transfer
19. The organizations engaged in similar development and transfer of technology in question.

20. The government's functional linkages with such organizations.

Transfer of technology or any new method, practice or innovation amounts to introducing of change in the client system. Here, we look into the effective ways and process in introducing change.

Introducing Change

The major problem in introducing social change is to secure enough local initiative and participation so that the enterprise will not be vulnerable as a foreign importation. The major questions we have to remember in this process of introducing changes are:

Who brings the change? What kind of change succeeds? And

How is it best done by what procedures and in what climate?

A. Who brings the change?

- Resistance will be less if administrators, change agents and community leaders feel that the project is their own-not one devised and operated by outsiders.
- Resistance will be less if the project clearly has whole-hearted support from top officials of the system.

B. What kind of change?

- Resistance will be less if participants see the change as reducing rather than increasing their present burdens.
- Resistance will be less if the project accords with values and ideals which have long been acknowledged by participants.
- Resistance will be less if the programme offers the kind of new experience which interests participants.
- Resistance will be less if participants feel that their autonomy and their security is not threatened.

C. Procedures in Instituting Change

- Resistance will be less if participants have joined in diagnostic efforts leading them to agree on the basic problems and to feel its importance.
- Resistance will be less if the project has been adopted by consensual group decision.
- Resistance will be reduced if proponents are able to empathize with opponents and to take steps to relieve unnecessary fears.
- Resistance will be reduced if it is recognized that innovations are likely to be misunderstood and misinterpreted and if provision is made for feedback of perceptions of the project and for further clarification as needed.
- Resistance will be reduced if participants experience acceptance, support, trust and confidence in their relations with one another.
- Resistance will be reduced if the project is kept open to revision and reconsideration if experience indicates that changes would be desirable.

D. Climate for Change

Readiness for change gradually becomes a characteristic of certain individuals, groups, and organizations. They no longer look nostalgically at a golden age in the past but anticipate their utopia in days to come. The spontaneity of youth is cherished and innovations are protected until they have had a chance to establish their worth. The ideal is more and more seen as possible.

It is relevant to mention some illustrious factors that affect our day-to-day life:

1. Necessity leads to change
2. Understanding leads to change
3. Appreciation leads to change

4. Scarcity leads to change
5. Abundance leads to change
6. Innovation leads to change
7. Deprivation leads to change
8. Affluence leads to change
9. Love leads to change
10. Motivation leads to change
11. Competition leads to change
12. Discovery leads to change
13. Force leads to change (may be for a short period)
14. Concern leads to change
15. Status leads to change
16. Jealousy leads to change
17. Situation leads to change
18. Change in Ideology leads to change.

16

THE PART PLAYED BY NGOs IN RURAL DEVELOPMENT

The rapid increase of state involvement in socio-economic development (loosely referred to as community development) during this century has been accompanied by a gradual consolidation of bureaucratic and technocratic specialization in each of the major development sectors. The result is that particular areas of development such as health, education and housing are now closely identified with government bureaucracies. Most developing countries have functionally specialized ministries which have primary responsibility for the formulation of policies and the implementation of state programmes in different sectors. Many governments have established what are variously known as Ministries or Departments of Social Welfare, Public Welfare, Social Services or Social Affairs. Their programmes are largely remedial in orientation, and are closely associated with the activities of professional social workers.

It is possible to formulate a typology of likely state responses to people's participation in development. This typology suggests that the state may act in several ways when eliciting people's participation. It may, firstly, suppress all attempts at people's participation; secondly, it may actively promote participation seeking to mobilize the whole community for social development and to encourage maximum involvement in decision-making. The state may, thirdly, attempt to use people' participation programmes with ulterior motives and seek to manipulate these programmes for its own ends. Finally, the state may have a vaguely formulated or poorly implemented policy on people's participation; while it does not seek to suppress participatory activities, it fails to provide adequate support. However, it is concluded that state sponsorship of people's participation has been largely incremental and manipulative in character and supports those who believe that state involvement in community participation is a contradiction in terms. It is believed that whether because of bureaucratic inefficiency or a determined effort to exploit particular programmes for ulterior ends, state involvement stifles authentic community responses and defeats the ideals of genuine people's participation in social development. This situation has allowed the proliferation of normative and ideological critiques of the prevalent model of development as perceived and initiated by the state (Haque *et al.,*1977).

There are also several new models being advanced at the abstract level of ideological alternatives to the prevalent model. But little or no attention has been paid to the numerous experiments, movements and organizational initiatives that struggle on the ground, to make "development" a relevant concept, a direct experience in the lives of the deprived, the oppressed and the impoverished populations which have either been "untouchables" of development or when touched are affected adversely and have become its victims. It is in these initiatives at the grassroots taking place generally outside the governmental and bureaucratic structure s and away from the normal political processes of parties and elections that another approach to rural development is becoming manifest. These are local actions that are basically initiated, nurtured and taken care by the native population.

Therefore, we observe that though the state assumes a greater share of responsibility for development government alone it is not in a position to build national identity, to institutionalize democracy and to keep up economic productivity. The private sector has an important role in mobilizing resources and in infusing efficiency through the market mechanism. The voluntary sector is an important source of developmental initiatives; in particular, the non-governmental organizations (NGOs) articulate more at the local level than at that of the state or regional level. Hence, the local administration bears a special responsibility as a listening post for incorporating people's views that are made available via NGOs.

NGOs in Asia

Depending on how tightly one draws the definition, there are reported to be somewhere one million development oriented NGOs in Asia. They are highly heterogeneous in character, varying considerably in character, geographic scope and sectoral interests. The overwhelming majority of the Asian NGOs are very small, employing generally only one or two staff, rarely more than ten. Frequently, they are the results of the efforts one – often charismatic-individual who draws together others for the purpose of ameliorating some social or economic need. The motivation is commonly charitable and the technical resources available are of a low order. The hope that such groups may make a contribution to development rests on the belief that it may be possible to reinforce them with insight (especially of social dynamics), appropriate intervention techniques and practice.

It is widely believed that non-governmental development organizations (NGDOs, or NGOs as referred to earlier) constitute a potentially important vehicle by which social and economic development can be promoted in developing countries, especially at the micro level. At the same time it is recognized that NGOs too depend largely on people's participation in accomplishing their objectives. Mid-1970s witnessed a revival of voluntary activity, largely attributable to:

(a) The failure of elective local democracy to satisfy the aspirations of the people;

(b) The sense of mission which imbued social workers for the betterment of the underprivileged and neglected classes;

(c) The need for intervention in areas of public life which were suffering from the effects of official apathy and evils associated with the misuse of power.

Since then we observe the birth of a number of praiseworthy voluntary ventures engaged in a variety of activities. A brief analysis of some of them will help in understanding the stimulant forces which gave them birth and the purposes for which they exist. To a casual observer, the strength of the NGOs lie in their ability to effectively motivate people to undertake some development initiatives at the village level, and serve as a intermediary for the government to understand people's needs and priorities.

Generally, the voluntary agencies fulfill several tasks apart from the usual service provision for the needy; these main tasks could be classified into two categories: animation and facilitation. In reality, one cannot clearly be distinguished from each other. Animation means, first of all, conscientisation of the poor. Animators help the poor to regain their self-confidence and self-assertiveness. Only when the poor regard themselves as equal human beings and citizens do they question the reasons behind their poverty, realize their rights, request changes, discover the abilities and capacities at their disposal, have the confidence to change established patterns of behaviour and dare to use their assets to promote their own interests.

Once the poor have been motivated and activated through a process of conscientisation, the animator changes into the role of the facilitator. He/she assists the poor in forming groups, in decision which measures should be taken and in executing the same. He/she acts as an intermediary to get access to governmental or commercial services. He/she, for example, manages to establish first contacts between the poor and the officials (e.g., banking sector) by facilitating to provide the securities banks require (i.e., seed money, incentive deposits or group guarantees), and by helping the banks to change their procedures in such a way that they meet the requirements and abilities of the poor.

NGOs also provide legal aid to the poor and their groups in their disputes with the rich and the government authorities, they encourage them to unite in federations or to take part in support networks in order to promote common interests collectively, and establish themselves as institutions at the service of those of the poor who have no access whatsoever to any services.

Those NGOs which are serious about grassroots development are aware that they themselves could not specifically predict the direction in which the poor will move. They present themselves, therefore, not as teachers and know-alls, but as equal partners and, by skilful questioning, make them conscious of their problems, prompt them to identify the causes and to propose solutions. Such a process provides a code of conduct for the organization rather than hierarchy that is conducive to participation. We can understand this by scrutinizing some movements in Asia.

People's Participation, Natural Resources and Protest Movements

People's participation is not a new concept in the Indian setting. The scope and content of it, of course, have been different at different times of history or in different regions or communities. For traditional communities, it was the management of communal properties and resources which extended to forestland, village land, water harvesting systems and village common cattle, grazing pastures, etc. For religious groups or communities it is a matter of providing and pooling labour and wealth for religious or even social functions. For patriotic groups, it is pooling people in movements such as Dandi March or, Quit India or electoral participation.

In the context of rural development, however, the term participation has a specific meaning. Participation is the introduction of a new set of people into the decision-making process with regard to resource allocation or distribution. By people we mean here those who have been victims of their exclusion from the development process and those who are likely to emerge as the beneficiaries of participation. In view of the complementary relationship between development and preservation of natural resources people's participation should involve the management of natural resources as well. From the history of traditional community organizations in India, people who were by and large concerned with common property resources, one can easily identify three minimal preconditions for such a group to emerge. *Firstly,* the community organizations should be able to reinforce the existing structures of authority as long as tradition and authority are upheld. *Secondly,* the community should feel empowered, and be independent of outsider's(including government) intervention. *Thirdly,* the set of rules and norms of cooperation should be such as to meet the felt-needs of the people.

The above concept and definition of participation in management of natural resources in a way, covers the entire gamut of development activities at the rural/village level. It may, however, operate at different levels of intensity, measured by the kind of activities in which the beneficiaries participate. When these are limited to information sharing and consultation, the level of participation is low. When beneficiaries become decision-makers or start initiating action on developmental activity, it can be surmised that participation has reached a higher level of intensity. All these, *i.e.,* consultation, information-sharing and initiating action on development activity are instances of participation (Bahuguna, 1983).

Though relevant in a wide spectrum of situations, participatory development is becoming growingly pertinent in the management of natural resources. Historically, the ownership and management of these resources always rested with the state, partly due to the failure of the market system and partly due to the eminent domain character of the state. But, due to the public goods nature of these resources, the preservation and policing costs to the government are prohibitively high. Secondly, natural resources qualify not only for preservation but also for their developmental use and as long as the management of the resources is with the government, it is the latter which is being revealed increasingly as the preference of the government. Multipurpose river valley projects such as Narmada, Kali, Nadi etc., are only some of the instances. Government's failure to preserve the natural resources together with their excessive exploitation for development purposes has led to serious degradation of the environment and hence its ecological repercussions (Aggarwal, *et.al;* 1985).

It is at this juncture that people's participation can be an alternative to government for providing development with preservation. People on their own may not perceive the preservation objective as a prime one due to their poverty, non-availability of alternative productive opportunities, lack of infrastructural facilities to reap the benefits from preservation, inability to possess private assets which are complementary to preservation of natural resources, lack of arrangements to participate and finally existing legal structures which are non-conducive to people's participation.

A Case Study of the *Chipko* and *Appiko* Movements

Policies and programmes of land-use as well as forest management, whenever they were put in place without consulting the local communities, have often resulted in "wastelands" and wasted human resources". We have a classic example of the *Chipko* movement in the Himalayan region in India where the people could no longer tolerate the inequity involved in transferring the benefits of the community resources to meet the needs of the people elsewhere. Since late 1970s, however, the people of the region acted together by adopting an unconventional approach and fully incorporating a new institution of people's participation which was totally devoid of bureaucratic and power politics.

The *Chipko*, or "Embrace (Hug) the Tree", Movement is essentially a Gandhian concept that espoused non-violent resistance to preserve the Himalaya's critical mountain-forest ecosystem. It began in Garhwal in the 1970s when women protected with their own bodies the trees that contractors were trying to remove. This message soon caused the *Chipko* struggle to grow into a national environmental movement. The struggles against limestone quarrying in Doon Valley, in the Haryana and Uttar Pradesh States of northern India, near the Himalayan range, is an extension of the original *Chipko* Movement. For the "last man" in the region, conservation has become a matter of life and death. Environmental destruction undermined the life support system of the poor, and their environmental struggles invite brutal attacks from truckloads of goondas hired by the contractor mafia (Bahuguna, 1983).

Chipko of Uttarakhand in the Himalayas inspired the villagers of the Uttara Kannada district of Karnataka Province in southern India to launch a similar movement to save their forests. In September 1983, men, women and children of Salkani "hugged the trees in Kalase forest (the local term for "hugging in Kannada is *Appiko*). *Appiko Andolan* gave birth to a new awareness all over southern India (Cultural Survival, 1989).

The story of Uttara Kannada region is different. In 1950, Uttara Kannada district's forest covered more than 81 per cent of its geographical area. The government, declaring this forest district a "backward" area, then initiated the process of "development". Three major industries-a pulp and paper mill, a plywood factory and a chain of hydro-electric dams constructed to harness the rivers – sprouted in the area. These industries have overexploited the forest resource, and the dams have submerged huge forest and agricultural area. The forest had shrunk to nearly 25 per cent of the district's area by 1980. The local population, especially the poorest groups, were displaced by the dams. The conversion of the natural mixed forests into teak and eucalyptus plantations dried up the water sources, directly affecting forest dwellers. In a nutshell, the three *p*'s – paper, plywood and power – which were intended for the development of the people, have resulted in a fourth *p*: poverty.

The *Appiko* Movement is trying to save the Western Ghats by spreading its roots all over southern India. The movement's objectives can be classified into three major areas. First, the *Appiko* Movement is struggling to save the remaining tropical forests in the Western Ghats. Second, it is making a modest attempt to restore the greenery to denuded area. Third, it is striving to propagate the idea of rational utilization in order to reduce the pressure on forest resources. To save, to grow and to use rationally – popularly known in Kannada as *Ubsu* (save), *Belesu* (grow) and *Balasu* (rational use) – is the movement's popular slogan.

The *Appiko* Movement used various techniques to raise awareness: foot marches in the interior forest, slide shows, folk dances, street plays and so on. The movement has achieved a fair amount of success: the State government has banned felling of green trees in some forest areas; only dead, dying and dry trees are felled to meet the local requirements. The movement has spread to the four hill districts of Karnataka State, and has the potential to spread to the Eastern Ghats in Tamil Nadu and Goa.

The objective of the *Appiko* Movement's work is to promote afforestation on denuded lands. In the past, *Appiko* activists have successfully motivated villagers to grow saplings. Individual families as well as village youth clubs have taken an active interest in growing decentralized nurseries. An all time record of 1.2 million saplings were grown by people in the Sirsi area in 1984-85. This was possible because the local Forest Department officials were forthcoming in eliciting the support of the people. The villagers initiated a process of regeneration in barren common land. The Youth Club has taken the responsibility for the project and the whole village has united to protect this land from grazing, lopping and fire. The experience shows that in those areas where soil is present, natural regeneration is the most efficient and least expensive method of bringing barren area under tree cover. In the areas in which topsoil is washed off, tree planting-especially of indigenous, fast-growing species- is done. The irony is that the forest department is resorting to the mechanized planting of exotic species, and also uses huge amounts of fertilizers on these exotic monoculture plantations. This would definitely harm the soil, and eventually the tree cover, in the area. Two obvious techniques of greening are being performed: one, the forest department's method, is capital intensive, and the other, the people's technique of growing through regeneration, is a natural process for sustainable development of the soil.

The other major area of activity in the *Appiko* Movement is related to rational use of the ecosphere through introduction of alternative energy sources to reduce the pressure on the forest. The activists have constructed about 5,000 fuel-efficient *chulas* (hearths) in the area, which save fuel wood consumption by almost 40 per cent. The activists do not wait for government subsidies or assistance, since there is spontaneous demand from the people. Even in towns and other urban areas, these *chulas* are installed in hotels, reducing firewood consumption.

Also, some people deter the regeneration process in the forest area through incorrect lopping practices. The *Appiko* Movement is trying to change people's attitudes so that they realize their mistake and stop this practice.

The thrust of the *Appiko* movement in carrying out its work reveals the constructive phase of the people's participation and movement. Through this constructive phase, depleted natural resources can be rebuilt. This process promotes sharing of resources in an egalitarian way, helping the forest dwellers. The movement's aim is to establish a harmonious relationship between people and nature, to redefine the term development so that ecological movements today form a basis for a sustainable, permanent economy in the future.

In the *Appiko* efforts a persistent leadership (as a catalytic institution) and some support from the government saw to it that what would have been a prisoner's dilemma with repeated non-cooperative game with sustainable development. By 1986, the extent of soil run-off had come down and average crop yield had gone up. Then two important socio-economic questions are raised while analyzing such a case example. *First*, what kinds of links between communal and private property resources are required so as to sustain such a participatory initiative. *Second*, to what extent are the production and distribution mechanisms evolved in such institutions independent of the market, an alternative institution. In Karnataka, increased cattle population, and improved land management are the two major thrust areas in the augmentation of private property resources. Afforestation, soil conservation, irrigation water from the community tanks, access to fodder and *bhabbar* grass on equitable basis etc., are instances of complementary flows of common property resources towards rural transformation on a sustained basis. The strength and nature of the link between these two types of resources is an empirical question, though theoretically there is no unique argument for their unilateral link as a pre-condition for rural development.

Even on the assumption that the market is less relevant in large rural parts of developing economies and the state is favourably inclined to the establishment of participatory institutions, existing property rights shall prevent spontaneous evolution of participation. Property rights emerge to help people to coordinate their productive activities and to avoid wasting time on conflicts, the result of which is purely distributive and not allocative. Since participatory institutions are bound to suggest a changed distribution, the possibility of their organic evolution is constrained by the existing institution of property rights. Such situation was observable in case of "milk revolution" in Gujarat. The group of households who owned land and cattle also monopolized control over the newly started institution of milk production and distribution i.e., AMUL Cooperative. To serve the interests, water from the irrigation tank was sold at a low price even in 1987-88, a year of acute scarcity. A breakthrough could be achieved only when a change in management with a new leadership was brought about in early

1988. It still remains to be seen how lasting the breakthrough will be. Therefore, as a process, participation shall spread only if it is designed so as to be in conformity with the norms that motivate people's social and economic behaviour in that particular society.

The *Chipko* and *Appiko* movements emerged as the consequence of an evolutionary process. People saw the consequences of the "tragedy of the environment" and worked out a set of rules for the management of forests and water from irrigation tanks. Their understanding of the issues involved did change the perception of the outside agencies who moved away from conventional solutions for soil erosion to a participatory approach. By now a large number of villages in the region seem to have followed these models, but with a difference, (UNESCO, 1992).

Summary

We observe that the voluntarism in Asia has passed through a number of stages.The Gandhian (peace loving, silent strugglers) and other types of voluntary agencies that existed prior to the phasing out of Colonialism in the region, on receiving government grants started working closely with and under the broad guidance of the government. They had lost the pioneering independent spirit that they had come to symbolize during the freedom struggle. In the second stage, there came a shift back to constructive work from "progress" or development work, as conceived by the government. The next phase saw a new genre of activist groups came up, ready to struggle on behalf of the poor, landless, *dalits* and other minority groups, against the State and dominant interests. There is a wide variety of such groups working in as different sectors as forestry, migrant labour, women, child labour and so on.

These few examples suggest the richness and diversity of local struggles by people trying to solve problems. The validity of each example, at this stage, resides probably in its specificity, and the fact-finding process has just started. It would be pointless to attempt any generalization. The purpose of this chapter is therefore, only to draw attention to the phenomenon, and endeavour to place it in the proper perspective.

There are various, essentially limited actions taken by groups of concerned men and women having or acquiring some control over their immediate environment and becoming able to define and carry out, in a self-reliant manner, solutions to their social and economic problems while modifying their relations with the State and/or market. They are either spontaneous or stem from encounters of a special kind with outsiders which have resulted in conscientisation. Their two major features are innovation and a certain transformation of social relations within the group and between the group and the larger environment (Guha, 1987).

The immediate result of the successful ones has been that fundamental needs are better met in the material sphere (often the prime mover) as well as in the political sphere, in its widest sense: taking action means self-confidence and reinforcing it; the moment people seize control of their own affairs, they cease to be passive and marginalized. They have started the process of development.

Thus a people-centred approach is not an utopia; it is the way out of poverty and underdevelopment. Already links appear with larger national struggles. One example is that of anti-nuclear popular actions in Asia. Local experiments with soft energies are also linked with a wider social movement which, in the final analysis, is challenging the whole system of values of the consumer society.

Local development action does not take place only in liberal or permissive political conditions. They also happen in the uncontrolled interstices of anti-popular regimes. They will be ignored or tolerated as long as they remain in their immediate locus-as long as they do not challenge the existing order. This is not a reason to remain passive; local actions are important in themselves and in them may be the seeds of larger movements.

REFERENCES

Agarwal, A., Narain,S. (editors)(1985), *India: The State of Environment 1984-85. A Citizen Report,* Centre for Science and Environment, New Delhi.

Bahuguna, S.(1983), *Walking with the Chipko Message,* Navjivan Ashram (Tehri Garhwal, India).

Guha, R. (1987), "Ideological Trends in Indian Environmentalism", *Economic and Political Weekly,* December 3, 1987.

W.Haque, N. Mehta, A. Rahaman and P. Wignaraja, (1977), "Towards a Theory of Rural Development", *Development Dialogue,* Vol.2.

Regional Unit for Social and Human Sciences, UNESCO (1992), *Forests and Cultures in Asia,* Bangkok.

17

JANMABHOOMI IN ANDHRA PRADESH – A CLINICAL APPROACH TO MULTI-SECTORAL AND SEGMENTAL DEVELOPMENT

Janmabhoomi is a movement imbued with principles of democracy, self-reliance and concerted coordinated community action for all round development in rural and urban areas. The programme carries with it an emotional and patriotic tone. It aims and stands for comprehensive community development, a massive people's planned movement with the stimulus provided by the Government. It works towards realizing the VISION-2020. It is not a one-time operation and one sector development but it is envisioned as a continuous and periodic collective activity focusing on one sector at a time.

During the past five decades there have been several programmes under the generic name of rural development. Though these programmes covered, of course, several development sectors and segments of population and despite efforts made, the results have not been encouraging. It was not only due to limited funds, lack of detailed planning and organization, but in a way the official machinery both at the planning, administrative and delivery level was not streamlined. The people also at the receiving end of the dividends of development were not properly mobilized in order to secure their participation in planning and carrying out development activities as partners with the administrative machinery. Based on the lessons learnt from the previous experience, the Government of Andhra Pradesh has come up with an innovative idea of sectoral and segmental development in a focused and concentrated way. They have christened the programme as *Janmabhoomi*. The first round was initiated on the 1st of January, 1997. In the beginning there were four rounds in a year, later on it was reduced to three and now it is two rounds per annum in January and July lasting for ten days. We may briefly go through the philosophy and imperatives of *Janmabhoomi* and the achievements of the programme.

Janmabhoomi is a movement imbued with principles of democracy, self-reliance and concerted coordinated community action for all round development in rural and urban areas. The programme caries with it an emotional and patriotic tone. It aims and stands for comprehensive community development, a massive people's planned movement with the stimulus provided by the Government. It works towards realizing the vision-2020. It is not a one-time operation and one sector development but it is envisioned as a continuous and periodic collective activity focusing on one sector at a time.

Prior to our spelling out the Imperatives of *Janmabhoomi*, it is relevant here to briefly look into the historic impetus behind *Janmabhoomi*.

Our freedom struggle is an epic saga of unparalleled martyrdom and a relentless battle of truth and non-violence fought under the leadership of the Father of the Nation, Mahatma Gandhi. A non-violent struggle aimed at political freedom, reinforced by tireless effort at social reform, represented a defining moment in the annals of world history. The Vision of an independent India, a strong committed leadership, and the fusion of the masses were the unique characteristics of India's freedom movement. Our struggle for freedom was a true example of mass mobilization cutting across the barriers of class, community, caste, creed, or occupation.

The mass mobilization of the people in the freedom

movement constituted only the first phase of democratic development. The founding fathers envisioned that democratic development has to bridge the gap between political equality and economic equality with social justice as mandated by the constitution.

What have we achieved?

While celebrating the Golden Jubilee of our Independence, we cannot but bow with gratitude and reverence to all those who fought selflessly and valiantly for our freedom. The leaders of the pre-independence era believed that political freedom would herald economic and social emancipation. To what extent have we achieved these aims? Do we stand up to their expectations?

We can justifiably feel proud of having preserved the democratic framework, as also the unity and integrity of the country despite several threats. We have tripled our agricultural production which has made us self-sufficient in food despite the pressures of growing population. Industrial production has grown manifold. We have built up a vast reserve of scientific, technological and managerial skills. After Independence, we undertook planned economic development through the instrument of five-year plans to fulfil the needs and aspirations of the people. Many welfare schemes were introduced to improve the living conditions of the people. When the 'trickle down' effect of the overall growth of the economy did not benefit the disadvantaged, we made special efforts, in recent years, to formulate programmes specifically directed at them.

But, when we evaluate our achievements against our expectations, we realize, to our dismay, that despite notable successes in certain sectors we are still extremely backward in several areas like literacy, health, employment-generation, etc. Even in sectors where we have achieved a measure of success, the fruits of success have been uneven and have not been distributed equitably. There is a wide gap between the aspirations of the people, particularly the poorest of the poor, and the achievements made so far.

The level of human development is an important indicator of the development of a Society. At the global level, the Human Development of the UNDP for the year 1996 ranks India as 138th out of 174 countries and classifies India as a country with "Low Human Development". This contrasts sharply with the remarkable progress made by and the enviable ranking of countries such as Japan (rank 7), South Korea (rank 32) and Malaysia (rank 61).

Countries that attained independence around the same time as we did have, overtaken us in improving the living standards of their peoples. For example,

- Japan, which was reduced to shambles in the Second World War, has emerged as a premier world economic power by dint of hard work, discipline and by the innovative adoption of technologies. Through a strong sense of loyalty, devotion to the nation and a keen urge to excel, the Japanese have succeeded in making their country an economic dynamo and a byword for quality and 'values' in an age of technology.
- Malaysia, which is also an agro-based economy like ours and which became independent ten years after us, has become an industrial giant in a span of 40 years mainly due to the team spirit of its people and a strong and visionary leadership.
- South Korea, which was backward and underdeveloped until the sixties, has been able to attain sustained economic growth through rapid strides in industry and exports. This was achieved through an innovative mass mobilization strategy that focused on internationalization of the core values of diligence, self-help and cooperation among the people and provision of intensive training.
- China, despite its large population, is poised to emerge as the economic giant of the 21st century, thanks to the spirit of hard work of its people and also the commitment of the Chinese Diaspora across the world.

Israel, which is a small country, has successfully illustrated how innovative approaches and appropriate technology can contribute to progress even in the face of several natural and man-made adversities.

Within India, the position of Andhra Pradesh is unfortunately below the national average in several key development indicators such as per-capita income, literacy and health status. The brunt of poverty and adversity is borne by our women and children and their condition continues to be a cause of serious concern for all of us. Environmental degradation has been posing a serious threat to sustainable development. Abysmal sanitation in the villages and towns is posing a serious threat to health.

This scenario in the human and physical development front is particularly distressing given that the State is endowed with rich natural and human resources. Our people, who have gone abroad, have achieved commendable success in their respective fields. However, here on native soil we have been unable to provide an environment whereby our people reach their full physical and intellectual potential.

What have we learnt?

What are the causes of this distressing scenario? Government institutions and local bodies could not succeed to the extent expected. The common man perceives the government as inaccessible. We have not succeeded in effectively harnessing the latent creativity of the people in formulating and implementing schemes for their own development. Instead of becoming 'partners in development', the people, particularly the poor, have become 'passive beneficiaries'. As the government acquired the role of 'doer' and 'direct provider', its paternalistic approach has driven people further towards dependency on government, even for small and sundry interventions. Lack of information about government programmes and procedures has made people dependent on intermediaries to intercede on their behalf in the Government.

Even though a few government programmes have

specifically sought to enlist people's participation, the effort got diluted in practice. The excessive centralization in planning and decision-making has dampened the initiative of the people. Access of people to government has been neither direct nor adequate. Government programmes and activities have remained largely ineffective in fostering the naturally positive elements of collective good, teamwork, honesty, dedication and hard work.

Values and principles, which once formed the core of the Indian ethos and which were so forcefully reflected in our freedom movement have got deeply eroded. The malaise we find ourselves in, today, is a result of this loss of values.

What should we do now?

The individual well-being of each one of us lies in restoring the health of the society and in promoting a healing process. No individual or group can prosper in the long run, at the expense of the society. As in the freedom struggle, each citizen is required to join hands with fellow citizens in finding a lasting solution to this crisis. The enemy is within. The fight should be directed at eradicating our internal enemies such as lethargy, despair, dishonesty, corruption, inequality, and moral degradation. We need wage another freedom struggle. This is the time to liberate our people from morass and despair, restore the lost values and build an egalitarian society based on the principles of equity and sustainability.

Towards a People's Movement

The struggle to be waged today by each one of us, individually and also collectively, is an important and perhaps more difficult one than the freedom struggle. *Janmabhoomi* is a people's movement for reconstruction and revitalization of the society. It is aimed at helping each one of us internalize the time-tested values of sacrifice, hard work, diligence, discipline, honesty, self-respect and the quest for excellence. Through this movement, every institution internalizes the guiding principles of participation, equity and equality, transparency and accountability, organizational excellence and sustainability. These principles will guide the policies, programmes and the day-to-day activities of all institutions.

Janmabhoomi–Values

The effort to be made by each one of us, individually and collectively, should be for restoration of these timeless values and for internalization of these values by each of one of us. Rejuvenating these core values is the pre-requisite for succeeding in our quest for excellence. Let us see how these values assume critical importance in our Janmabhoomi philosophy.

Spirit of Sacrifice

The spirit of sacrifice, which was the dominant quality that spurred the people of our country during the freedom struggle, needs to be revived. The Gandhian thought of simple living and high thinking will help every individual to lead a happy life devoid of greed and also enthuse him to contribute to the welfare of his fellow beings. The idea of living for others and for a cause, by sacrificing the 'self' should be the guiding principle. It is through the spirit of sacrifice that team spirit is nurtured and teamwork built up.

Diligence

Everybody should work hard. Anything is possible through hard work, dedication, determination and consistent effort. Consistent effort leads to success and sustainable development. Diligence coupled with dedication plays an instrumental role in achieving one's goals and ideals in life.

Honesty

Honesty and integrity are the two cardinal principles of life. Honesty means no contradictions or discrepancies in thought, word or deed. To be honest to one's self and to the purpose of a task earns trust and inspires faith in others. Honesty is the basis for cooperation between individuals and institutions. It is also the basis for transparency.

Self-help

The spirit of self-help enables one to solve one's own problems with one's own efforts. Solving problems with one's own efforts imbues one with a sense of pride and achievement. It also gives dignity of life.

Self-respect

To know one's own worth and to honour the worth of others is the true meaning of self-respect. Self-respect and belief in one's own ability are essential for achieving one's goals. Self-respect also means respect for honest labour. Physical or manual labour should be looked upon with respect..

Quest for Excellence

Quest for excellence should be the motto of every individual in his or her respective filed of activity. Only then will the society advance. One should never be satisfied with one's current standards of achievement but constantly strive for perfection. There should be pride in doing a job well. A scientific outlook can make a significant contribution towards our pursuit of excellence. Scientific progress is a harbinger of change in the modern world. Imbibing scientific temper promotes excellence.

Sense of Fulfillment

One can attain a sense of fulfillment through achieving something useful. A person with a sense of fulfillment is at peace with himself. Acquisition of wealth or achievements on the material plane does not necessarily lead to happiness. One should therefore aspire for spiritual fulfillment.

Janmabhoomi–Principles

In addition to rejuvenating values, *Janmabhoomi* seeks to radically reorient the way we do things. Such a shift is essential not only to accelerate the pace of development but also to sustain the same through equitable distribution of benefits. Towards this end each one of our institutions should be restructured and realigned with the core principles of *Janmabhoomi*, namely, people's participation, equity & equality, transparency and accountability, innovation and sustainability. The institutions will then be able to promote *Janmabhoomi* values among every citizen in the Society. These basic principles have the potential to enrich the life of every citizen irrespective of gender, age, profession, status, caste, creed, community or location. Let us see how.

Operationalisation of Janmabhoomi

The conduct of Prajala Vaddaku Paalana, Sramadanam and *Janmabhoomi* has positively reaffirmed the power of these time tested values and basic principles. Armed with exemplary grit, determination and commitment, our people have demonstrated the immense potential of *Janmabhoomi.*

Janmabhoomi essentially means a people centred participatory development process. The institutional framework for *Janmabhoomi* should therefore facilitate such a process wherein the Government, the democratic institutions of the people, the grassroots people's institutions, the facilitating agencies (including NGOs, academic institutions, etc.) and the people themselves can participate as equal partners. All these Institutions would be imbued with the core principles of *Janmabhoomi* to enable them to carry out their tasks effectively.

We are conscious that a movement of this magnitude would have wide ramifications for all of us. Accordingly we should gear ourselves through the following interventions:

- Environment building
- Promotion of grassroots people's institutions
- Strengthening local bodies
- Training and orientation
- Administrative reforms.

Environment building

A massive environment building will be one of the activities for sensitization and for inculcating the values and principles of *Janmabhoomi*. The philosophy of *Janmabhoomi* would be widely disseminated, through all the institutions – academic, government institutions, youth associations, women's organizations, voluntary organizations, grassroots people's institution, local bodies, industrial establishments, etc. Eminent citizens, freedom fighters, professionals and experts in various fields will be requested to take an active part and lend their time and effort in this process. Voluntary Organizations will play an active role and their services will be fully utilized, particularly in training the grassroots people's institutions and community volunteers. The media, industrial establishments – private and public, financial institutions, research bodies will be motivated to define a clear role for themselves and participate in the *Janmabhoomi* processes.

Promotion of Grassroots People's Institutions

Janmabhoomi will induce, develop and nurture social mobilization of people, particularly the poor, organizing the community around specific interests such as women thrift and credit groups, youth groups (CMEY), Vana Samrakshana Samithis, water users associations, watershed development committees, village education committees, etc. This will be achieved through sensitization, awareness building, organizing grassroots people's institutions (GPIs), organizing women into thrift and credit groups (self help groups), building up the capability of the leaders of these people's institutions and promoting the consolidation of the groups on a sustained basis. *Janmabhoomi* will provide for capacity building of these groups to enable them to access and manage the resources, to articulate their requirements in the Gram Sabha, to sensitize them on issues affecting the people and to train them to take up participatory planning. *Janmabhoomi* will build up people's skills through intensive training. *Janmabhoomi* will foster leadership at the grassroots level and the grassroots people's institutions shall act as the nurseries for the growth of leadership.

Janmabhoomi will develop appropriate support structures for achieving social mobilization and capacity building. The support structures are intended to provide necessary training and technical guidance, exposure, as well as to develop suitable literature for different sectors. There will be a system of regular feedback and discussions in the workshops where the best experiences within and outside our State would be considered for adoption. At the State level, appropriate structures will be established for overseeing this as well as to look after the training needs including development of literature.

Strengthening Local Bodies

Janmabhoomi will strengthen local bodies through a policy of decentralization and develop a framework for a larger role for the local bodies. The guiding principle will be that what can be done at the grassroots level would be done only at that level. For this, each department will analyze and draw up a list of activities in each sector that can be decentralized, including the powers necessary at appropriate levels for effective decentralized decision-making. Necessary financial devolution will also be made. At the same time, full accountability to people will be ensured. *Janmabhoomi* will build up the mechanism of an active and vibrant Gram Sabha, which will not only decide on various issues but also monitor development programmes. *Janmabhoomi* will also develop a system by which information and knowledge are constantly made available to people.

Janmabhoomi will enable participatory planning at the grassroots level. Towards this end, individuals, members of the local bodies, representatives of the grassroots people's institutions will be sensitized about the significance and modalities of participatory planning. The Gram Panchayat would be the unit for planning in those sectors where it can act. For other sectors, the Mandal or the District will be the unit for planning. Suitable units will be identified in the urban sector. Training would be provided to enable the grassroots level institutions to take up planning and preparation of action plans. These will be implemented by the people and monitored constantly by the Gram Sabha, which would also take up evaluation of the programmes at their level.

Training and Orientation

Training shall be organized for government functionaries, elected representatives, voluntary organizations, representatives of grassroots people's institutions, community volunteers and all those involved in the implementation of Janmabhoomi at various levels. Expert groups constituted at various levels shall prepare training modules. The existing training infrastructure available shall be utilized for providing training. Similar training programmes shall be organized at the village level in schools and colleges.

Academic institutions will participate in the *Janmabhoomi* movement, as part of socially useful and relevant work experience. It is proposed to integrate the *Janmabhoomi* experience into the academic programme by allotting a specific number of hours for this purpose. The *Janmabhoomi* philosophy will be incorporated in the curriculum. The daily Assembly time in schools and colleges will be utilized for inculcating the values of *Janmabhoomi*. Specialized training for staff and students will also be given.

Administrative Reforms

In contrast to its current role of a 'provider' and 'doer', the Government's role would be transformed into that of a 'facilitator' and enabler of self-governance. Towards that goal of a transparent and people friendly Government, administration would be simplified and demystified through a comprehensive set of reforms. This would include a thorough reorientation of the government functionaries to enable them to adopt their redefined roles and make the system service oriented. *Janmabhoomi* will institutionalize the process of the governmental actions being transparent and the government machinery being accountable to the people. All activities of public bodies shall be subjected to Social Audit. Each Department shall have a Citizen's Charter presenting the standards of services to be provided to the citizens.

Emphasis will be laid on building awareness among the people. *Janmabhoomi* will also develop a process by which information and knowledge are constantly made available to the people. Janmabhoomi will seek to provide the people with all the relevant information through appropriate channels.

The task ahead....

Janmabhoomi is a people-centred development process aimed at establishing an ideal society, which embodies and cherishes the principles of people's participation, equality, transparency and accountability leading to sustained economic development and excellence in all walks of life. The goal is an enhanced quality of life for every man, woman and child in the State.

As the children of this beloved land, *'Janmabhoomi'*, it is our privilege to be proud of our heritage. At the same time, it is our responsibility to contribute our might to enhance the glory of this land. *Janmabhoomi* is our collective effort for achieving and sustaining such a glory.

Janmabhoomi–Rural Development

Janmabhoomi as conceived and introduced by the Chief Minister Nara Chandra Babu Naidu, though primarily relates to Shramadan (Gift of Labour) on the part of the people, it is to be reckoned as significant movement with economic, social, cultural and psychological ingredients educating, appealing, inviting and encouraging people to plan, organize and develop in order to accomplish community needs and infrastructure on their own. It is not simply educating one individual but it is a very effective education to the entire community which is to become a tradition and value system of the community for its development. *Janmabhoomi* as a movement goes with emotional tone instilling activity and pride on the part of the members of the community. In the course of the last five years it has drawn the attention not only of the people but the entire administration, and the personnel at different levels. The *Janmabhoomi* as a people's movement initiated and augmented by the Government is expected to be a continuous periodic movement towards development. The expectation is that this movement should become a part of the socio-cultural value system to be observed and carried on in action for all-round development in the rural and urban communities. It is envisaged that it should be something sacred as in the case of certain traditional and religious observances.

It is interesting to see that the concept of *Janmabhoomi* is akin to 'SAEMAUL UNDONG' a South Korean model of community development. It may be relevant here to briefly look into SAEMAUL UNDONG as it was adopted by the South Korean Government. This has been a nation-wide development movement under the slogan of diligence, cooperation and self-help. The first nation-wide community development programme in Korea was launched in the late 1950s after the Korean War, another trial was made in 1960s under the name of National Reconstruction. But these two attempts were not much of success and so in 1970s SAEMAUL UNDONG succeeded in achieving the people's voluntary participation and active public support. The community development projects in Korea were carried out by community people themselves who were led by elected SAEMAUL leaders. Integrated planning (Bottom-up and Top-down mixed) were made democratically. Adequate administrative and financial support and supervision were made with the priority of hardworking communities.

Generally speaking, integrated community development projects are designed to improve the standard of living and social welfare of people living in communities through effective cooperative utilization of all available physical and human resources. Every community has a different historical, social and economic background, which must be taken for project planning and implementation. The community development in the name of SAEMAUL UNDONG can be largely divided into three categories: spiritual reform, social development and economic development. SAEMAUL UNDONG based its action on the following principles: Firstly, the movement relied on integrated participation of the whole nation. Everyone in the community can take part in its development plans and programmes with common agreement by the community members. Secondly, the SAEMAUL spirit of diligence (self-help) and cooperation has to reflect people's aspirations and visible in the everyday life. Thirdly, all the activities must be undertaken in the interest and for the benefit of the community. The members of the community should be involved directly or indirectly in the increase of production and income. The Korean model of community development though emphasizes on community action it is always to be encouraged and supported by the State.

As one could see, in the case of *Janmabhoomi*, it is being initiated by the State Government, mobilizing all the administrative resources and soliciting, motivating and encouraging the people to participate in the chosen programme. As mentioned earlier, the communities though they are interested in their development, may not maintain the same momentum of spirit and seriousness in their efforts to meet their needs. A constant and a periodic awakening of the community is essential to carry on self-help community development. More often, a community may not realize its own resources, the potential it has and the way in which the potential could be utilized for its development. There is need for some body like the State authority to remind the people what they could do for themselves with partial assistance from the government. In this kind of development, the people play a major role and the state a supportive role. It should become an established tradition of continuous improvement in the quality of life in rural and urban communities. The *Janmabhoomi* as a popular and pragmatic movement is committed to generate enthusiasm and action on the part of the community for its overall and comprehensive development towards a richer life.

A Brief Review of Janmabhoomi Programmes

The *Janmabhoomi* Programme as a people's movement for development is highly imaginative in motivating and stimulating action on the part of the people towards bettering their way of life. And thus for the following have been the focal areas:-

1. Micro Level Planning
2. Health and Sanitation
3. Education
4. Community Organization
5. Artisan Development
6. Empowerment of women
7. Decentralization of Administration
8. Development of Local Bodies
9. Constitution of People's Functional Associations
10. The environmental protection
11. Upgrading of Artisans
12. Focus on aged and disabled and
13. The focus on Farm Development, in terms of increased production and profitable marketing of produce within and outside the country.

It is needless to say that all the programmes initiated thus far under *Janmabhoomi* are quite relevant for the overall development of rural communities. In one sense, some of them are initial motivating activities. Some try to meet solve certain local problems and local needs. Some needs are of a perennial nature. In a larger sense, the major objective of *Janmabhoomi* as a People's Movement is to build self-reliant, self-generating, progressive little dynamic, democratic communities.

In brief, the *Janmabhoomi* movement has created awareness among the people, it drew their attention to the basic minimum needs of life. And in a sense, made them aware of the physical, natural, material and human resources they are endowed with. It also made them feel their own potential, what they could do and accomplish if they want to. The periodic programmes to a considerable extent, tapped new human resources, talents of the leadership and initiative among the various age groups in the villages and organized several self-help associations to manage certain sectoral and segmental needs of the rural community. These are newly organized social, operational, functional sub-systems within the rural community. The credit goes to *Janmabhoomi* Programmes in motivating, mobilizing and organizing these individuals both men and women. The programmes have created social support systems, and social infrastructure to initiate and manage certain interests of the community. We may mention here the rejuvenation of the Grama Sabha by the *Janmabhoomi* movement. Though it has been the statutory, people's association at the community level, in many cases, the Grama Sabha has been dormant and non-functional. The *Janmabhoomi* movement through its stipulated programmes activated and regenerated the periodic assembly of the Grama Sabha. The *Janmabhoomi* programmes educated the people and drew their attention to the Grama Sabha, how it is the statutory fundamental forum of the community wherein the development ideas, needs, issues and problems could be discussed and to forward the needs and plans of action to the Grama Panchayat which may be described as the executive wing of the Grama Sabha. Further, interestingly and very importantly, *Janmabhoomi* drew the attention of the community and all wings of administration at the state, district and mandal level to the primacy of women welfare. It does not mean women's development did not figure in the earlier movements but *Janmabhoomi* specifically devoted to what is called *Mahila Janmabhoomi* and also focused attention on the minorities and of course on the larger segment of the society the farmers. Creation of awareness and reinforcement through motivation and practical programmes of action are necessary and this has appreciably manifested in the *Mahila Janmabhoomi*.

The officials operating at the village level promoting developmental activities may acquaint themselves with the indigenous knowledge system which has been developed over a period of time for meeting local needs and solving local problems. The indigenous knowledge system comprises the ways, the means, the methods and the techniques which the rural people have been using for decades in the past. At the operational level, one may make use of the indigenous knowledge system also along with new ways of development. Sometimes, in our enthusiasm we introduce new methods and technologies, ignoring the norms and the mechanisms, people have developed in solving their political, economical and social issues. By now, 14 rounds of Janmabhoomi programmes have been carried out and it has been recently decided by the Government that hereafter there will be 3 rounds, one devoted to Farmers, and the second one to Women, and the third one to the Minorities.

We may briefly focus on the 14th Janmabhoomi aptly called Rythu Janmabhoomi (Farmer's Janmabhoomi) 2-8, January, 2001, since the farmers and agriculture are the backbone of India or any other country.

The commitment, dedication and hard-work of the farmer who toils year-round in the field often does not get appropriately rewarded in the market. Farmers are not adequately compensated, and they do not get competitive prices for their produce.

Therefore, the government of Andhra Pradesh has stepped forward to strengthen the agricultural sector and empower farmers by helping them fetch the highest possible prices for their produce; and to also provide solutions to all their problems.

Since the farmer is the mainstay of progress of the State, the government has dedicated this Janmabhoomi to them.

To alleviate the hardships faced by the farmers during the summer season, the government has launched *Neeru-Meeru* Programme. Despite cyclones and other natural calamities which befell Andhra Pradesh last year, it is creditable that the State nonetheless recorded an increase in agricultural production as a result of the previous Janmabhoomi's agriculture development programmes.

The government understands the needs, limitations, trials,

and tribulations on the part of the farmers and the Government is with the farmers.

Rythu Janmabhoomi targeted on the following activities:

- Improving the water levels of canals and ponds,
- The use of dry crops during the Rabi Season
- Keeping the shortage of electricity in mind
- Timely decisions to be taken in all related matters
- Creating awareness about the harmful effects of using spurious pesticides.

The farmer is the base and the foundation, there will be no State, no progress, no promise for a better future without the farmer.

We may just mention here the priority issues that have been covered thus far during the past Janmabhoomi Programmes:

- Neeru-Meeru
- Veterinary Camps
- Distribution of Revolving Fund to DWCRA Groups
- Eradication of Superstitions
- Health Camps – Special emphasis on Prevention of AIDS, Pulse Polio
- Awareness about sanitation
- Distribution of Pensions
- Akshara Sankranthi
- Distribution of Gas Connections

GRAMA SABHAS

- Grievance redressal
- Problem solving

ACTIVITIES THAT HAVE BEEN COVERED UP TO THE SIXTEENTH ROUND UNDER JANMABHOOMI PROGRAMMES

Round	*Period*	*Theme*
First Round	1-8 January, '97	Janmabhoomi Concept and Micro Level Planning.
Second Round	1-7 May, '97	Constitution of HLCs/WLCs, Community Infrastructure Development Works.
Third Round	1-7 August, '97	Janmabhoomi Janachaitanyam – Immunization and Health Camps
Fourth Round	1-7 October, '97	Clean Village/Town Concept. Free Veterinary Camps, Campaign on Save Energy and Small Savings
Fifth Round	1-7 January, '98	Participation of Students and Lecturers along with the Habitation/Ward Level Committees and the people in activities promoting Clean Village/Ward concept and creation of Community assets.
Sixth Round	1-7 May, '98	Free Health Camps with focus on TB and Blindness control. Works Programmes through Self-Help Groups.
Seventh Round	1-7 August, '98	"Cheyutha" for Disabled. Pollution Control in Urban Areas.
Eighth Round	3-9 October, '98	Free Health Camps with focus on AIDS, TB, Eye Care, Dental Care and Reproductive health care.
Ninth Round	2-8 January, '99	Micro Level Planning Free

		Health Camps with focus on curative and preventive aspects of AIDS, TB, Eye Care, Dental Care and Reproductive health care.
Tenth Round	1-7 May, '99	Mahila Janmabhoomi
Eleventh Round	3-11 Jan., 2000	Micro Level Planning & Evaluation of Gram Panchayats/ Wards and Nodal Officers.
Twelfth Round	1-7 May, 2000	Neeru – Meeru – Focus on Health Drought and Water Conservation.
Thirteenth Round	1-7 August, 2000	Mahila Janmabhoomi
Fourteenth Round	2-8 January, 2001	Rythu Janmabhoomi
Fifteenth Round	1-10th June, 2001	Mahila and Sishu Janmabhoomi
Sixteenth Round	2-11th Jan, 2002	Welfare of the Weaker Sections

JANMABHOOMI-CUMULATIVE ACHIEVEMENTS FOR THIRTEEN ROUNDS (FROM JAN 1997 TO AUG 2000)

1. Habitations And Wards Covered (in every round)	58,753
2. No. of Teams Constituted	1,347
3. A). No. of Grama Sabhas Held In Each Round	53,625
B). No. of Grama Sabhas Held in Twelfth Round	25,762
4. PRIMARY EDUCATION	
Additional enrolment in Primary Schools during 1997-98	6.31 lakh

No. of children identified for enrolment in 1998-99	7.90 lakh
Additional enrolment in Primary Schools during 1998-99	5.71 lakh

5. PRIMARY HEALTH AND FAMILY WELFARE

No. of eligible couples motivated for Family Planning Operations	9.84 lakh
No. of Free Health Camps organized	3.16 lakh
Patients Treated	147.49 lakh
Malaria treated	43,953
AIDS awareness Camps conducted	2.07 lakh
Dental Camps organized	11,876
School Children Treated in Dental camps	3.64 lakh
Women Medical camps conducted in Mahila Janmabhoomi	10,062
Women examined under reproductive health care	7.12 lakh
Children Immunized	8.11 lakh
No. of TB patients identified for treatment	69,240
No. of persons identified with eye problems	2.25 lakh
No. of operations done	1,70,541
➢ Conventional	1,00,491
➢ IOL	70,050
No. of persons with cataract	4,44,542
Free Spectacles distributed for refractive errors	83,201
Glaucoma cases identified	1,644
Glaucoma cases operated	77
No. of cases identified for GE treatment	2,430

6. ENVIRONMENTAL CONSERVATION	
Trees planted	1087.06 lakh
Individual Sanitary latrines sanctioned	19.50 lakh
Individual Sanitary Latrines completed	12.27 lakh
Repairs to Soak-pits and Platforms of drinking water sources	62,130
Cleaning and Chlorination of drinking water sources (no. per round)	89,390
Adoption of Smokeless chulhas	1.76 lakh
Special sanitation driver under taken in public institutions (no. per round)	40,948
Pollution check-upNo. of vehicles	25.16 lakh
P.V.C. Certificates issued	15.97 lakh
7. REDRESSAL OF FELT NEEDS (1st – 12th rounds)	
INDIVIDUAL FAMILY NEEDS (Nos.)	
Received	42.43 lakh
Solved	16.18 lakh
Ineligible	24.52 lakh
Balance	1.73 lakh
NON-FINANCIAL COMMUNITY NEEDS (Nos.)	
Received	1.78 lakh
Solved	1.14 lakh
Ineligible	0.57 lakh
Balance	0.01 lakh
8. **COMMUNITY WORKS**	(Rs. in crores)
Received in Grama Sabhas - 1,22,572	1937.47
Grounded - 1,18,194	814.53
Completed - 1.01,539	1627.85

Government share required for works grounded	1337.34
Funds released (including those released in April, 2000)	1117.03
Expenditure	1091.12

9. FREE VETERINARY CAMPS (1st – 12th rounds)

No. organized	3.45 lakh
Animals treated	1294.13 lakh
Sheep Dewormed (Jan '99 round)	127.16 lakh
Sheep Dewormed (Jan '2000 round)	90.89 lakh
Cattle vaccinated against Foot & Mouth Disease (Jan'99 round)	15.68 lakh
Calf Dewormed (May '99 round)	19.69 lakh
Farmers assisted in 12th round	15.68 lakh

10. DISABLED WELFARE (Distributed upto May 2000)

Marriage Incentives issued	6,173
Scholarships	99,374
Pre-Matric	34,248
Post-Matric	17,558
Aids/Appliances distributed	62,583
No. of persons economically assisted	31,873
Issue of Certificates (Non-Financial benefits)	8,06,087

11. MICRO LEVEL PLANNING DURING ELEVENTH ROUND OF JANMABHOOMI

Total No. of students drafted
1,26,852

No. of students actually participated	1,22,216
No. of GRPs attended	22,854

No. of WRPs attended	3,985
No. of Mandal/Municipal Resource Persons attended	1,299
No. of households surveyed (excluding part of Hyderabad city and other urban areas)	1,71,50,761

ANNAPURNA SCHEME (During 12th Round)

Beneficiaries covered	58,843
Rice distributed (in M.Ts.) 160.75	

DROUGHT – INPUT SUBSIDY (During 12th Round)

Farmers covered	32,28,806
Amount distributed (Rs. in lakhs)	2421.14

PENSIONS DISTRIBUTED DURING 12th ROUND

No. of pensions distributed	8,55,233
Amount distributed (Rs. in lakhs)	1270.98

Note:- The detailed figures of achievements under various heads are available upto 13th Round of Janmabhoomi and in respect to the 14th, 15th and 16th Rounds, a brief description as to what has been achieved in general is provided below.

The 13th round of Janmabhoomi programme focused on distribution of 4 lakh LPG connections under 'Deepam' Scheme, granting of revolving funds/matching grants to thrift groups, pension distribution to various groups like Old age, Widow, Landless, agriculture labour etc; distribution of smokeless Chulhas, formation of new thrift groups, construction of 'DWCRA' Bhavans, distribution of Bank Loans to 'DWCRA' groups, free health camps, enrolment of girl children in schools, campaign for equal wages for equal work etc., was held from 1st August to 7th August, 2000, all over the State.

In the 14th round of Janmabhoomi, 886 proposals for works at an estimated cost of Rs 15.47 crores were sanctioned under

50:50 pattern. The Government share for these works comes to Rs 7.73 crores and an amount of Rs. 2.19 crores has been released by the Government so far. Out of 886 works sanctioned, 807 works have already been grounded.

Evaluation of the Gram Panchayat / Ward / Mandal / Municipality is done to introduce a system of incentive for the local bodies linked to their performance. The Nodal Team is also being evaluated. Achievement during last financial year will be the basis for evaluation.

An elaborate analysis is made to identify the pending Grievances department-wise. The mandal register is updated and computerization of the grievances is done at the mandal / municipality level.

Feedback workshops were organized from 15th to 20th June 2001 at the Mandal level for village / mandal officials and at the district level for Nodal Officers, Divisional Resource Persons and District Level Officials to identify the problem areas of the last round of Janmabhoomi for improvements in the future.

The fifteenth round of Janmabhoomi was conducted for ten days, for the first time in the history of Janmabhoomi. Two gram Sabhas were conducted per day. 1263 Nodal Teams were constituted to conduct 26172 Gram/Ward sabhas. 25787 Gram / Ward sabhas were actually held during this round of Janmabhoomi. Only 385 (1.47%) Gram / Ward sabhas could not be held due to various reasons like drinking water problem, electricity problem, non-redressal of pending grievances and extremist activities. The number of boycotts in this round is the least in the last five years.

This round of Janmabhoomi provided an excellent opportunity for effective convergence of Self Help groups and Gram Panchayats. The participation of women was quite encouraging. It resulted in increased awareness among the people on health, education and small family norms. The distribution of assets was done in a transparent manner. During this round, JANANI for women and children (integrated health care) was launched.

Village level exhibitions were organized for the first time. The themes covered in the exhibition were women and child welfare, Neeru-Meeru, population control, literacy and agriculture. The exhibition mainly focused on the achievements made in the village on the above-mentioned themes and inter comparison with other villages.

Funds amounting to Rs. 340 Crores were sanctioned for carrying out various activities in this round of Janmabhoomi. Rs. 52 Crores were released towards revolving fund to DWCRA/ DWCUA. A provision of Rs 30 Crores was made for girl child protection scheme and Rs. 37 Crores for distribution of pensions. Funds to the tune of Rs. 120 Crores were earmarked by the SC/ST/BC/Minorities/Women Finance corporations out of the marginal money available with them for group based economic support programmes for the women. An amount of Rs. 46 Crores (Rs. 2 Crores per district) was released for decentralized planning to fill the gaps as untied funds. Rs. 40 Crores was released for giving 4 lakh as connections under DEEPAM Scheme.

41673 DWCRA/DWCUA groups were sanctioned revolving funds. An amount Rs 45 Crores was distributed as pensions to 12.31 lakh beneficiaries. 36695 women were provided assistance under National Maternity Benefit Scheme and 3365 beneficiaries under National Family Benefit Scheme. 20521 ' girls were provided assistance under Girl Child Protection Scheme. 1.91 lakh gas connections were released to women beneficiaries under Deepam Scheme. 34420 beneficiaries were provided assistance under Cheyutha and 7649 aids and appliances were distributed to disabled beneficiaries.

During the 15th round, the total number of grievances received under IFN and NFCN are 2,22,351 and 16,522 respectively. Including the number of grievances pending before 15th round, the number pending redressal under IFN and NFCN are 2,36,097 and 17,241 respectively.

Free Health Camps organized during this round were 28052 in which 20.45 lakh patients were treated. In addition, 6607

Special Camps were conducted for women and 2.11 lakh patients were treated. Medicines worth Rs. 107.84 lakhs were given to the patients in these camps.

Free Veterinary Camps organized were 36587 and 89.98 lakh animals were treated. The total number of farmers assisted during these camps is 16.01 lakhs. Medicines worth Rs.191 lakhs were used during these camps.

Proposals for .12309 works at an estimated cost of Rs.198.65 Crores were received during 15th round under the sharing pattern of 70:30 pattern. The Government share for these works amounts to Rs. 139 Crores where as the people's share comes to Rs. 59.59 Crores. So far, Rs. 68 Crores has been deposited by the people and there is an assurance for depositing Rs. 25.77 Crores. In addition, 171 proposals costing Rs. 5.13 Crores under 50:50 pattern were received. Only Rs. 1.81 lakhs have been deposited so far. There is an assurance for depositing Rs. 2.08 Crores.

The Sixteenth Round of Janmabhoomi was conducted from the 2nd of Jan to the 11th of Jan 2002, focusing on the welfare of the weaker sections.

By now 19 rounds of Janmabhoomi were carried out through out the state focusing as mentioned earlier on women, children, minorities and farmers. *Janmabhoomi* focuses on several development and welfare activities, it will take time for some of the programmes to bear fruits. It may be briefly mentioned here apart from sensitizing and motivating people, *Janmabhoomi* has to its credit tangible results in physical and material development. Though, the official machinery is there, it is the people and the people's leaders who have to move forward and shoulder the responsibility as partners in development. One can easily say that it is a failure, that so much of time and lot of money and large amount of human resources both on the administrative side and from the people have been invested during the last rounds of *Janmabhoomi*. Development is time related. One cannot expect instantaneous results. *Janmabhoomi* is not a miracle or a magic to bring about instantaneous changes for better. No one can call the past 19 rounds of *Janmabhoomi* as total success, because as mentioned earlier you are dealing with diversity of people at different levels of motivation, potential and capability and even in the case of officials who are drawn into the *Janmabhoomi* programme as Nodal Officers and others are not just stereo type of human tools doing exactly what was expected of them. In the case of the officials also you find differences in terms of commitment, sincerity, knowledge and skills in planning and in working with the people. There is mild criticism also. The creation and the support provided to self-help groups in the rural communities is highly desirable and it has gone in the right direction in organizing the community into viable functional units. Though, it was a desirable kind of community organization in terms of specific activities, it has rather minimized the importance and the role that is expected of the village panchayats.

The State of Andhra Pradesh has started the journey of comprehensive rural development with Janmabhoomi as an emotional, motivating factor. And it is a long way to go for accomplishing the overall development of rural communities wherein every individual is ensured of the basic minimum needs and leads a happy life. In this context, while we refer to the journey of development one could recall the famous lines of Robert Frost, the National Poet of the United States of America,

"The woods are lovely dark and deep

I have promises to keep

And miles to go before I sleep

And miles to go before I sleep".

REFERENCES

1. Setty, E.D., "*A Model for Securing People's Participation in Janmabhoomi-Rural Development*", published by Dr.MCR HRD Institute of AP, Hyderabad, Govt. of Andhra Pradesh, 2001.

2. www.andhrapradesh.com

18

CASTE DYNAMICS IN RURAL DEVELOPMENT

Of several affinities that foster unity, bonds of enduring relationship, solidarity and concerted social action on the part of the people such as territorial, regional, racial, ethnic, political, ideological, religious, sectarian, lingual, occupational and professional, the social institution of caste is a strong and enduring one. The institution of caste is unique in India. It is an unchanging ascribed status and identity for an individual. One may change his political and ideological views and change his religious faith and move from one region to another, but one's caste identity does not change. Caste is both a unifying and divisive force. The forces of caste for and against are apparent in every field. One could witness the caste dynamics operating in the villages creating enmity, cliques, factions, and rivalries, one caste group fighting against another. Caste generates competition, both subtle and vibrant with expression of emotions. Competition by itself is not negative. It promotes improvement and advancement. A healthy competition is a welcome factor in order to make the caste groups in the villages compete with one another and excel and improve their lives.

When it comes to helping people caste promotes favouritism helping the group that belongs to the political leaders and administrators although we have all the rules, regulations and specifications as to whom the help should reach yet caste factors influence the delivery of goods and services to the deserving minority caste groups.

It is well-nigh impossible to eliminate the negative and detrimental caste born attitudes from some caste groups. The problem with caste system is its rigidity in attitude. Caste discriminations are more visible and active in rural areas. One may come across instances wherein numerically dominant and politically influential caste groups are barriers in assistance reaching the lower caste groups or downtrodden ones. One may speak at length about the dynamics and the historical tradition and hereditarily inherited patterns of behaviour associated with different caste groups. As we discuss below there are positive and negative elements in the institution.

In the context of rural development with multiple development and welfare programmes, the development workers at the field level should have some understanding of the caste dynamics. They have to keep in mind the forces that are in operation and manoeuvre over these forces to see that help reaches the deserving and they should also work as effective social change agents to bring about harmony in the rural communities to work towards development of the entire community.

Here, we may mention that it is not only the field workers who are to be sensitive to these forces but the entire administration in the field of rural development should be sensitive and wise-enough to operate in such a way that over a period of time we succeed and gradually reduce the prejudices and stereotypes attributed to different caste groups. In this context, a brief understanding of the emergence operation and slowly declining caste system in India is relevant and interesting.

It is much easier to say what caste is not than what caste is. It is not class, for it consists of rich and poor, literate and illiterate and of high and low mental calibre. It is not colour. An upper-caste man may be black and a Harijan quite fair in complexion. It is not Aryan and non-Aryan, conqueror and conquered. It is not even occupation. Many occupations, mostly of artisans, overwhelmingly identify themselves with particular castes, but the main occupation, agriculture is open to all.

Hundreds of castes and sub-castes live on the plough. So occupation alone has not caused caste. Occupational distribution is not now based on caste.

Caste is not exclusively Hindu or exclusively Indian. It obtains elsewhere too in a modified form. Nor does the present caste structure bear much relation to the traditional four *varnas*.

> Each caste embodies in itself its rites, taboos, do's and don'ts in food, drinking and matrimony.

Whatever sets off a group in any way may be sufficient to make it a caste in India. If groups diverge within an established caste they become recognized as sub-castes, perhaps finally to develop into wholly separate castes. Caste is a way of thought that the Hindu has tried to universalize.

Castes are Endogamous

All Indian castes are in theory strictly endogamous; intermarriage is intolerable. All possess an intrinsic, unchangeable worth. Thus they automatically rank themselves. Caste embraces one's life activities in their entirety from cradle to grave. Each possesses an occupation, a mode of life and customs, a set of prescribed rituals, inherently peculiar to it. The greater the restriction and prohibition incumbent upon it, the less it relaxes to comfort and indifference, the more spiritual it is, the higher its grade. In consequence it is also more pollutable, and so its restrictions are drawn closer. The wider the gap with the lower classes, the greater becomes its purity.

Life cannot be lived in parts or compartments; it is an integrated whole. So, religion, man's spiritual food, is fused with caste or the other way about.

The *Rig Veda*, the most ancient and sacred of Hindu hymns, does not talk of the caste system. Caste existed during the epic period. Caste is a hierarchy and has no bearing to the original four *varnas* in its content and functions. Hundreds of castes are sub-divided into sub-castes and sub-castes run into thousands. Among Brahmins alone there are over two thousand sub-castes and even among the so-called untouchables, over five hundred. It is the sub-castes which give Hindu society its character. Each caste embodies in itself its rites, taboos, do's and don'ts in food, drink and matrimony.

Caste not only governs one's manner of life, it also fixes the place in society in which one lives. Caste structure, to a larger extent, conditions human relationships and sentiments. "Caste gives its directions for recognition, acceptance, consecration, and sacramental dedication, and *vice versa*, of a human being on his appearance in this world. It has for infancy, pupilage, and manhood, its ordained methods of sucking, sipping, drinking, eating, and voiding; of washing, rinsing, anointing, and smearing; of clothing, dressing and ornamenting; of sitting, rising and reclining; of moving, visiting and traveling; of speaking, reading, listening, and reciting; and of meditating, singing, working, playing, and fighting. It has its laws for social and religious rights, privileges, and occupations; for instructing, training and educating; for obligation, duty, and ceremony; for errors, sins and transgressions; for intercommunication, avoidance, and ex-communication; for defilement, ablution, and purification; for fines, chastisements, imprisonments, mutilations, banishments, and capital executions. It deals with death, burial and burning; and with commemoration, assistance, and injury after death. It interferes, in short, with all the relations, and events of life and with what precedes and follows...life".

> This winding has been going on for centuries and to unwind the whole thing in a span of few decades would demand a basic change in people's attitudes.

Caste hierarchy was built on inter-caste relationships. It was the elaborate proliferation of the rules governing inter-caste relationships and the meticulous enforcement of them that guaranteed the separateness and integrity of each caste. It was this complete separation of the various social strata which made India's class structure unique.

Caste grew with the sanction of the society. Conditions such as geographical isolation, static society, foreign aggression, rural social structure, influence of the religion, differences of races, and lack of education, have favoured the continued existence of the caste system. However arbitrary it is, it was spontaneous in the growth. It has played a positive cementing role. It has been a unifying force. In the long chequered history of India, it has held together the fabric of Indian society. Caste in unison with Hinduism resisted the onslaught of successive foreign invasions and centuries of alien rule and preserved the content of Hindu culture.

Caste reveals itself most obviously and most rigidly in everyday life, through the concept of pollution, a concept fundamental to the Hindu way of life. Caste which begins with pollution develops into a way of life. The concept of pollution is simply maddening, carried to meaningless, illogical and incomprehensible extremities. How fantastic are its magnitude and ramifications! There is pollution by sight, pollution by approach, pollution by touch, pollution by drink, pollution by food, pollution by matrimony, pollution by travel over sea and so on. The faith or the belief works in this way; God has ordained everything and caste too is His making and so preserve and live the tenets, rituals, taboos and everything that go with each caste.

Caste functions in a multitude of ways, diet regulations for every occasion; ritual bathing, caste deities, the manner of worship, fasts, the colour of one's clothes, the colour of the flowers one wears, the shape of one's ornaments, the pattern of one's rituals, decoration, ancestral worship etc. Further we have the Indian village structure and during festive and ceremonious occasions the distribution of work or division of labour is assigned to each sub-caste and each attends to a specific item of work arranged in gradation underlying prestige and privilege.

Changes Despite Rigidity

Despite the rigidity, conservatism and complexity of caste,

changes have been taking place in the system. Many forces opposed the evils of caste system, Jainism, Buddhism, Lingayatism, Sikhism, Christianity and the movements of Arya Samaj and Brahma Samaj and social reformers have proclaimed their opposition to caste. Modern education with its democratic ideals and values, industrialization and urbanization, money power, various movements of social emancipation, increase in the means of communication, political awakening, the emergence of legal machinery, appearance of new social classes and most important the universal adult franchise have tended to weaken the caste system.

Opposition to the caste system works in two ways. People do not believe in either predestined superiority or predestined inferiority. With all these things, the change in the villages is obviously very slow. Caste breathes quite healthily even today in the rural areas.

But, on the other hand, by the very nature and composition of the social structure in towns and cities, caste is ineffective; it does not raise its head, does not make much ado and is fast sinking. Here, no segregation, no discrimination in buses, trains, restaurants and other public places is possible. It is dying a slow and a natural death.

The villager's contact with the town slowly undermines the hold of caste on his thought. As a result of modern education and industrialization, the sanctity of caste has begun to be questioned. The caste hierarchy is slowly crumbling down.

The Constitution forbids the practice of untouchability and does not recognize caste. Though law holds itself against caste and untouchability, yet does not operate by itself but in a social environment. Transformation must take place in the attitude and beliefs of people.

The political parties in their own pursuit for power are reviving the disintegrating caste system. The slow dying embers of casteism are kindled by the politicians at every level during the elections.

The process of democracy is changing the old order; the old structure is being restructured, the functions are changing, power is redistributed, and the whole fabric of the socio-economic order is reconditioned, in a manner unthought of and unheard of before.

Caste differences were accepted as cultural and social norms. So long as it was not challenged, it flourished. Had it been challenged in the earlier centuries, it would have crumbled long ago. Many factors made this institution thrive for a pretty long period. This winding has been going on for centuries and to unwind the whole thing in a matter of few decades would demand a basic change in people's attitudes. For caste lies in the mind of man. Let us hope that at least in the years and decades to come it will become a thing of the past and a primitive institution.

Source:- E. Desingu Setty, "Caste Hierarchy : The Crumbling Edifice", *Social Welfare*, Vol. xxv, No.9, December 1978, New Delhi.

19

RURAL SANITATION - NEED FOR A PERSPECTIVE PLAN

> "The causes for the bad sanitary conditions in the villages are physical, economic, socio-cultural and psychological."

The sanitation in most of the villages in India presents a dismal picture. It has been a perennial problem, so complex in its character posing a threat to public health. The situation deserves utmost attention and consideration of every individual, local institutions, corporate bodies and the Government at large, for it affects our health and living.

The Japanese are said to be meticulous in their personal and environmental cleanliness. They take as much care of the precincts of their dwellings as they do in the case of their drawing room and bedroom. After a picnic party is over, the Americans do take pretty care to see that they do not leave any litter behind. They leave the place as clean as it was before. What an appreciable civic sense it is! And what do we do here? And what is the environmental sanitary condition in the Indian village?

By sanitary environment we mean a place or village where the residential quarters, cattle sheds, the village precincts, lanes and streets, are regularly swept and kept clean, free from open ditches, pools or slushes, dungheaps or garbage and faecal matter fouling the whole surroundings. A clean village is one free from the above and enjoying drainage facilities and arrangements for regular disposal of refuse. But today most villages in India present a dismal picture. Indiscriminately deposited dung and garbage heaps in various stages of decomposition, ditches and unwanted dirty water pools, ugly looking lanes and streets are some of the characteristic features of the villages. The insanitary conditions pose a constant threat to public health, being the root causes of innumerable diseases and spread of epidemics.

The Multiple Causes

The causes for the bad sanitary conditions in the villages are physical, economic, socio-cultural and psychological. In regard to the patterns of settlement of Indian villages, there are mainly three types – the dispersed or scattered type, the nucleated or the cluster type and linear type i.e., houses built on either side of a road in rows. The nucleated or the cluster type poses many sanitary problems in regard to space for drinking water wells, drainage, bathing and lavatory facilities, disposal of refuse and for sinking of soakage pits. Many of the villages were unplanned houses clustered together with narrow lanes or no lanes at all. Some ancient villages are walled around as a measure of protection from wild animals and thieves. And there will be fields around the village narrowing down the residential quarters. Where the houses are congested and where the villages are situated in low-lying areas, drainage is a problem. So, the very pattern of village settlements, the narrowness and physical or spatial limitations on the expansion of some villages, the topographical features of villages lead to bad sanitary conditions.

In a broad sense, occupation or economic activities of the people also decide the type of environment they live in. India is predominantly an agricultural country. Agriculture in India means use of cattle for draft, milk and manurial purposes which mean housing the cattle in separate sheds and the collection and depositing of dung and other waste materials. Lack of improved cattle-sheds and sheep-pens is a problem in the villages. Either as a matter of convenience or due to socio-cultural and religious attitude of the villagers, the cattle sheds are located near the living quarters and there may not be any wall separating the living quarters and the cattle shed. In many cases the cattle dung and urine are not properly collected. The droppings of cattle, sheep, goats and of poultry strewn all over are usually not taken care of. Even though each household attends to its own immediate surroundings, the village lanes and streets are nobody's responsibility. The villagers also dump indiscriminately cattle dung and all waste material of considerable manurial value around the house and the immediate surroundings of the village. This is due to congestion of space, feeling of difficulty in carrying the matter over a long distance to the fields or outskirts of the village. The indiscriminately dumped dungheaps are seldom covered as a measure to conserve the nitrogenous content in the matter or to prevent foul or stinking smell emanating from them.

Lack of drainage facilities in the villages and the habit of open defaecation on the part of the villagers are other common causes for disgusting sanitary conditions. The open defaecation is a psycho-cultural problem. The villagers are used to it. A change in this habit is long overdue. Either the villagers could use sanitary type of latrines or the centuries old habit of open defaecation persists. The simple fact is that over 90 per cent of the villagers were not used to a flushout latrine in their lives.

Illiteracy, poverty and lack of contract with the outside world contribute to the low civic sense among the villagers.

Another source of insanitation is the drinking water well that lacks raised platforms and causes cesspools making the place dirty.

The Bleak Background

Illiteracy, poverty and lack of contact with the outside world contribute to the low civic sense among the villagers. Further, the places where shandies and weekly markets are held, when not maintained properly, add to the insanitation of the area. Chewing and indiscriminate spitting is another common social phenomenon.

Having been used to a bad sanitary environment, the villagers do not shudder at anything dirty. The tendency is to take things easy.

There are over 5,80,000 villages in India – just one village per two square miles over the surface of this sub-continent. Now all the villages in India come under the village Panchayat administration. The Panchayats vary in geographical, topographical and economic conditions and cultural practices. Each area in view of its diversity needs a special treatment to solve the problem of environmental sanitation.

In the case of those panchayats which have adequate income, water facilities and have a permanent establishment for sweeping and scavenging, the question of village sanitation is not serious. But the problem becomes acute only with the minor panchayats which cannot or do not have sweeping and other facilities, nor do the villagers in such panachayat areas attend to general sanitation of the village.

Thus we find small villages suffering from (or enduring) a distressing and disease-producing sanitation. Most villagers are aware of the problem, but a remedy is beyond them.

Rural sanitation finds a prominent place of importance in Gandhiji's constructive programme. He often emphasised the magnitude and importance of village sanitation. He practised what he preached. He himself swept the streets and cleaned the latrines. He introduced the *wardha* latrine (trench type) which is beneficial in two ways – preservation of night soil (for manurial purposes) and preventing the fouling of village surroundings through indiscriminate defaecation.

Low Priority

Civil amenities and environmental sanitation are statutory functions of the village panchayat. But apparently the order of priority goes to items like water supply and street lighting and mostly sanitation is not accorded the importance it deserves.

Programmes to improve rural sanitation find a place in the Five Year Plans. Individual and mass sanitary drives were targeted items in the community development extension programmes. These drives in the initial stages were effective and successful and attained a great degree of publicity. The villagers and the school children participated in the drive enthusiastically. Local leaders, officials, men, women and children held brooms in their hands and cleaned the streets. In this, an attempt was made to drive home the dignity of labour and to create among the villagers a new awareness as to the prime importance of the upkeep of the village.

Civil amenities and environmental sanitation are statutory functions of the village panchayat. But apparently the order of priority goes to items like water supply and street lighting and mostly sanitation is not accorded the importance it deserves.

Allied to the sanitation programme are the propagation of sanitary type of latrines, sinking of soakage pits where there are no drainage facilities, construction of *kacha or pucca* drains, improved cattle yards, urinal trenches, scientific methods of compost making, provision of refuse bins, pavement of lanes and streets. This integrated approach is aimed at promoting sanitary conditions in the villages.

Some of the officially sponsored programmes could not make any headway. There were certain inherent shortcomings. Strictly speaking there was no scientific approach on the part of the extension and public health personnel in introducing innovations. The rural workers dictated by a conceptual frame of modern sanitary amenities and accessories as provided by the agencies tried to implant new ideas and habits in the rural communities. For instance, the construction of public lavatories (flushout latrines) in the villages at a considerable public cost was a thorough failure. First, there was no sufficient involvement and commitment of the villagers in this programme. There was the problem of water scarcity. While we discuss the question of rural sanitation water should not be treated as an isolated factor. Above all, the failure in the use of the public latrines was mainly due to the villager's attitude and habits. An attitudinal change is what is desired.

The second factor is limited governmental allocations for programmes connected with village sanitation. Thirdly, poor and inadequate finances of the panchayts and lastly the general apathy of the villagers towards sanitary measures.

As observed earlier, rural sanitation is a complex problem warranting a perspective plan and short-range specific measures to promote better sanitary conditions. The Rural Development Agency, the village panchayat, the village school and the voluntary organizations such as youth clubs and mahila mandals could play a significant role in this respect.

The supply of technique, personnel and funds depends on the Government. The programmes towards better sanitary conditions in the villages should be flexible enough so that they could be modified in accordance with the local conditions. A survey of attitudes, felt-needs and specific problems of the villagers should precede on scientific lines before the programmes are formulated. In introducing innovations, the approach should be scientific and institutional. The techniques of group-involvement, group-commitment, propaganda, publicity, demonstration, etc., must be made use of. In other words, the extension methods must be fully employed so as to motivate the villager to use a sanitary latrine and keep the precincts of his house clean. This is a slow, painstaking process. It must be gone through. There is no short cut to it.

In each rural area the vulnerable areas of insanitation and the factors causing unclean conditions are to be located, studied and remedied. The dungheaps should be taken care of. If the villagers are educated on scientific lines of compost making, the ever exposed heaps will not foul the village with stinking odour and become a breeding source for flies and insects. Wherever possible a common compost yard a little away from the village could be established. This could be done by the village panchayat. Drainage depends mainly on two things – the physical feasibility of constructing drains and financial resources. Wherever these two are positive, depending on the size of the village, *kucha or pucca* drains could be constructed as a phased programme. Areas where either of the two is absent, soakage pits are better substitutes. It falls to the lot of the individual householder. Sinking of soakage-pits is cheap and is within the capacity of the commonest man in any village. The only limitations in digging soakage pits are availability of space within the housesite and the composition of the ground soil in the house site. In case of loose soil the soakage pit is not to be located close to the draw-well because of percolation of impure or contaminated water from the soakage pit to the draw-well.

Strictly speaking, the panchayat is responsible for ensuring better sanitary conditions in the panchayat area. In the budgetary allocations of the panchayat enough provision must be made for water supply, drainage, public latrines and refuse bins and recurring expenditure towards sweeping, scavenging, etc. Every panchayat has its annual and Five Year Plans. The panchayats which could not afford full-time sweepers for daily sweeping of the village, could at least appoint either a less number of full-time or more number of part-time sweepers, in order that the villages are kept clean at lest once a week. It is desirable that this minimum programme is carried out by every panchayat.

In regard to the using of sanitary type of latrines by each family, the panchayat should take the initiative and lead in their introduction not only as a civic measure but as a persuasive step creating facilities and favourable public opinion in the use of latrines. In achieving the above-mentioned ends the panchayat can enlist the cooperation of the village school, youth club and mahila mandal and work in unison with them.

The voluntary organizations in the villages could take up village sanitation as one of their main activities and arrange periodical mass sanitary drives. The mass sanitation drives, if carried out sincerely over a period of time, are bound to influence the general public and change their attitude, make them sane to keep their surroundings clean.

The village school as one of the three basic institutions in the village could take the lead and function as a pioneer and model in sanitation programmes. It could function as an experimental and demonstration centre for a soakage pit, a lavatory, a compost pit and for environmental sanitation. The school children could be very easily trained to make use of a sanitary latrine, providing one at the school. They carry their ideas and habits to their homes and it may result in a flush-out latrine in their homes. Further, under the guidance of the school teacher the children learn the importance of environmental sanitation and could even participate in the periodical mass sanitary drives organized in the villages.

Public Health Cess

Some of the corporate bodies at present are engaged in rural developmental programmes. It is a welcome sign that they have assumed this role as partners in rural development. Their role in rural uplift will become more significant and pointed if they could concentrate on rural sanitation. They may take up programmes such as provision of drinking water, sanitation which will include drainage, latrines and gobar gas plants. The Government may also consider income tax relief to the corporate bodies in respect of the amount they spend towards rural sanitation. Further, the nationalized and scheduled banks which have adopted some villages for development may lay emphasis on programmes of rural sanitation. The Government may also bring in legislation towards what may be called public cess. The public health cess as a certain percentage of land revenue will go to the village panchayat and the amount will be utilized exclusively for rural sanitation.

Thus, we see the problems of rural sanitation in India today are deep-rooted, complex and important demanding the attention, cooperation and coordination of the Government, statutory bodies, educational institutions, voluntary organizations and above all the understanding of the general public.

[*Source*:-Dr. E. Desingu Setty, 'Rural Sanitation – Need for a Perspective Plan', *Social Welfare*, April-May, 1981.]

20

PROSPECTS AND PROBLEMS IN RURAL COMMUNITIES LEAD TO URBANIZATION IN INDIA

Urbanization in India has been the consequence of large-scale production, introduction of machinery and the growth of industrial civilization. In India the process of urbanization did not take place as it happened in the West. The process of urbanization in India during the nineteenth and the first half of the twentieth century has been the result of the following factors:

i) Growth of railways meant diversion of trade through important stations. The development of railways was necessitated in India either to meet the needs of administration or to collect goods and raw materials at important commercial centres for export.

ii) Widespread occurrence of famines during the nineteenth century meant large-scale agricultural unemployment. As there was no work in the rural areas, the population was driven by economic forces to seek employment in towns.

iii) The creation of a class of landless labourers also helped to promote urbanization, though negatively.

iv) The tendency of the wealthy landlords to settle in urban areas because city life offers certain attractions which are non-existent in rural areas, and v). The establishment of new industries or the expansion of old industries resulted in the absorption of the rural labour force in urban areas.

"Of all these different causes," says Professor D.R. Gadgil (*Industrial Evolution in India*, p.148), "the growth of industries has been at any rate in all other countries, the most important one. But in India its influence has certainly not been as powerful. Indeed there are very few towns in India which are the creation of new industries." The definite impact of industrialization in stimulating migration from rural to urban areas has not so strongly been felt in India. This is evidenced by the fact that there has been simultaneous growth of agricultural and non-agricultural workers along with a general increase in total proportion of agricultural workers vis-à-vis non-agricultural workers, whereas in 1901, 67.5 per cent of total working force consisted of agricultural workers in 1971, this ratio was 65.6 per cent.

The Criteria

The definition of "Urban" area adopted in the 1971 census is as follows:

(a). All places with a Municipality, Corporation or Cantonment or notified town area, (b) all other places which satisfied the following criteria:

i) a minimum population of 5,000.

ii) at least 75 percent of the male working population is non-agricultural, and

iii) a density of population of at least 400 per sq. km (Japan, 30,000 population defined as urban)

Based on the above criteria there are 2,921 towns in India as against 5,66,878 villages. Of these towns the largest number of towns (931) are in the category of 10,000 to 20,000 population followed by 617 towns in the category of 20,000 to 50,000; 198 in the category of 50,000 to 1,00,000 and 142 with 100,000 and above population. Nine cities in India (Greater Calcutta 7.00

million, Greater Bombay 5.90 million, Delhi 3.63 million, Madras 2.47 million, Hyderabad 1.80 million, Bangalore 1.65 million, Ahmedabad 1.59 million, Kanpur 1.27 million) and Pune have each a population over one million. One in five lives in an urban area (urban 19.9 per cent, rural 80.1 per cent).

Urbanization (it subsumes industrialization) as a complex phenomenon is fraught with positive and negative effects. These effects (positive or negative) are relative judgments based on certain values of the group. The effects could be thought in terms of absolute good and absolutely deleterious or harmful to the individual and the community. Again the changes desirable and undesirable could be analyzed in terms of physical, political, economic and socio-cultural realms of a group or in terms of various social institutions such as family kinship, caste, community, etc. And further, the effects of urbanization could be discussed at two levels – at the urban centres themselves and in the rural communities influenced by the former. The developed world is confronted with problems of urban renewal, pollution, the decay of the central city (as the affluent have moved out to the suburbs), class and ethnic tensions, crime, the energy crisis and the rest. The developing world faces all these problems of metropolitan urbanization plus the problems of transition in the rural areas.

Economic growth is positively correlated with the rate of urbanization both in the developed and developing countries, but with a difference. In the case of developed countries it was/is the "pull factor" generated by mass production and technological innovations and advancement and on the other hand, in the case of developing countries it was/is the "push factor" consequent upon mass poverty and population pressure over the land.

"Pushed Out"

Comparatively speaking, Western urban centres are economically viable and could absorb the population that they have drawn to them and we may say that there is overpopulation in the cities there, in a social sense, creating social problems.

But the picture in India is entirely different, the cities in India are overpopulated both in economic and social sense, they lack the economic potential to absorb the rural "pushed out" population and so you find a twin phenomenon in India—urban misery and rural poverty.

When any change is brought about in any aspect of culture which is a logically integrated, functional, sense-making whole there is a corresponding change in other parts of the culture too. Often when this process of change is very quick, the various parts of the culture fail to adjust in the same pace, resulting in the disruption of culture which is manifest in the various forms of social problems. Associated with every technical and material change, there is a corresponding change in the attitudes, thoughts, values, beliefs and the behaviour of the people who are affected by the material change.

We may very briefly examine some of the merits and demerits and social problems of urbanization-industrialization in general and with special reference to India.

From the standpoint of village life, urbanization creates greater political consciousness among the rural folk and develops functional leadership. It brings the rural elite in closer contact with the urban leaders and people. The modern rise of urban life has greatly accelerated the movement towards the assumption of more responsibility by government in providing educational facilities, safeguarding health, creating parks, playgrounds for recreation and operate utilities such as water, gas, electricity and transport system. On the other hand, the traditional pattern of leadership based on age, social and ritual hierarchy and the traditional village councils are relegated to a secondary position. Village communities get permeated with politics, cliques and factions.

Urbanization opened a vista of new markets, goods, services and improved farm in-puts. It results in occupational, territorial and social mobility and in the increase of transport and communication facilities, increase in employment opportunities, specialization and division of labour. But, on the other hand, in the context of Indian economy especially in respect of the rural socio-economic structure it brought in disorganization. Urbanization /industrialization broke up and continues to break up the Hindu Jajmani system resulting in the unemployment and underemployment in the case of servicing and occupational castes. The Jajmani system is closely linked with the institution of caste. It is centred round the values of honour, pride and prestige. It is a reciprocal socio-economic relationship of exchange of goods and services. This formed a sort of social and economic boundary for the village communities in India. This barter-economy in a limited sense stands disrupted today, though it is a passing phenomenon. This process of economic change has resulted in competition.

The Impersonal Mass Society

The impersonal mass society in urban centres affords the individual a degree of freedom which he cannot have in the smaller, more agrarian community. Urbanization gives access to a wide variety of social contact, mobility in spatial and social sense. It affords a chance to the individual to seek the type of work that will be compatible with his own temperament and training. In the urban setting individual gains anonymity. But, on the other hand, individual loses identity, and personal disorganization sets in, owing to loneliness and isolation. Life becomes impersonal. Life is mechanized and the mode of leisure spending in an urban setting is different. Contact with the members of the family and others become limited and segmental. The term 'neighbour' has lost any real meaning in city life. Urbanization robs family life of its traditional social and economic functions. Family becomes a consuming agency, not a working unit. It also results in the reduction of the size of the family dwelling. Time-honoured social functions of family life, religious experience, instruction of the young, recreation, sociability are now, to a very large extent, centre outside the home and this itself may well be a contributing factor to the personal disorganization. Urbanization fosters secondary group of life and controls. It affords less security of association with other individuals. Urban life tends to be swift moving, impersonal and fragmented.

In India, we find the same process at work. The traditional joint family is breaking down rapidly giving rise to nuclear family. In the urban set-up this brings a significant change in the role of the wife. On the one hand, the young housewife has to do her household and other duties such as child care and training all by herself, which often in the joint-family were being shared by the mother-in-law or any other elderly woman of the same generation, and, on the other hand, she has often to help her husband in harnessing the family income by joining some service since the accelerating pace with which the standard of living is increasing has brought economic strain on the family. The emergence of career women as a class is to be reckoned with. No doubt, economic freedom has helped raise her position and status but it has at the same time brought to her problems which were hitherto unknown to her. These are complex social and psychological problems and may be said to have assumed a universal distribution though their nature and intensity may vary depending on the extent of women's advancement and the state of industrialization attained by the society.

Disproportionate Sex Ratio

The industrial and urban areas are noted for the high disproportion of sex ratio in which male population outnumbers the female population in great numbers. Thus in the three townships at Durgapur it has been found that single number units who live only by themselves without any kinsfolk constitute less than two thirds of the total number of households surveyed. Again another survey reveals that about a quarter of the population of Calcutta city live single life without their families and they form more than half of the households. Most of those single people are males, married and migrants. Presence of such a high number of single persons is often a threat to the social health of the community as they are liable to create many serious problems. In 1957-58 the city's population consisted of about 35 per cent women and 60 per cent men. The consequence has been a steady high rate of social crimes and unhealthy pattern of behaviour in slum region surrounding the factories.

The situation often becomes worse with the presence of a large number of women, mostly unmarried migrants who come to the cities far from their homes for earning their livelihood. Thus the working girls' hostels aided by the Central Social Welfare Board alone accommodate over 2,000 such girls in the cities where parents or guardians live far off from them. As much of the social relations in urban areas are impersonal where the community has little or no control at all, much of these unhealthful patterns of behaviour tend to be encouraged. Very closely associated with this is the problem of immoral traffic in women.

Many sociologists have associated urbanization with rising rates of juvenile delinquency and crimes. A survey of crimes in India which includes murder, kidnapping and abduction, decoity, robbery, house-breaking thefts, rioting, criminal breach of trust, cheating, counterfeiting, and miscellaneous crimes in 1956 shows that of a total of 130,682 convicted cases, the crimes in 7 big cities of India alone constitute 10 per cent (13,653) which is quite significant. The decay of community feeling in urban areas due to rapid urbanization, culture conflict leading to maladjustment resulting from industrialization with modern technological tools etc., are some of the factors responsible for rising rates of delinquency in the urban and industrial centres of India.

High Rate of Alcoholism

The rising rate of alcoholism is another misgiving of urbanization/industrialization. Change of values, availability of cash money and decay of community control explain to a great degree the rise of alcoholism in urban and industrial area. Again the educated middle class youth often falls a prey to this when he migrates to urban centres and it becomes easier for him when he is aware that he is far beyond the control of his community and family.

Caste-wise settlement is one of the characteristics of the Indian rural ecology and the most significant factor is that higher castes always maintain some distance from the lower castes or the so-called untouchables. Urbanization has often helped to a large extent to break up this traditional pattern and the lower castes often share the localities of the higher castes in the urban centres. Urbanization has also brought amity between the high and the low castes. Peripheral changes are taking place in the caste system though the core of caste system, its endogamous nature remains almost intact. It is, however, interesting to note that while urbanization and industrialization often destroy some caste differences, it often fosters communal loyalties on the basis of either language, religion, culture or sometimes even on common economic interest.

Changes in the Rural Community

Improvement in communication has considerably reduced the isolation of the rural community. Radio, for instance, is a tremendous factor in broadcasting the horizons of activity and ideas. Farmers are more and more compelled to match their old ways of doing and thinking against new ones. The farmer, like the town dweller, is made at least a passive participant in the affairs of the world beyond his own community. Modern communication facilities have also brought about a great invasion of rural life by city standards of consumption. The intrusion of urban service and ideas into rural areas, then, undoubtedly has broken down much of old-time unity of farm community life. Villagers are becoming like their town brothers in matters of dress, home equipment, food consumption, recreational activities and even production and marketing techniques. Nevertheless, the character of agricultural production still requires that farmers live in relatively isolated communities where primary neighbourhood relationships remain prevalent. In this the distinctive characteristics of the rural community are not being submerged by urban influence.

India is now probably at the infant stage of urbanization and industrialization, or in other words the process has just set in. In the near future the tempo of this urbanization/ industrialization process is expected to increase, thereby involving a considerable shift of population rural to urban areas. There is need for developing the rural communities. Providing them civic amenities and institutional facilities and revamping the towns and cities with the strengthening of community and family life. The approach to this is an integrated area development approach, establishing productive, exchange and consumptive links and institutions between the rural and urban areas and thereby building viable rural-urban communities.

[*Note:*- The above article written by the author was published in Social Welfare, December, 1979, *Central Social* Welfare Board, Govt. of India, and the data mentioned in respect to the villages and towns in India relate to the period when it was published.]

INDEX

A

Africa, 56

Agricultural marketing,
  extension education in aid of, 210-234

Agricultural products,
  marketing of, 226

Agricultural research and development,
  role of PTD in, 133

Agricultural yields,
  actions steps for increasing, 247

AID/OCEAC, 56

Alcoholism,

Amul Cooperative, 302

Andhra Pradesh, 2, 4
  land and water situation in, 6
  irrigation scenario in, 6
  water conservation mission,16

Appiko Andolan, 299, 300, 301

Asia, 111, 112

B

Bahuguna, Sunderlal, 294

Bay of Bengal, 112

Behaviour modification, 165

Bhattacharya, 65

Bihar, 69

Boulding, 80

Bruneau, 73

C

Cameroon, 56, 57

Career planning,
  and development, 160

Caste,
  endogamous, 337
  changes despite rigidity, 339

Cernea, 71

Chadwick, 62, 63

China, 112, 113, 309

Chipko movement, 298, 299

Christian Missionaries, 188

CMEY, 315

Communities,
  concept of, 234

Community organization, 41
  and programme planning, 87-106
  benefits of, 46
  central objective, 43
  conditions for successful facilitation of, 50
  definition, 42
  facilitating, 46
  measure of, 45

Community,
  cultural patterns, 179
  information about, 52
  political structure of, 182

Consumer credit, 221

D

Deforestation, 110, 111
Drainage, 4
Drucker, Peter, 154
Dube, 76, 79
Durgapur, 355
DWACRA, 46
DWCUA, 332

E

Employment opportunities, 257
  action steps for increasing, 252
Ensminger, Douglas, 284
Entrepreneurs, 201
  characteristics of, 197
Entrepreneurship,
  assumptions, 176
  organization, 192
  sociological aspects 175
  strategies for developing, 172-209
Extension
  education, 210
  main components of, 215
  philosophy of 212
  principles of, 213

F

FAO, 70, 110
Farmers,
Empowering for self-sustaining development, 134
Formal R&D system, 134, 135
Freire, 65
Frost, Robert, 334
FSDP-EV, 139, 140, 142
Fugui, 76

G

Gadgil, D.R., 351
Green Revolution, 125, 126
Grievance handling, 169
Groundwater, 23
  rechange structures, 24
  methods of artificial recharge, 25
Guha, R. 304
Gujarat, 302

H

Hanumantha Rao Committee, 16
Haque, W, 293
HRD initiative, 153, 154
  training as a principal factor of, 151-171
HRD, 157, 158, 159
  training efforts for, 169
  elements, 160
  OD, 157, 158, 162
HRIS, 168
HRM, 155
  nature of, 155
Human resources, 180
Humidity, 4
Hydrology, 3

I

IADS, 68
Image, 63, 64
  led participation, 69
India, 65, 175, 176
Indigenous knowledge, 81
Infrastructure, 195
Israel, 310

J

Janmabhoomi, 22

brief review of programmes, 320
in Andhra Pradesh, 306-336
operationalisation of, 314
principles, 313
rural development, 310
values, 312-315
Japan, 309
Joint Forest Management Bodies, 11

K

Karnataka, 302
KVIC, 230

L

Lakson, 76
Land tenure,
security of, 118
Laos, 113
Lincoln, Abraham, 215

M

Madhya Pradesh, 2
Mahabharata, 152
Maharashtra, 2
Malaysia, 74, 309
Mass media, 231
Mass society,
impersonal, 354
Mayfield, 75
MBRLC, 142
McClelland, 198
Miller, 62

N

Naidu, Nara Chandra Babu, 318
Natural resources
and protest movements, 290
Neeru-Meeru Programme, 14, 15, 132
philosophy of, 10-13
Nepal, 71, 113
NGDO, 294
NGOs,
in Asia 294
Nyerere, 73

O

Oakley, 70, 71, 83
Organisational commitment,
and development of
leadership, 103

P

Pakistan, 113
Panchayat Samithi, 241
Perception,
and image, 61
Performance appraisal, 166
Phillippines, 78, 126, 139, 144
Planning Commission,65
Pradhan, 71
Programme planning, 101
guides to, 103
professional abilities, 104
PSSP, 74, 75
PTD, 127, 128,136, 137, 138
experiences in, 139
Public health cess, 349
Rainwater,
advantages of harvesting, 33
operational means in
harvesting, 23-36
Rao, S. Vanaja, 229
Raper, 67
Rigveda, 11
ROAP, 70
Romm, Jeff, 72
Royal Watershed Management

Projects (Thailand), 114
Rural areas,
application of appropriate technology to, 285-292
Rural community,
changes in, 357
Rural development,
caste dynamics in, 337-342
field approach to integrated, 359-380
part played by NGOs in, 292-305
people's image of, 60-87
village as a unit of, 233-241
Rural sanitation,
perspective plan for, 342-349
Rural Industries products, 229

S

SAEMAUL UNDON, 319
Sanitation,
bleak background, 344
multiple causes, 343
Sarawak, 112, 113
Schumacher, 80
Schumpeter, 197
Sectoral development,
guidelines for, 241-285
Self Help Groups, 46
Sen, D. 72
Setty, E.D., 61, 65
Sex ratio,355
SIRSDP, 144
Smith, John Guy, 218
Social institutions, 99
local, 98
South Korea, 309
Storage facilities, 224
Sustainable agriculture,
and participatory technology developments, 125-151

T

Taiwan, 67
Taylor, 240
Technologies, 285
profile of, 288
Tilakaratna, 70-71
Toynbee, Arnold, 154
Training , 151, 171
Transfer of Technology (TOT), 120

U

UHRIS, 168
UNDP, 309
UNESCO, 303
Upland conservation,
current approaches to, 113
education, 117
extension services, 117
people's participation in 107-125
promotion of local organizations, 119
role of Govt. in enhancing 115
role of NGOs, 122
training of staff, 116
Uplands
and uplanders, 107-124
deforestation and degradation of, 10
Urbanization in India, 350-358
USAID, 139
Uttara Kannada, 299
Uttarakhand 299

V

Vegetation, 4